SENIORS HOUSING

RESEARCH ISSUES IN REAL ESTATE

Sponsored by
The American Real Estate Society

Volume I

APPRAISAL, MARKET ANALYSIS, AND
PUBLIC POLICY IN REAL ESTATE
   edited by
   James R. DeLisle and J. Sa-Aadu

Volume II

ALTERNATIVE IDEAS IN
REAL ESTATE INVESTMENT
   edited by
   Arthur L. Schwartz, Jr. and
   Stephen D. Kapplin

Volume III

MEGATRENDS IN RETAIL REAL ESTATE
   edited by
   John D. Benjamin

Volume IV

SENIORS HOUSING
   edited by
   Michael A. Anikeeff and
   Glenn R. Mueller

SENIORS HOUSING

edited by

Michael A. Anikeeff

and

Glenn R. Mueller

KLUWER ACADEMIC PUBLISHERS
DORDRECHT • BOSTON • LONDON

Distributors for North America:
Kluwer Academic Publishers
101 Philip Drive
Assinippi Park
Norwell, Massachusetts 02061 USA

Distributors for all other countries:
Kluwer Academic Publishers Group
Distribution Centre
Post Office Box 322
3300 AH Dordrecht, THE NETHERLANDS

Library of Congress Cataloging-in-Publication Data

Senior housing / edited by Michael A. Anikeeff and Glenn R. Mueller.
      p. cm. -- (Research issues in real estate ; v. 4)
  "National Investment Conference Board and The American Real Estate Society."
  Includes bibliographical references.
  ISBN 0-7923-8012-6
  1. Aged--Housing--United States. 2. Aged--Dwellings--United States--Finance. 3. Retirees--Housing--United States. 4. Real estate business--United States.   I. Anikeeff, Michael A.
II. Mueller, Glenn R.   III. National Investment Conference Board.
IV. American Real Estate Society.   V. Series: Real estate research issues ; v. 4.
HD7287.92.U5S45   1997
363.5'946'0973--dc21   97-35809
                                                             CIP

Copyright © 1998 by Kluwer Academic Publishers

All rights reserved. No part of this publication may be reproduced, stored in a retrieval system or transmitted in any form or by any means, mechanical, photo-copying, recording, or otherwise, without the prior written permission of the publisher, Kluwer Academic Publishers, 101 Philip Drive, Assinippi Park, Norwell, Massachusetts 02061

Printed on acid-free paper.

Printed in the United States of America

1997 AMERICAN REAL ESTATE SOCIETY

PRESIDENT'S COUNCIL
Appraisal Institute
ERE-Yarmouth
Federal National Mortgage Association Foundation
Institutional Real Estate, Inc.
International Association of Corporate Real Estate Executives (NACORE)
LaSalle Advisors Limited
Price Waterhouse
Prudential Real Estate Investors
The RREEF Funds

REGENTS
F. W. Dodge/McGraw-Hill
John Hancock Real Estate Investment Group*
Heitman Capital Management Corporation
International Council of Shopping Centers (ICSC)
MIG Realty Advisors
National Association of Real Estate Investment Trusts (NAREIT)
The Roulac Group

SPONSORS
ALLEGIS Realty Investors
Association of Foreign Investors in U. S. Real Estate (AFIRE)*
BOMA International*
Boston Financial Group
CIGNA Investments
Citadel Realty
Citicorp Real Estate
Cornerstone Real Estate Advisers
Counselors of Real Estate (CRE)
Dearborn Financial Publishing
The Dorchester Group
E & Y Kenneth Leventhal Real Estate Group
Freddie Mac
GE Capital*
Government of Singapore Investment Corporation (GSIC)
Hancock Agricultural Investment Group
Hendricks, Vella, Weber, Williams
Richard D. Irwin and Irwin Professional Publishing
Jones Lang Wootton USA*
Koll
Korpaca & Associates
Legg Mason Wood Walker*
MetLife Real Estate Investments
Metric Realty
Mortgage Banker's Association
National Association of Industrial and Office Properties (NAIOP)
National Association of REALTORS® (SIOR)
SSR Realty Advisors
SynerMark Investments
Texas Instruments
Torto Wheaton Research
Urban Land Institute
Westmark Realty Advisors*

*New for 1997

1997 AMERICAN REAL ESTATE SOCIETY

Officers

1997 President	Willard McIntosh,
	Prudential Real Estate Investors
President Elect	Glenn R. Mueller,
	Legg Mason Wood Walker
Vice President and	Karl L. Gunterman
Program Chairman	Arizona State University
Executive Director	James R. Webb*
	Cleveland Sate University
Secretary/Treasurer	Theron R. Nelson*
	University of North Dakota
Editor, JRERG	Donald Jud
	University of North Carolina at Greensboro
Co-Editors, JREL	James B. Kau
	University of Georgia
	C. F. Sirmans
	University of Connecticut
Editor, JREPM	John T. Emery
	Louisiana Tech University
Editor, JREPPE	Donald R. Epley
Newsletter	Washington State University
Editor, ARES	Stephen A. Pyhrr,
	SynerMark Investments
Director of Public	Roy T. Black
Relations	Georgia State University
Ombudsperson	Larry E. Wofford
	C&L Systems

Board of Directors

Christopher Bettin (1996-97)
Appraisal Institute
Roy T. Black (1997)
Georgia State University
James Carr (1997-01)
FNMA Foundation
Deborah Jo Cunningham (1997-01)
Citicorp Real Estate
James R. DeLisle (1995-97)
ERE-Yarmouth
Geoffrey Dohrmann (1997-99)
Institutional Real State, Inc.
Terry V. Grissom (1997-00)
Georgia Sate University
Jacques Gordon (1997-00)
LaSalle Advisors
Steven D. Kapplin* (1996-98)
University of South Florida

Karen E. Lahey (1996-98)
University of Akron
Joseph Lipscomb (1996-98)
Texas Christian University
Christopher A. Manning (1997-99)
Loyola Marymount University
Norman G. Miller (1997-00)
University of Cincinnati
Stephen E. Roulac* (1997-01)
The Roulac Group
Arthur L. Schwartz, Jr.* (1995-97)
University of South Florida
Gordon Wyllie (1996-98)
NACORE
John Williams (1997-99)
Morehouse College
Michael S. Young (1997-01)
The RREEF Funds

*Past President

1997 Fellows of the American Real Estate Society

Joseph D. Albert
James Madison University
Michael A. Anikeeff
Johns Hopkins University
Paul K. Asabere
Temple University
John S. Baen
University of North Texas
Stan Banton
Banton Roach & Beasley
John D. Benjamin
American University
J. Thomas Black
Urban Land Institute
Roy T. Black
Georgia State University
Donald H. Bleich
California State University at Northridge
Waldo L. Born
Eastern Illinois University
Suzanne E. Cannon
DePaul University
James Carr
FNMA Foundation
James R. Cooper
Georgia State University
Glenn E. Crellin
Washington State University
Deborah Jo Cunningham
Citicorp Real Estate
John A. Dalkowski III
Phoenix Real Estate Advisors
Charles G. Dannis
Crosson Dannis, Inc.
James R. DeLisle
ERE-Yarmouth
Gene Dilmore
Realty Researchers
Mark G. Dotzour
Wichita State University
John T. Emery
Louisiana Tech University
Donald R. Epley
Washington State University
S. Michael Giliberto
J. P. Morgan Investment Management
John L. Glascock
University of Connecticut
Richard B. Gold
Boston Financial Group
William C. Goolsby
University of Arkansas at Little Rock
Jacques Gordon
LaSalle Partners Limited
G. Hayden Green
University of Alaska at Anchorage
D. Wylie Greig
The RREEF Funds

Terry V. Grissom
Georgia State University
Karl L. Guntermann
Arizona State University
Jun Han
John Hancock Real Estate Investments Group
Richard L. Haney
Texas A&M University
William G. Hardin III
Morehouse College
Chao-I Hsieh
National Taipei University
William Hughes
MIG Realty Advisors
Jerome R. Jakubovitz
MAI
Linda L. Johnson
Miller & Johnson
Ted C. Jones
Texas A&M University
G. Donald Jud
University of North Carolina at Greensboro
Steven D. Kapplin
University of South Florida
George R. Karvel
University of Saint Thomas
James B. Kau
University of Georgia
William N. Kinnard, Jr.
Real Estate Counseling Group of Connecticut
Karen E. Lahey
University of Akron
Paul D. Lapides
Kennesaw State University
Donald R. Levi
Wichita State University
Yougou Liang
Prudential Real Estate Investors
Joseph B. Lipscomb
Texas Christian University
Marc A. Louargand
Cornerstone Realty Advisors
Christopher A. Manning
Loyola Marymount University
Willard McIntosh
Prudential Real Estate Investors
Isaac Megbolugbe
Price Waterhouse
Ivan J. Miestchovich, Jr.
University of New Orleans
Norman G. Miller
University of Cincinnati
Philip S. Mitchell
Mitchell & Associates
Glenn R. Mueller
Legg Mason Wood Walker
William Mundy
Mundy Jarvis & Associates

F. C. Neil Myer
Cleveland State University
Theron R. Nelson
University of North Dakota
George A. Overstreet, Jr.
University of Virginia
Joseph L. Pagliari, Jr.
Citadel Realty
Thomas D. Pearson
The Thomas D. Pearson Company
Steven A. Pyhrr
SynerMark Investments
Stephen E. Roulac
The Roulac Group
Ronald C. Rutherford
University of Texas at San Antonio
Karl-Werner Schulte
European Business School
Arthur L. Schwartz, Jr.
University of South Florida
M. Atef Sharkawy
Texas A&M University
Robert Simons
Cleveland State University
C. F. Sirmans
University of Connecticut
Petros Sivitanides
Westmark Realty Advisors
Almon R. "Bud" Smith
National Association of REALTORS
C. Ray Smith
University of Virginia
Halbert C. Smith
University of Florida
Rocky Tarantello
Tarantello & Company
Stephen F. Thode
Lehigh University
Ko Wang
Chinese University of Hong Kong
James R. Webb
Cleveland State University
John E. Williams
Morehouse College
Larry E. Wofford
C&L Systems Corporation
Andrew Wood
ERE-Yarmouth
Elaine M. Worzala
Colorado State University
Charles H. Wurtzebach
Heitman Capital Management
Tyler Yang
Price Waterhouse
Michael S. Young
The RREEF Funds
Alan J. Ziobrowski
Lander University

1997 NATIONAL INVESTMENT CONFERENCE BOARD OF DIRECTORS

OFFICERS

William E. Shine .... President
Raymond J. Lewis .... Vice President
Andrew J. Ward .... Treasurer
Robert G. Kramer .... Secretary

EXECUTIVE COMMITTEE

Robert T. Eramian, President, Consulco, Inc.
Al Holbrook, President, EdenCare Senior Living Services
Robert G. Kramer, President, Kramer•Crosby, Inc.
Anthony J. Mullen, Managing Partner, Traditions of America, G.P.
William E. Shine (Conference Chair), Executive Vice President, GMAC Commercial Mortgage Corp.
Peter Sidoti, Senior Vice President, Schroder Wertheim & Co.
Arnold J. Whitman (Conference Co-chair), President, PRN Mortgage Capital, L.L.C.

RESEARCH PROJECTS COMMITTEE

Anthony J. Mullen (Committee Chair), Managing Partner, Traditions of America, G.P.
Harvey N. Singer, NIC Research Director
Geoffrey Dohrmann, President, Institutional Real Estate, Inc.
Raymond J. Lewis, Senior VP, Product Manager, Heller Financial, Inc.

OTHER DIRECTORS

R. Bruce Andrews, President & CEO, Nationwide Health Properties, Inc.
Raymond M. Anthony, Managing Director, Nomura Securities International, Inc.
Rick Anthony, Senior Vice President, SouthTrust Capital Funding
John W. Dark, Vice President, Prudential Real Estate Investors
Abraham D. Gosman, Chairman & CEO, Meditrust
Rick K. Price, VP-Housing Finance, Ziegler Securities
Andrew J. Ward, Partner, Coopers & Lybrand, L.L.P.

EDITORIAL REVIEW BOARD

RESEARCH ISSUES IN REAL ESTATE: VOLUME 4 SENIORS HOUSING

John D. Benjamin
American University

Lewis Bolan
Bolan Smart Associates

David Fick
Legg Mason Wood Walker Inc.

Jay H. Gouline
Springlake Corporation

Karl L. Guntermann
Arizona State University

John H. Haas
Senior Campus Living

Robert R. Kramer
National Investment Conference for the Senior and Long Term Care Industries

M. Shawn Krantz
NationsBank

Stephen Laposa
Price Waterhouse LLP

Emil Malizia
University of North Carolina at Chapel Hill

R. Paul Mehlman
Landmark Realty Advisors LLC

Anthony J. Mullen
Traditions of America, G.P.

Stephen E. Roulac
The Roulac Group

David Scribner, Jr.
Scribner & Partners, Inc.

David J. Segmiller
Cochran, Stephenson & Donkervoet Inc.

Harvey Singer
National Investment Conference for the Senior Living and Long Term Care Industries

Glen A. Tipton
Cochran, Stephenson & Donkervoet Inc.

David S. Schless
American Seniors Housing Association

James R. Webb
Cleveland State University

CONTENTS

ABOUT THE EDITORS XIII

FOREWORD XV

INTRODUCTION 1
Michael A. Anikeeff and Glenn R. Mueller

1   PRIMER ON KEY ISSUES IN SENIORS HOUSING 5
John D. Benjamin and Michael A. Anikeeff

2   OVERVIEW OF SENIORS HOUSING 21
Charles M. Sexton

3   VALUE INFLUENCES PAST, PRESENT AND FUTURE 45
Mark D. Roth, Charles J. Herman, Jr., and Christopher Urban

4   1996 ACQUISITION MARKETS SENIOR HOUSING AND LONG-
TERM CARE INDUSTRIES 63
American Seniors Housing Association and Capital Research Group

5   THE EVOLUTION AND STATUS OF SENIORS HOUSING
TERMINOLOGY: A REVIEW AND ANALYSIS BY SERVICES,
PRODUCT TYPES, AND POLITICAL JURISDICTIONS 73
David Scribner, Jr., and John A. Dalkowski, III

6   TOWARD STANDARDIZING SENIORS HOUSING: INDUSTRY
DEFINITIONS BY PROJECT TYPE 89
Michael A. Anikeeff and Glenn R. Mueller

7   RETIREMENT HOUSING AND LONG-TERM HEALTH CARE:
ATTITUDES OF THE ELDERLY 109
Karen Marten Gibler, James R. Lumpkin, and George P. Moschis

8	ADAPTING DEMAND METHODOLOGIES FOR ASSISTED LIVING MARKET ANALYSIS 131
	Susan B. Brecht
9	SENIORS HOUSING INVESTMENT: HOW PENSION FUNDS CAN OBTAIN SUPERIOR RETURNS, ACHIEVE PORTFOLIO DIVERSIFICATION, AND PROVIDE FUNDS FOR A NEEDED HOUSING PRODUCT 153
	L. Robin DuBrin
10	PENSIONS AND SENIORS HOUSING 167
	Stephen Roulac
11	THE INVESTMENT CASE FOR SENIOR LIVING AND LONG TERM CARE PROPERTIES IN AN INSTITUTIONAL REAL ESTATE PORTFOLIO 171
	Glenn R. Mueller and Steven P. Laposa
12	QUANTIFYING THE SUPPLY OF SENIOR HOUSING 183
	Michael A. Anikeeff and James E. Novitzki
13	FORECASTING SENIORS HOUSING DEMAND..205
	Robert H. Edelstein and Allan J. Lacayo
14	THE RELATIONSHIP BETWEEN HEALTH CARE REITs AND HEALTH CARE STOCKS..237
	Darcy D. Terris and F.C. Neil Myers

ABOUT THE EDITORS

MICHAEL A. ANIKEEFF

Michael A. Anikeeff is chairman of the real estate department and director of the Allan L. Berman Real Estate Institute at Johns Hopkins University. His research interests and publications are in the areas of seniors housing, location theory, and the strategic management of development firms. He has published in the *Journal of Real Estate Research* and the *Journal of Managerial Issues*.

Prior to joining Hopkins in 1991, Dr. Anikeeff was a senior associate in research and education at the Urban Land Institute in Washington, DC. He also served as assistant professor in the graduate planning program in the School of Architecture, University of Arkansas, legislative assistant to Congressman Charles Bennett (D-FL), and assistant professor of sociology at the University of North Florida.

Dr. Anikeeff received his AB from University of California at Berkeley in social science, a Masters in City Planning from the School of Architecture, Ohio State University, and a Ph.D. in sociology and planning from Ohio State, as well as an MBA in finance from American University.

GLENN R. MUELLER

Glenn R. Mueller oversees research activities for the Legg Mason Wood Walker, Inc. real estate groups, and is a faculty member of The Johns Hopkins Berman Real estate Institute.

Dr. Mueller has 22 years of experience in the real estate industry, including 13 years of research. Mueller's research experience includes: market cycle analysis, real estate securities analysis, portfolio and diversification analysis, and both public and private market investment strategies. In addition, he has performed specific macro- and micro-economic level analyses, both nationally and internationally, of office, industrial, apartment, retail, hotel, single family residential and senior housing property types.

Mueller has written more than fifty articles that have appeared in top industry publications such as: The *Journal of Real Estate Research, Real Estate Finance, Institutional Real Estate Securities, Real Estate Review, The Journal of Real Estate Portfolio Management, Urban Land,* and has won three national awards for his some of his articles. Most recently Mueller's article, "Interest Rate Movement's Effects on Real Estate Investment Trusts", co-authored with Keith Pauley of LaSalle Securities won "Best Article of the Year 1995" in the Journal of Real Estate Research. He is also a member of the editorial board of a number of major real estate industry publications, including: the *Journal of Real Estate Research,* the *Journal of Real Estate Portfolio Management,* the *Real Estate Capital Markets Report, Institutional Real Estate Securities, The Journal of Applied Real Property Analysis, PREA Digest,* and the *Journal of Real Estate Literature.* In addition, he is a contributing editor to *Real Estate Finance, Forecast Magazine,* and *The Handbook of Real Estate Portfolio Management.* He is a frequent presenter of research at national and international conferences on topics ranging from market cycle analysis, to real estate securities, to portfolio strategies, to investment analysis.

Prior to Legg Mason Mueller has held top research positions at Price Waterhouse, ABKB/LaSalle Securities, and Prudential. He was also, an assistant professor of real estate & construction management at the University of Denver and a developer/builder in New England.

Mueller holds a Ph.D. in Real Estate from Georgia State University, an MBA from Babson College, and a B.S.B.A. from the University of Denver and is a Fellow of the Homer Hoyt Advanced Studies Institute.

He is currently on the faculty at The Allan L. Berman Real Estate Institute, Johns Hopkins University.

Mueller is the 1998 president elect of the American Real Estate Society (ARES)

Chairman of the research committee at the Pension Real Estate Association (PREA) and a

Director of the American Real Estate & Urban Economics Association (AREUEA)

FOREWORD

Any growing market needs research-based information to ensure that sound financial investment takes place. Certainly, the senior living and long term care industry—ever expanding and diversifying—has a growing need for reliable data and performance benchmarks. As such, The National Investment Conference for the Senior Living and Long Term Care Industries (NIC) is pleased to co-sponsor this special issue monograph of the *Journal of Real Estate Research* with the American Real Estate Society.

Devoted solely to senior living and long term care topics, this monograph features articles based on original research, both theoretical and empirical. We believe these articles will stimulate dialogue between the academic and institutional real estate communities and examination of other important industry issues. A range of timely topics—from forecasting demand to acquisition markets to the case for institutional investment—is addressed by some of the industry's most respected analysts.

Sponsoring this special issue monograph also supports NIC's mission. Founded in 1991 as a nonprofit, 501(c)3 educational forum, NIC serves as an information resource for lenders, investors, developers, owners/operators, and others interested in meeting the housing and healthcare needs of America's aging population.

NIC's Annual Conference, held each October, attracts more than 1,000 executive-level decision-makers, bringing the financial and development sectors together in productive exchange. Proceeds from the conference are used to fund research efforts—both in-house and in strategic alliance with leading institutions—to provide better information and investment benchmarks to stimulate efficient capital formation in the senior living and long term care industries. The results of these research efforts—from consumer awareness and preferences to investment risks and returns, from tax incentives to trends in both the retirement housing markets and the capital markets—are published and made available through NIC's own publications and through a variety of other sources.

We hope you find this research information useful in assessing this growing market niche. And NIC looks forward to being an information bridge between capital markets and the senior living and long term care industries. For more information about NIC, please call (410) 267-0504.

Robert G. Kramer
Executive Director

Anthony J. Mullen
Chairman, Research Projects Committee

Harvey N. Singer
Research Director

INTRODUCTION

Seniors housing improves the quality of life for an increasingly significant segment of the population. The number of people in the United States over 65 years of age is projected to double in the next thirty years. However, the number of individuals most in need of seniors housing—those age eighty-five and over—is projected to increase three times. Businessman/author Pete Peterson, in his latest book, *Will America Grow Up Before it Grows Old,* points out that this growth in the seniors population is equivalent to adding an entire New York City of people over eighty-five to the population.

The business implications of this demographic change are significant. Peterson says that one safe prediction is that aging baby boomers will redouble their demand for health services. He also suggests that the greatest payoffs are likely to go to businesses specializing in lower-cost, more efficient, healthcare–like, cost-effective alternatives to nursing home care. The private sector will play the major role in meeting this significant social need. The institutional investment-quality seniors housing market is currently valued at $86 billion—already larger than the public REIT market. It is predicted to grow by $16 billion in the next four years, and grow to $490 billion in the next 35 years.

The American Real Estate Society (ARES), in cooperation with and supported by the National Investment Conference for the Senior Living and Long Term Care Industries (NIC), sponsored this monograph dedicated to seniors housing. The primary purpose of this monograph is to stimulate research on seniors housing and long-term care—topics of interest to the institutional real estate community. The research should be of interest to several audiences. Industry researchers should find base line information useful for analysis. Developers and investors will find articles that will assist them in decision making. Finally, academics will find a fertile area for further research.

We have attempted to collect the basic data for an industry analysis to provide a source for understanding the industry to the individual new to the industry—with the ultimate goal of expediting needed investment. We provide articles for industry analysts on product lines, complementary products, and substitute products. Further, the monograph investigates buyers and their behavior, the growth potential of the industry, the growth pattern and the determinants of growth, the economics of the different product types, and market analysis techniques. Finally, although the industry is fragmented, with few large participants, we include an article on healthcare REITs and healthcare stocks that investigates the performance of the larger players in the industry.

The monograph begins with the John Benjamin and Michael A. Anikeeff article "Primer on Key Issues in Seniors Housing." This chapter offers the novice highlights of research and industry expert views on trends and issues.

The next chapter, written by Charles M. Sexton, Director of Real Estate Research at Unum Life Insurance, provides the "Overview of Seniors Housing." This is a broad summary of the seniors housing industry in the United States. Sexton provides a discussion of the types of products available. He also details the demographic and economic picture of American seniors as well as their current housing arrangements. The chapter finally points out key facts and trends in property types, healthcare, legislation, and financing.

"Value Influences Past, Present and Future," a paper by Mark D. Roth, Charles J. Herman, Jr., and Christopher Urban, examines four product categories of long-term care: independent or congregate living, assisted living, nursing, and subacute care. The paper explains the asset value of these products in terms of the evolution of managed care, buyer motivations, seller motivations, opportunities, and threats. The authors provide data on unit sale prices and capitalization rates for the period from 1990 to 1996. Their findings support a low-cost quality producer strategy.

The Capital Valuation Group and American Seniors Housing Association have provided an update and expansion of their previous studies in "1996 Acquisition Markets: Seniors Housing and Long Term Care Industries." Their previous studies considered only seniors housing transactions and not skilled nursing. However, since the distinctions are blurring, this current study considers congregate housing, assisted living, and skilled nursing. The data cover these product types for the time period 1993 to 1996 and include sales price per bed, gross income multiplier, capitalization rate or cash flow multiple, and price per square foot.

The next few chapters examine the problem of definitions in the seniors housing industry. In "The Evolution and Status of Seniors Housing Terminology: A Review and Analysis by Services, Product Types, and Political Jurisdictions," David Scribner, Jr. and John A. Dalkowski, III demonstrate the considerable confusion regarding the types of housing that exist and the terms by which they are known. According to the authors, the industry is far from achieving any meaningful standardization of terminology and no government agency, medical group, or professional organizations have been able to successfully standardize the terminology. They predict that the problem will escalate as states impose new regulations on seniors-living alternatives, particularly assisted living.

In "Toward Standardizing Seniors Housing Industry Definitions by Product Type," Michael A. Anikeeff and Glenn R. Mueller take a different approach to the definitions problem. They utilize a model that says that aging is a process of decreasing function, and that seniors housing is a means of helping to maintain function. The authors call for using operational definitions that explain the functional needs that each particular facility meets. Toward this end, the functional needs of the elderly as defined in the medical literature are reviewed. Some of these functional need-based definitions are already utilized in the seniors housing industry, including the two most widely-used terms—activities of daily living (ADLs) and instrumental activities of daily living (IADLs). The chapter concludes with the presentation of a potential functional scale to be applied to real estate project types.

Buyers and their behavior are the topic of "Retirement Housing and Long-Term Health Care: Attitudes of the Elderly." This paper is based on data from a well-known study funded by the American Association for Retired Persons (AARP). Karen Martin Gibler, James R. Lumpkin, and George P. Moschis used focus groups and a mail survey to determine the attitudes of the elderly. The study found that many elderly persons are uninformed about their housing and care options, and that they would prefer to age in place in a mixed neighborhood. According to the study, the preferred mode of retirement housing offers cheerful facilities, high-quality food, understanding staff, and reasonable monthly charges for a range of services.

Susan B. Brecht's article "Adapting Demand Methodologies for Assisted Living Market Analysis" examines each component of the market feasibility study for assisted living. This article illustrates how this particular feasibility study differs from the market study for traditional seniors housing as described in her earlier book *Retirement Housing Market*s. Brecht also identifies analytical issues that need further research and calls for improved methodological techniques and standards.

L. Robin DuBrin, in "Seniors Housing Investment: How Pension Funds Can Obtain Superior Returns, Achieve Portfolio Diversification, and Provide Funds for a Needed Housing Product," sets a research agenda. She illustrates the investment potential for the seniors housing product and explains why pension funds have been reluctant to invest. To increase activity, she calls for research to define the merits of the business, and to develop methods to classify assets, to quantify risk, and to evaluate investments. She argues that the industry must provide standardized information to facilitate institutional investment.

To emphasis the role of the institutional investor and provide transition from the DuBrin article and the Mueller and Laposa article, we have inserted a research note by Stephen E. Roulac titled "Pensions and Seniors Housing."

"The Investment Case for Senior Living and Long-Term Care Properties in an Institutional Real Estate Portfolio" by Glenn R. Mueller and Steven P. Laposa is a summary of their report prepared for NIC. This study uses industry definition categories based on function (as also called for by Anikeeff and Mueller) to provide estimates of future potential demand. It also attempts to refine estimates of the supply of seniors housing. The study reviews industry risks and returns and concludes with reasons for investors to choose seniors housing as an attractive investment alternative, including an estimate of the amount of capital that may be required—$16 billion in the next four years!

Michael A. Anikeeff and James Novitzki, in "Quantifying the Supply of Seniors Housing," use previously unpublished data from the 1991 National Health Provider Inventory to give detailed analysis on nursing homes and board and care homes on a state-by-state basis. State-level data is provided for number of facilities, number of residents, facility size by number of beds, occupancy rates, for-profit and nonprofit ownership, beds per population over age 65, and usage of long-term care facilities by those over 65.

The Mueller and Laposa findings are supported by Robert H. Edelstein and Allan J. Lacayo, in "Forecasting Seniors Housing Demand." They use a statistical analysis of PUMS data (public use microdata samples), which contains housing unit and personal data from the U.S. Census. The data suggests that predicting demand for seniors housing is complex because it combines the demand for shelter with varying degrees of nonhousing personal service. To complicate matters, the needs of the household are functionally dependent upon household location, age, and physical and mental condition. The authors used a statistical analysis to forecast demand for five-year intervals through the year 2020 for different age groups and different geographic regions. They found that the fastest growing area will be assisted living; the residents of which, they assert, need relatively low levels of nonhousing services and tend to age in place.

"The Relationship between Healthcare REITs and Healthcare Stocks" is a reprint of an article that appeared in the *Journal of Real Estate Research* published by ARES. The authors are Darcey D. Terris and F.C. Neil Myer. We include this article here because of its relevance to the question of viewing seniors housing as real estate or operating-service company. The authors' findings suggest that perhaps the retail real estate industry could offer models for studying the seniors housing industry.

It is our sincere hope that these chapters addressing the present and future of seniors housing can help developers, investors, and researchers gain insight into this dynamic industry. We would like to acknowledge Kelly Hall Williams for her work in administering this project and to Les Williams for his editorial assistance. Finally, we as editors of this monograph accept responsibility for this publication.

—Michael A. Anikeeff
—Glenn R. Mueller

1

PRIMER ON KEY ISSUES IN SENIORS HOUSING

John D. Benjamin
Department of Finance and Real Estate
Kogod College of Business Administration
The American University

Michael A. Anikeeff
The Allan L. Berman Real Estate Institute
Johns Hopkins University

ABSTRACT

This chapter presents ten interesting observations about fundamentals shaping seniors housing, based on an extensive review of the seniors housing literature and on discussions with leading seniors housing developers and managers. Literature reviewed includes items from recent academic research, the American Seniors Housing Association (ASHA) files, and from LEXIS/NEXIS.

Utilizing the ten-point format of Goodman and Grupe (1995), we present the following observations:

1. Demographic analysis must further document the subcohorts of persons over age 65.

2. Ethnic and location preferences will have prominent impact on seniors housing.

3. Many baby boomers—now entering their 50s—will retire or are planning to retire before age 65.

4. Seniors prefer remaining in their homes, but often move either resulting from desire for independence or a change in life circumstance.

5. Seventy percent of seniors' households own their own homes, but studies disagree on whether the majority will have saved enough to maintain its pre-retirement lifestyle during retirement.

6. Seniors housing options are varied and will likely evolve to meet the desires of future generations. Home health care shows major growth.

7. Assisted living facilities will continue to fill a unique niche in the spectrum of seniors housing.

8. Seniors housing regulation varies significantly by state and impacts market segmentation of products.

9. Seniors housing involves relatively few large companies as compared to the conventional multifamily business. Consolidation and expansion provide opportunities for institutional investment.

10. Seniors housing has a surprisingly long history of meeting the needs of the elderly.

The market for seniors housing is growing, and suppliers will surely need to recognize the characteristics of senior consumers and of the business itself—an amalgamation of the health care, hospitality, and real estate industries.

TEN OBSERVATIONS ABOUT SENIORS HOUSING

Americans who will retire between now and 2010 are readily identifiable. Their gross numbers, ages, and ethnicity can be determined. In addition, their household characteristics, incomes, and geographic distribution can be projected. Nevertheless, understanding the demand and supply for seniors housing is a daunting task. According to the U.S. Bureau of the Census (1995), there are already more than 33 million seniors (those persons age 65 years or older) in the U.S., and this cohort of the domestic population is growing rapidly. Further, the retirement cohort is segmented into many smaller subcohorts based on ethnicity, age, and location attributes.

For this cohort, seniors housing is an innovative and efficient long-term care option that combines residential multifamily housing with direct access to needed sup-

PRIMER ON KEY ISSUES IN SENIORS HOUSING

portive services and health care.[1] Seniors housing can be a practical, cost-effective, and consumer-friendly long-term care option, although it largely has been overshadowed by the nursing home industry. Given the dearth of academic articles on seniors housing, we include in this chapter an extensive review of other available seniors housing literature, including items from the American Seniors Housing Association (ASHA) files and a popular media review, including a broad Lexis/Nexis search to identify articles about seniors housing. This chapter highlights a range of issues that will affect the future supply and demand for seniors housing. We utilize the format of Goodman and Grupe (1995) to capsulize the available literature on seniors housing into ten informative and interesting observations about seniors housing.[2]

1. Demographic analysis must further document the subcohorts of persons over age 65.

According to the U.S. Census Bureau, U.S. population growth (defined as births plus immigration, less deaths and emigration) is only about 1% per year and decreasing.[3] The characteristics of the population cohorts, however, are changing quite rapidly due to lengthening life expectancies and the impact of the baby boomers (those born from the post-World War II period to 1964). As indicated in Table 1, persons over age 65 will comprise a growing share of the total population. While the growth of the seniors population (now comprising around 12.8% of the U.S. population) will be stagnant for the next decade, by the year 2030, older adults are expected to comprise 20.1% of the U.S. population.

Demographic analysis must be sensitive to differences in age subcohorts. Overall, the number of persons over 65 is increasing at an increasing rate. The rate of increase is 1.05% for the years 1994-2000, 2.14% for the period from 2000-2010, and 4.8% for the decade from 2010-2020. The first member of the baby boom turns 65 in 2013. However, within the overall 65+ cohort, there is a subcohort of individuals born between World War I and World War II that will show a decline in numbers. The subcohort from age 65-69 will decline from 1994-2006, and the subcohort from 70-74 will decline from 1996 to 2010. Seniors housing projects dependent on attracting

---

[1] Because these residences and associated services are typically not reimbursed by federal or state funding sources, consumer preference and choice have defined this long-term care option. This attribute has fueled the development of market-driven products. The unique characteristics of seniors housing include:
  1. Residential community-based settings
  2. Opportunities for social interaction and recreation
  3. Security
  4. Access to supportive services and health care
  5. Individualized personal care and economic efficiency
  6. Personal choice of housing
  7. Special accessibility design features

[2] Goodman and Grupe (1995) used a top ten format to discuss the market for multifamily housing. We also want to note that all of the revelations discussed in this chapter require a careful analysis at the local level for implications concerning specific seniors housing formats.

[3] See U.S. Bureau of the Census, *Statistical Abstract of the United States: 1994* (114th edition).

individuals in these groups should plan carefully (see Sexton in Chapter Two for more details).

Table 1: Seniors' Share of the U.S. Population

Year	Age 65 and Over
2000	12.8%
2005	12.8%
2010	13.3%
2020	16.4%
2030	20.1%
2040	20.7%
2050	20.4%

Source: J.C. Day (1993)

Longer life expectancy and the aging of baby boomers will require the provision of housing and supportive care services for an increasingly larger older population. By 2030, the number of seniors will exceed the number of young children, and the trend will not reverse itself until 2050. The baby boomers are now just entering middle age in large numbers, and life expectancy is increasing. The large baby boomer cohort's impact will hit in 2013 when the cohort begins to reach age 65. Thus, most of the important cohort population growth over the next several decades will be in the older age cohorts. Immediate demand for seniors housing in the period from 1994-2010 is generated by the increasing proportion of older seniors seeking assistance as they age. During this decade and a half, the number of seniors over 75 will increase by 34 percent. Within this cohort, 20 percent require assistance with activities of daily living (ADLs). In addition, within this period, the number of those over age 85 will increase 73 percent to 2.5 million, and in this group, over 50 percent require assistance with ADLs.

2. Ethnic and location preferences will have prominent impact on seniors housing.

An aging population will likely translate into greater demand for seniors housing. Seniors will want retirement housing formats that cater specifically to their needs and preferences. The tremendous diversity of the older adult population will likely give developers and operators vast opportunities to meet a variety of different seniors housing niches. According to Gibler and Moschis (1996) and data from the American Seniors Housing Association, the typical seniors housing resident today is a single, widowed, Caucasian female, with relatively-high annual income and assets. This senior typically will have moved from a house or condominium she owned.

However, if the future distribution of the seniors population is overlaid with variations in income, race/ethnicity, and household characteristics, a large number of discrete target markets becomes apparent. In determining the demand for seniors housing development opportunities, the nature and composition of the seniors population and its proclivity to use seniors care services are as important as its total size. In the future, a retiree will be increasingly likely to be a member of a discrete group whose tastes may not be the same as those of the current standard.

Today, seniors' use of healthcare services differs significantly by region of residence (see the Anikeeff and Novitski chapter). Although the national average for individuals over 65 using nursing home, board and care, and home health care is 77 individuals per 1,000, the use varies from 91 per 1,000 in the Northeast to 57 per 1,000 in the West. The Western senior also differed in the quantity and type of service—using more board and care than nursing home or home care.

Ethnic population growth arises primarily from immigration. According to Day (1993), Hispanics are the fastest-growing minority group and will represent 13.5% of the U.S. population by the year 2010. The Census Bureau assumes net future yearly immigration to be 880,000 immigrants, of which persons of Hispanic origin will comprise 37%, while persons of Asian origin will comprise 34%.[4] Further, there are many different types of Asian and Hispanic immigrants within these categories with separate tastes and preferences for housing.

These minority populations are often concentrated within specific metropolitan and state areas. As an example, approximately 22% of California's population is foreign born as compared to only 7.95% of the overall U.S. population. It is clear that ethnic-targeted seniors housing will be important in a number of states, including Arizona, California, Texas, and Florida, which are among the fastest-growing states. According to the U.S. Bureau of the Census (1995), Florida's population had the highest concentration of seniors with 18.4% of the state population, followed by Pennsylvania (15.7%) and Iowa (15.4%).

Seniors housing developers and property managers can benefit from greater sensitivity to the different cultural norms reflected in seniors housing choices. Astute retirement developers and managers of properties should closely monitor not only age cohorts and subcohorts, household composition, and income characteristics, but also ethnicity and geographic area to determine the impact on demand for seniors housing.

3. Many baby boomers—now entering their 50s—will retire or are planning to retire before 65.

Despite the changes in demographics cited above, the real crunch in seniors housing supply for baby-boomers-turned-seniors is likely more than 20 years away.[5] Various U.S. Census Bureau demographic data document the changing needs of this

---

[4] See Day (1993) for more extensive analysis.
[5] In fact, as Schless (1996) reasons, because the age of residents of seniors housing is on average 75 or older, the impact of the large baby boomer cohort on seniors housing will probably not occur until at least 25 years from now.

segment of the U.S. population. Baby boomers comprise the largest segment of the population ever in American history. Between 1946 and 1964, 76 million babies were born in the U.S.. Beginning in 1996, the first of these post-World-War-II babies will be celebrating her 50th birthday and has started to think about her retirement options, including housing. According to Mergenhagen (1994), the median retirement age was 63 during the period from 1985-1990, and is expected to remain the same as baby boomers approach retirement.

Given that the median baby boomer is now only 41, she will have nearly 22 years before retirement in the year 2018 at an expected age of 63. The expected retirement age is increasing overall, although many people choose to retire sooner than age 63. While the great need for service-enriched retirement housing will not occur until well into the next century, baby boomers will begin to have a notable impact on the retirement housing market before the year 2010.

Baby boomer desires for leisure and housing amenities will likely have strong effects on demand for trade-up homes and, at least initially, will create an intensified demand for active adult retirement communities. The U.S. Census Bureau, for example, expects the number of move-up buyers to increase from 2.7 million to 3.1 million by the year 2000, due to the aging of the baby boomers. Many of these future retirees will seek to buy homes closer to their roots and families, though it is difficult to predict exactly which types of housing they will prefer. One likely preference is that a large number of these retirees will move to warmer-weather states, including traditional Sunbelt states such as Florida and Arizona, as well as the Carolinas, Arkansas, Nevada, and elsewhere. According to the Census Bureau, persons aged 55 and over will make up over 45% of Florida's population by the year 2010.[6] Other states, including California, Texas, and New York, expect a growth in their 55-and-over population of up to 30 percent of total residents by 2010.

4. Seniors prefer remaining in their homes, but often move resulting from desire for independence or change in life circumstance.

According to Gibler and Moschis (1996), most senior Americans prefer to live out their lives in the homes they purchased during middle age. The 1992 American Association of Retired Persons (AARP) National Housing Consumer Survey (a telephone survey of 1,507 Americans age 55 and older) revealed that 85% of respondents will prefer to remain in their present homes during retirement and more than three quarters believe that their current residence is where they will always live. Additionally, only 13% of respondents expressed the desire to move and only 8% believe that they will relocate following retirement.

Despite liking where they live, many seniors do move, either resulting from desire or a change in life circumstance. Litwak and Longino (1987) reported that over a preceding 5-year period, approximately 5% of the U.S. population age 60 or over made a long distance move. Many more seniors make local moves, according to

---

[6] See the American Association of Retired Persons' "Understanding Seniors Housing for the 1990s" for additional information on demand.

Gibler and Moschis (1996), to supportive or less maintenance-intensive housing. Creating additional pressures on the need to relocate is the fact that many senior Americans live alone. Saluter (1991) reported that, of the 32 million then-living senior Americans, 30% lived alone. Many of these seniors living alone have supportive-care needs and may not have family- and friend-based support networks. According to Kichen and Roche (1990), the most important factors influencing the decision to move into a retirement residence are the desire to remain independent coupled with the need for health maintenance and other services.[7]

5. Seventy percent of senior households own their own homes, but studies disagree on whether the majority will have saved enough to maintain its preretirement lifestyle during retirement.

There is no clear consensus as to whether or not baby boomers have saved enough for their retirement years. Mitchell (1994) reports that the aggregate net worth of persons over the age of 60 approaches as much as $10 trillion dollars. This large amount of wealth is segmented, however, at the top decile of the retirement population. Although the costs of seniors housing are less than many persons believe, the demand for seniors housing may be reduced by the inability of some people to save for retirement or by the collective delay in beginning retirement saving.

Thurow (1996) describes the "double forty whammy." He points out that, on average, those over 65 receive just over 40 percent of their income from government. And slightly less than 40 percent of the elderly receive 80 percent of their income from government. Thurow also reports that 62 percent receive over half of their income from government and only 35 percent receive money from private pensions.

There are fewer poor people among the elderly than among any other age group in the population. For many, the standard of living improves in retirement because the decline in income is less than the savings from not working. Adjusting for household size, capital gains, taxes (state and federal), noncash benefits like health insurance, and imputed returns on equity in owner-occupied housing, the elderly have a per capita income 67 percent above that of the population as a whole. The average 70-year old is spending 20 percent more in cash income than the average 30 year old. Government spending on the elderly—by itself—gives the elderly per capita income equal to 60 percent of the American average (Thurow, 1996).

According to the American Seniors Housing Association, monthly resident costs in the form of rental fees for congregate seniors housing and assisted living may range from $1,000 to $3,000 ($12,000 to $36,000 annually) or more, including a

---

[7] Although long-term care options are ever present, more than half of the population is not aware of facilities other than nursing homes. Schless (1996) cites a study by the Harvard School of Public Health in cooperation with Louis Harris and Associates that found "that over 60% of the population aged 50 years or older had not heard of a continuing care retirement community, while about half were unfamiliar with assisted living." A further study by the American Seniors Housing Association and Coopers & Lybrand, LLP asserts that those professionals responsible for giving care-giving counseling do not know enough about seniors housing options.

private apartment, meals, and support/care services.[8] The prices for seniors housing vary, of course, by market area and resident care needs. While the median senior household income in 1993 was $17,751 (U.S. Bureau of the Census, 1995), almost 70% of all elderly households are homeowners, and 82% of these households own their homes free and clear, which further bolsters their ability to pay for seniors housing.[9] Covering the costs for seniors housing may be within the means of many of these individuals.

The willingness of baby boomers to purchase or rent relatively-affordable seniors housing is uncertain. A recent poll taken by Del Webb Corporation, for example, found that two thirds of baby boomers believe that they are not yet financially able to retire (U.S. News and World Report, 1996). Other studies contend that baby boomers are saving at only one third the rate necessary to maintain their level of consumption and lifestyle during their retirement years. One explanation for the slow savings rate is that baby boomers typically do not know how much money they will need for retirement years. Increased job insecurity, college tuition payments, and support for elderly parents have led to credit-card debt and high mortgage payments (Cohen, 1996). Pulse Surveys of America discovered that the average American between the ages of 45 and 64 can look forward to an income of just $20,000 a year in retirement including Social Security and pension benefits (Cruz, 1996). Americans fear, furthermore, that Social Security benefits may not be available when it comes time for them to retire. Forty-six percent of baby boomers expect less than one tenth of their retirement income to come from Social Security (U.S. News and World Report, 1996), and 54% do not believe that they will receive any Social Security benefits during retirement (Russell, 1996).

In contrast, some studies contend that baby boomers are saving more than their parents did at the same age. The Federal Reserve Bank of New York found that baby boomers are saving more and their income is considerably larger on an "income per adult-equivalent" basis than that of their parents at the same age (Russell, 1996). A possible explanation may be that baby boomers have had fewer children than their parents, and that baby boomer women are more likely to work than their mothers. Baby boomers are expected to maintain a retirement standard of living comparable to that of their parents, though it may be a lower standard than during their working years.[10]

It has been determined that as the average life expectancy increases, retirees must accumulate more during their working years or may have to continue working through some of their retirement years. In fact, 13% of baby boomers intend to pursue a new full-time career after retiring (U.S. News and World Report, 1996). Life in

---

[8] Entrance fees are sometimes charged in addition to the normal monthly service fees. Entrance fees can be as high as $100,000 for certain continuing care retirement communities, but are usually partially or wholly refundable when the senior dies or leaves the facility. Entrance fees are typically used to reduce the debt load for the retirement facility.

[9] See U.S. Department of Commerce & U.S. Department of Housing and Urban Development (1995).

[10] Russell (1996) comments that "Hard data reveal that Baby Boomers are better prepared for retirement than had been expected by most people except the Boomers themselves. Despite what the headlines say, Baby Boomers are saving money for retirement. This little-known fact is not often reported by the media."

retirement for baby boomers may be expected to last between 25 and 30 years. Baby boomers who expect this increased retirement period are not saving less, but may be struggling in order to save the amounts necessary to maintain their current lifestyles over a longer period of time. If housing wealth is taken into account, they are saving at 84 percent of the rate necessary to maintain their lifestyle during retirement, a rate which is better than many analysts expected (Cohen, 1996).

6. Seniors housing options are varied and will likely evolve to meet the desires of future generations. Home health care shows major growth.

The uncertainty of what kind of housing will appeal to the baby boomer generation in the next 10 to 30 years arises from likely but unpredictable changes in lifestyles and living patterns. Additionally, government policies and programs may shift, leaving seniors with different needs.

According to Gibler and Moschis (1996), desired features in retirement housing include two bedrooms, health care, transportation options, emergency call system, similar-aged residents, and one meal per day. Early in the retirement stage, many seniors may opt for some form of single-family-type home. In fact, retirees are expected to comprise the largest group of home buyers after the turn of the century (Kuhn, 1995). The proportion of elderly who own their homes is expected to increase from 70% to 80% by 2030. Many retirees, however, may elect to move from a larger house because they are no longer raising children in their home, and wish to take advantage of the one-time capital gains tax exclusion opportunity.[11] Many seniors may want space in their homes for home-office use, including computers and other modern office equipment. Some may prefer condos, townhouses, or apartments rather than detached, single-family homes in early retirement. Older seniors (those 75 years and older) will likely choose from among the following service-enriched options:[12]

1. Congregate Seniors Housing—Congregate seniors housing is multifamily housing designed for seniors who pay for some services (such as housekeeping, transportation, and meals) as part of the monthly fee or rental rate, but

---

[11] Many do not choose to move into a continuing care retirement community because current tax law (IRA Revenue Ruling 67-135) precludes deferring some or all of the capital proceeds from the sale of a prior resident when the next move is into a CCRC (Schless, 1996).

[12] Some subcategories of seniors housing that are being developed or have already been developed are:
  1. Congregate housing, without assisted living
  2. Congregate housing, with assisted living
  3. Continuing care retirement community (CCRC)
  4. Stand alone assisted living communities
  5. Assisted living with nursing
  6. Assisted living services for independent living residents
  7. Active adult retirement communities
  8. Alzheimer's/Special care
  9. Nursing homes
  10. Home care agency

who require little, if any, assistance with the activities of daily living. Units have kitchens, but the facility may have a common dining room. Some residents of congregate seniors housing will likely have supportive-care services provided to them by in-house staff or an outside organization, such as a visiting nurses association or home health agency. Congregate seniors housing is not regulated by the federal government, and may or may not be licensed at the state level.

2. Assisted Living—Assisted living residences are designed for frail seniors who need significant assistance with the activities of daily living, but do not require continuous skilled nursing care. Assisted living units may be part of a congregate seniors housing residence or continuing care retirement community (CCRC), or may be contained in a property that supports assisted living units and nursing beds, or may be a freestanding assisted living residence. Residents may have kitchenettes in their apartments, although most residents will receive three meals a day in a common dining area. Assisted living is currently not regulated by the federal government, but is subject to more stringent state licensing and regulation than congregate seniors housing.

3. Continuing Care Retirement Community—Continuing care retirement communities (CCRCs) are senior living complexes which provide a continuum of care including housing, health care, and various supportive services. Healthcare (i.e., nursing) services may be provided directly or through access to affiliated health care facilities. Fees are structured as either refundable (or partially-refundable) entrance fees plus a monthly fee, or as a rental program. Some CCRCs are offered as either condominiums or cooperatives. Continuing care retirement communities are not regulated by the federal government, but are subject to state licensing and regulation in most states.

4. Unlike the previous service-enhanced seniors housing options, active adult retirement communities tend to attract recent retirees, generally aged 55 to 65. These developments primarily focus on amenities such as golf, tennis, swimming, and walking trails, and are geared toward those who are active, fully independent, and affluent. These communities are most prevalent in traditional Sunbelt states where weather permits year-round activity, but are also found in several Mid-Atlantic states and elsewhere in the U.S. (Hogan, 1994).

A recent phenomenon in seniors housing has been the development of new retirement housing in conjunction with special affinity groups, such as retired military officers or retired college faculty/alumni. Since 25 percent of baby boomers attended college—making them more highly educated than other generations—it is quite possible that university-based retirement housing will continue to flourish (Ernest, 1995). Developments with affinity groups tend to be popular with developers and operators

PRIMER ON KEY ISSUES IN SENIORS HOUSING   15

because they may make the marketing and lease-up phase relatively easier than projects without such specialized relationships.[13]

7. Assisted living facilities will continue to fill a unique niche in the spectrum of seniors housing.

The fastest growing category of seniors housing today is the assisted-living segment, which caters to the frail elderly who need assistance with one or more activities of daily living, but do not require continuous nursing care. Hogan (1994) reports that

> experts in this field view the key to assisted living as a combination of small-scale facilities, personal-care options, and a feeling of independence. Successful projects make each resident believe he or she is at home and not in a nursing home.

Many of these residences contain sizable common areas, dining rooms, activity rooms, libraries, and hair salons, and are distinctively non-institutional in appearance.

Hogan (1994) stresses that approximately 21% of people older than 75 years of age require some form of ongoing physical or health-related assistance. Of that number, 65% do not require nursing home services, but need some assistance based on general physical or mental impairments. A great advantage of assisted living is its ability to provide basic services in an environment that is pleasant for the residents and allows them to choose from the various amenities offered.[14]

8. Seniors housing regulation varies significantly by state and impacts market segmentation of products.

Seniors housing is regulated (and in some instances, licensed) at the state level, but is not specifically regulated by the Federal government at this time.[15] The variability across the states has contributed to the lack of a standard nomenclature for seniors housing. Scribner and Dalkowski, in their chapter herein on housing terminology, point out that assisted living (or its equivalent), for example, is regulated

---

[13] Further innovation could include making elderly housing part of a neighborhood infrastructure with service centers for the elderly, much like the role that schools play for children. Such hybrids have led to new classifications for facilities, such as that in Oregon, which has a new code category called "special residential," differing from "institutional" or "residential." Such creative thinking extends into the actual design of amenities for the elderly, such as in a Veterans Affairs nursing home in Virginia, where design for safety and ease of use takes precedence in bathroom design (Brecht, 1996).

[14] ASHA's 1995 Report prints survey results which show that 49 percent of executives indicate that their companies plan to develop stand-alone assisted living communities in 1996, and 31 percent plan to incorporate nursing or independent living residences with assisted living (Brecht, 1996).

[15] It is true, however, as Schless (1996) explains, that federal OSHA requirements related to employees as well as the federal Fair Housing/Americans With Disabilities Act requirements related to residents both compel compliance from seniors housing operators. In its quest to make sure state legislators distinguish between regulation for institutions and non-regulation for seniors housing, ASHA continually provides information to state legislators about the distinctions.

across the country by a host of different state agencies (from Social Service Agencies to Public Health Departments) and is called a plethora of different names such as "supportive residential living centers" (Arizona), "rest homes" (Delaware), "boarding homes" (Maine), "adult residential shelter care homes" (New Mexico), and "personal care facilities" (Texas). In general, the greater the care needs of residents, the more stringent the state regulatory/licenser environment.

Anikeeff and Mueller, in the chapter herein on standardizing housing definitions, show that the definitions for nursing homes in two states—Washington and Oregon—differ and significantly impact the market for less-institutionalized care. If Washington's definitions were applied to the U.S. nursing home population, 15 % of residents could be moved to a lower level of care. However, if Oregon's standards were applied to the U.S. nursing home population, 75 percent of the residents could be served by facilities offering less-intensive care.

Although the federal government does not specifically regulate seniors housing, there are a number of regulatory issues that ultimately affect the construction and operation of these properties. The Americans with Disabilities Act and the Fair Housing Amendments Act, for example, are two federal laws that are quite pertinent to seniors housing. In addition, federal oversight of seniors housing also occurs in the context of environmental issues (such as the reporting of job-related illnesses and injuries), as well as oversight by the U.S. Department of Housing and Urban Development. Many observers believe that increased federal oversight of seniors housing is likely, as more public funds will be used to pay for assisted living.[16] Today, the vast majority of resident days in seniors housing are paid for privately.

9. Seniors housing involves relatively few large companies as compared to the conventional multifamily business. Consolidation and expansion provide opportunities for institutional investment.

Although there are a number of seniors housing owners and managers whose portfolios have grown markedly in the past several years, the industry still has a relatively-small number of owner/operators with national portfolios.[17] The most recent (July 1, 1995) American Seniors Housing Association ranking of the largest 25 owners and managers of market-rate seniors housing, for example, reveals just one owner (Holiday Retirement Corp./Colson & Colson of Salem, OR) with a portfolio in ex-

---

[16] A recent trend is for states to approve Medicaid reimbursements for assisted living services through Medicaid waivers. By doing this the states believe that they can limit the rising cost to Medicaid for nursing home care and will help control overall long-term care costs (Brecht, 1996).

[17] The journal *Contemporary Long Term Care* reports a 1995 study that shows a census of 916 retirement communities with 124,699 units, up from 1986 with 563 communities and 71,985 units (Brecht, 1996). Difficulties in the industry include a growing trend toward smaller groups of independent units, a high turnover as seniors grow into the need for more assisted living, and projection difficulties when an ever-older population delays entrance into continual care communities (Brecht, 1996). Furthermore, as Anikeeff (1996) notes, investment opportunities in the seniors housing market are not without considerable concern because the industry lacks quantifiable risks, standards, and guidelines.

cess of 17,000 units. This same company also has the largest portfolio of seniors housing units managed—just over 18,000 units. The conventional apartment industry, by contrast, features a number of firms with owned portfolios in excess of 50,000 units, and the largest apartment owner—Insignia Financial Group, Inc. of Greenville, SC—has a portfolio of more than 135,000 units. Insignia Financial Group is also the apartment industry's largest manager, with a portfolio in excess of 270,000 units, according to the National Multi Housing Council.

Mueller and Laposa, in their chapter herein on demand for seniors housing, estimate that the current institutional-quality seniors housing market is $86 billion—already greater than the public REIT market. It is predicted to grow by $16 billion in the next four years and grow to $490 billion in the next 35 years.

10. Seniors housing has a surprisingly long history of meeting the needs of the elderly.

Seniors housing is not a new business. In reality, seniors housing has existed in the U.S. for almost 100 years. And while most of the earliest operators were not-for-profit organizations, even the presence of for-profit operators can be traced back at least thirty years. According to the ASHA, religiously-affiliated organizations (not for profit) first met the housing and health needs of older Americans. Beginning in the late 1800s, these religious and fraternal organizations developed long-term care facilities, including the "care for life" concept—now generally referred to as "turnover of assets." Under this model, a resident would bequeath all of her personal assets in exchange for shelter, necessities, and health care to be provided for the remainder of the person's life.

During the Great Depression many of the religious-sponsored retirement homes were closed due to financial pressures. Counties and cities stepped in to fill the need and provided minimal shelter and services for the low-income elderly. According to ASHA, "these almshouses, poor houses, and county homes were espoused as the caring way of utilizing modest tax dollars for the aged" during the Depression (ASHA, *Senior Housing Finance: Trends and Prospects*, p. 7).

From the end of the Second World War through the 1970s, seniors communities sponsored by church-related and other not-for-profit organizations continued to account for the vast majority of non-government-sponsored seniors housing. Beginning in the early 1970s, however, seniors housing has increasingly been developed and operated by proprietary seniors housing firms.

CONCLUSION AND SUMMARY

Seniors housing is a practical, cost-effective, and consumer-friendly version of long-term care that is often overlooked. A significant number of aging Americans have the means today to pay for seniors housing, but due to limited familiarity with these communities or the false assumption that the related costs are prohibitive, those requiring long-term care often overlook seniors housing.

The influences of the baby boom age cohort imply that the number of U.S. seniors is increasing at a growing rate. The group is more diverse and is relatively affluent. The challenge for seniors housing developers is to identify and target specific submarkets based on careful market analysis. Thriving in the segmented markets of the 21st century will demand this careful analysis and customer targeting by seniors housing developers. In sum, seniors housing is a need-driven—not finance-driven—business seen as an extension of the hospital (health care) and hotel (service) industries.

ACKNOWLEDGMENTS

The authors gratefully acknowledge the helpful comments, criticisms, and suggestions of David S. Schless, executive director of the American Seniors Housing Association, along with the research work of Karen Bartashunas, Jan Deihl, and Lissa Horowitz, as well as participants of a session on seniors housing at the 1996 American Real Estate Society (ARES) meetings.

REFERENCES

American Association of Retired Persons (AARP), Understanding Seniors Housing for the 1990s, Washington, DC: AARP, 1992.
Anikeeff, Michael A., "Seniors Housing—Defining the Business," The REIT Report, Autumn 1996, 38-41.
"Baby Boomers," *U.S. News and World Report*, February 19, 1996, 22.
Birkett, Charles, "Moving into Assisted Living," *Nursing Homes* 45:2 (February 1996), 22.
Brecht, Susan B., "Trends in the Retirement Housing Industry," Urban Land, November 1996, 33-39.
Cohen, Susan, "The American Anxiety Dream," *The Washington Post Magazine*, February 25, 1996, 13-31.
Cruz, Humberto, "Saving a Generation; Baby Boomers Face Dearth of Savings on Road to Retirement," *Sun-Sentinel*, Fort Lauderdale, FL, January 7, 1996, 1F.
Day, J. C., Population Projections for States by Age, Sex, Race, and Hispanic Origin: 1993 to 2020, U. S. Bureau of the Census, Current Population Reports, U. S. Government Print Office, Washington, DC, 1993.
Ernest, Judy, "Boomers Reach the Big 5-0; When This 76-Million-Strong Group Itches, the Country Scratches," *The Plain Dealer*, December 31, 1995, 11.
Gamzon, M., "Emerging Seniors Housing Industry Depends on Political Scene, Expects Growth in 21st Century," *National Real Estate Investor*, February, 1995.
Gibler, K. M. and G. Moschis, "What Do Senior Citizens Want? A Review of the 1992 AARP National Housing Consumer Survey," Working paper presented at the 1996 ARES Annual Meeting.
Goodman, J. L. and M. R. Grupe, "Top Ten Surprises About Ownership and Financing of Rental Housing," *Real Estate Finance* 11:4 (Winter 1995), 42-48.
Hogan, John J., "An Overview of the Senior Housing Market," *Appraisal Journal* 62:1 (January 1994), 47.

Keating, D. M. and G. L. Brace, "Appraising Continuing Care Retirement Centers: The Income Approach," *Appraisal Journal* 62:4 (October 1994), 546.

Keefe, Robert, "Senior Group Housing Industry Comes of Age," *St. Petersburg Times,* January 14, 1996, 1H.

Kelleher, Nancy, "Elder Care Comes of Age; Assisted Living Facilities are Wave of Future," *The Boston Herald*, April 7, 1995.

Kichen, J. M. and J. L. Roche, "Life-Care Resident Preferences,": In R. D. Chellis and P. J. Grayson (eds.), Life-Care: A Long-Term Solution?, (1987) Lexington, MA: Lexington, 49-60.

Kuhn, Susan E., "Where to Move When You're Ready to Kick Back," *Fortune*, July 24, 1995, 86.

Litwak, E. and C. F. Longino, Jr., "Migration Patterns among the Elderly," *Gerontologist* 27 (1987), 266-272.

Lehman, H. Jane, "Aging Baby Boomers' Housing Problems; Existing Homes Can't Meet Needs of Tomorrow's Elderly," *The Washington Post*, September 30, 1989, F3.

Lehman, H. Jane, "Rules Changing For Seniors-Only Housing," *The Orlando Sentinel*, April 9, 1995, J1.

Mergenhagen, H., "Rethinking Retirement," American Demographics (June 1994), 28-34.

"Mixed Prospects for Baby Boomers in Retirement," *Research Alert,* September, 16, 1994.

Mitchell, Susan, "How Boomers Save," *American Demographics* (September 1994), 27-28.

Russell, Cheryl, "Baby Boomers on Target for Retirement Savings," *The Times Union*, Albany, NY, January 7, 1996, G1.

Saluter, A. F., U.S. Bureau of the Census (1991), Marital Status and Living Arrangements, March 1990, Current Population Reports, Series P-20, no. 450, Washington, DC: U.S. GPO.

Schless, David S., "Challenging 100 Commonly Held Assumptions About Seniors Housing," National Real Estate Investor, November 1996.

Thurow, L.C., The Future of Capitalism: How Today's Economic Forces Shape Tomorrow's World, New York: William Morrow and Company, 1996.

U. S. Bureau of the Census (1993), Profiles of America's Elderly, Living Arrangements of the Elderly, Washington, DC: U.S. GPO.

U.S. Bureau of the Census, Statistical Abstract of the United States: 1994 (114th edition) U.S. Government Printing Office, Washington, DC, 1994.

U.S. Bureau of the Census, Statistical Abstract of the United States: 1995 (115th edition) U.S. Government Printing Office, Washington, DC, 1995.

U.S. Department of Commerce & U.S. Department of Housing and Urban Development, American Housing Survey for the United States in 1993 (1995), current Housing Reports H150/93), Washington, DC: U.S. Government Printing Office.

2

OVERVIEW OF SENIORS HOUSING

Charles M. Sexton
Director of Real Estate Research
Unum Life Insurance Company of America

ABSTRACT:

The purpose of this chapter is to give a broad overview of seniors housing in the U.S. An acronym nomenclature is suggested to sort out the wide variety of seniors housing offerings. A statistical snapshot of the seniors is set forth. A brief description of the seniors housing industry is given, including history, governmental regulation, and current resident costs. Key facts and trends in seniors housing are identified, including demographics, property types, healthcare, legislation, and financing. Finally, there is a very brief statement of broad conclusions.

1. VARIETIES OF SENIORS HOUSING

A bewildering array of seniors housing options and acronyms dots the landscape and is evolving rapidly, filling the continuum from so-called independent living (just an apartment) to hospice. Here is a fairly common classification scheme:

ILF-Independent Living Facility

A seniors-restricted multifamily apartment complex. When ILFs were first developed, minimal or no services beyond building and grounds maintenance were provided. Subsequently, the Fair Housing Act required that certain unspecified facilities and services be provided for seniors in order to maintain an otherwise illegal age restriction limiting residents to those 55 and over. This created confusion and litigation over what sorts of facilities and services were necessary. The "Housing for Older Persons Act of 1995" amended the Fair Housing Act to remove the facilities and services requirement, and permits residency restriction to persons 55 and older, provided that at least 80% of the occupied units are occupied by at least one person who is 55 or older. Nonetheless, seniors market forces have caused many ILFs to bolster their array of services, short of providing a common dining facility, which is the recategorization threshold to CSH, as noted below.

CSH-Congregate Seniors Housing

A seniors multifamily complex with kitchens or kitchenettes in the units as well as a common dining facility. Limited services such as housekeeping, transportation, and recreational activities are usually provided. Also known as ACLF (Adult Congregate Living Facility).

ALF-Assisted Living Facility

A seniors living complex designed to accommodate the frail elderly, with staff and programs that assist residents with Activities of Daily Living (ADLs). There are many indices and lists of activities used to define and assess ADLs, and most include getting out of bed, bathing, dressing, mobility, feeding oneself, and continence. In addition, there are Instrumental Activities of Daily Living (IADLs)—more complex tasks than ADLs. IADLs usually include handling personal finances, preparing meals, shopping, housework, getting outside, using the telephone, and taking medications. ALF units may have a small refrigerator, but usually no kitchen, as there is a common dining facility.

SNF-Skilled Nursing Facility

Commonly known as nursing homes, these are institutions which provide licensed skilled nursing care and related services for patients who require nursing or rehabilitative services.

OVERVIEW OF SENIORS HOUSING 23

CCRC-Continuing Care Retirement Community

A seniors living complex designed to provide a continuum of living accommodations and care—from independent living through skilled nursing—within a single community.

The foregoing have a large real estate or housing element to them, and are generally known and used in the seniors housing industry today to categorize (and regulate) what is really a continuum. They are listed in order of decreasing magnitudes of the real estate element and increasing magnitudes of the service and care elements, from ILF to CCRC. This arrangement also results in a listing by increasing order of government regulation. Appendix A contains a table of selected data on the seniors housing industry, organized by these property types. The seniors housing industry is represented by a number of associations, which are excellent sources of further information. These are listed in Appendix B.

Not listed above are adult day care, home health care, sub-acute care facilities, hospitals (including rehabilitation hospitals), and hospices. These businesses compete with seniors housing at various points in the continuum, but are not listed here as varieties of seniors housing because they are primarily service businesses—not real estate—and their residential element is usually quite temporary.

2. SNAPSHOT OF THE SENIORS

Seniors have been defined for quite some time by the Bureau of the Census—and by most of the rest of us—as persons 65 years of age and older. The age 65 break point apparently derives from the U.S. Social Security Act of 1935.

As of July 1, 1994, the resident U.S. population was 260 million, and 12.7% of us—a little more than 33 million—were seniors, age 65 or older (Bureau of the Census, 1995, table 14).[1] That is the population equivalent of a California (31.4 million) plus a Maine (1.2 million) or two, all full of seniors (table 27)—except that seniors were spread out, living all around the U.S.. The largest number of seniors were in California (3.35 million), but they comprised only 10.6% of California's population (table 34). The highest concentration of seniors was in Florida, at 18.4% of that state's total population, and the lowest concentration was in Alaska, at 4.6% of its total population (table 34). Here is a table of the top 11 states by percent of seniors:

Table 1: Seniors as a percentage of state population, 1994, top 11 states

State:	FL	PA	IA	RI	WV	AK	SD	ND	NE	MO	MA
% seniors	18.4%	15.7%	15.4%	15.2%	15.2%	14.9%	14.7%	14.6%	14.1%	14.1%	14.1%

Source: Bureau of the Census, 1995, table 34.

---

[1] The most easily accessible and reliable current U.S. demographic numbers are found in the *Statistical Abstract of the United States 1995* (Bureau of the Census, 1995). All of the demographic information in this overview is from that source when a numbered table is referenced without further explanation.

The 1993 median household income of seniors was $17,751 in contrast to the overall 1993 median household income (including seniors) of $31,241 (table 725). 11.1% of seniors' households had incomes of $50,000 or more in contrast to 28.6% of total households (including seniors) (table 725). 24.8% of seniors households had incomes of $10,000 or less in contrast to 14.3% of total households (including seniors) (table 725). Another way of understanding the income paucity of seniors is the statistic that in 1993, fully 35.9% of seniors households were in the lowest income quintile (20%) of U.S. households while only 7.8% were in the highest income quintile (table 728). Also in 1993, only 10.3% of independently-living seniors households had savings and investments (not including their homes) of more than $25,000 (U.S. Department of Commerce & U.S. Department of Housing and Urban Development, 1995, table 7-12).

These income and wealth statistics indicate that seniors as a group are not an affluent market, although their significantly lower incomes may be more stable than the general population, because of the social security and pension elements, and their living expenses may be less, given their post child-raising, household formation, and mortgage status. In addition, they may be more willing to spend down their assets than younger age groups. So they probably have relatively more purchasing power than their low income and savings suggest.

Here is a convenient breakdown of seniors age groups:

Table 2: Seniors age groups, 1994

Age Group	% of Total Population	#	% female
65 to 74	7.2%	18,712,000	55.7%
75 to 84	4.2%	10,925,000	61.5%
85+	1.4%	3,522,000	72.2%

Sources: table 14; author

What about seniors housing? The Bureau of the Census and HUD jointly publish their American Housing Survey every odd year about 2 years after their survey. The latest available edition is called the American Housing Survey for the United States in 1993, and it reveals that seniors who were not institutionalized (i.e., not living in "group quarters," including nursing homes, assisted living, congregate and other facilities where common meals are provided to unrelated residents) lived in 22,329,000 housing units (U.S. Department of Commerce & U.S. Department of Housing and Urban Development, 1995, table 2-9). Here is a breakdown of those units:

Table 3: Housing Arrangements of Non-Institutionalized Seniors, 1993

Units with senior NOT head of household (5%):[2]			1,891,000
Units OWNED by senior head of household (70%):			15,767,000
physical structure		ownership structure	
single-family, detached	12,776,000	co-ops	137,000
single-family, attached	699,000	condos	781,000
2 to 49 unit structure	896,000	fee	14,849,000
50+ unit structure	235,000		
mobile home	1,161,000		
Units RENTED by senior head of household (20%):			4,671,000
physical structure		subsidized/non-subsidized	
single-family, detached	906,000	government subsidized	1,350,000
single-family, attached	300,000	non-subsidized	3,321,000
2 to 49 unit structure	2,321,000		
50+ unit structure	1,039,000		
mobile home	105,000		

Sources: U.S. Department of Commerce & U.S. Department of Housing and Urban Development, 1995, tables 2-9, 7-1 and 7-12.

In addition to the seniors living in the 22,329,000 housing units listed above, in 1990 there were 1,590,763 seniors living in nursing homes (Bureau of the Census, 1993). Further, in 1991 there were 900,000 seniors living in assisted living units, 186,000 seniors living in continuing care retirement communities, and 281,000 seniors living in congregate living communities (Feinberg, 1993).

Regarding mobility, over 4% of the seniors' households—884,000 of them—moved into their housing unit within the last year, and 78% of those moved within the same state (U.S. Department of Commerce & U.S. Department of Housing and Urban Development, 1995, table 7-10).

The average annual shelter expenditure of a senior consumer unit in 1993 was $3,440, which is the lowest average annual shelter expenditure of any age cohort over age 25 (table 718). Shelter expenditure is ownership or rental cost, not including utilities or household operations, supplies, furnishings, or appliances.

---

[2] Presumably the senior is living in the home of a younger relative.

3. THE SENIORS HOUSING INDUSTRY

A. History

In the 1800s, religiously-affiliated non-profit groups first recognized a need in this country for facilities for seniors who could no longer live in their own homes or apartments and were not being cared for by their families. They began "turnover of assets" homes where a participant would turn over all of his or her assets in exchange for shelter and care for the balance of his or her life. The majority of these homes closed during the Great Depression for financial reasons, and cities and counties began to take up the slack with almshouses, poor houses, and county homes for the aged. State governments and then the federal government entered the field, with HUD section 8 independent living seniors housing and section 202 residential care facilities loan guarantees proliferating in the 1970s and being utilized by for-profit entities. Until the late 1970s, the vast majority of non-government-sponsored seniors housing continued to be church related or sponsored by other non-profit organizations (American Seniors Housing Association, 1992).

In the 1980s a boom in seniors housing production by for-profit entities accompanied the boom in other commercial real estate. And just as other commercial real estate crashed in the late 1980s and early 1990s, so did seniors housing. The RTC has only recently liquidated most of its holdings of seniors housing, most of which were congregate housing—one of the hottest trends and biggest failures of the 1980s (Bergsman, 1995). This phenomenon is succinctly summarized by the American Seniors Housing Association (ASHA) (1994):

> Beginning in the early 1980s, profit-motivated companies began to develop and manage a wide range of seniors housing residences. Congregate seniors housing ... became the predominant property type of these for-profit firms. The rapid development of new congregate residences in the early-to-mid-1980s highlighted several serious conceptual flaws that led to numerous troubled seniors housing properties across the U.S.. The most basic problem was that few of these residences were able to attract the 65-to-75 year old, recently-retired couples that most had counted on to comprise the majority of their tenant base.... Many properties were overbuilt and overleveraged, and experienced significantly longer than anticipated lease-up periods.... By the late 1980s, a plethora of seniors housing residences were financially troubled, and an industry-wide shakeout began in earnest.

The seniors housing industry has now realized that seniors housing is predominantly driven by the needs of seniors who have lost a spouse or some ADL competencies. Seniors housing has become a combination of housing, services, personal care (assistance with ADLs), and healthcare, instigated by the needs of seniors who are being compelled by their changing circumstances to change their lives. For the most part, seniors housing is now marketed to the families of seniors, or to other controllers such as hospital discharge administrators or HMOs, rather than to the seniors themselves.

B. Federal Regulation

The federal government regulates seniors housing either through civil rights legislation (the Fair Housing Act), direct rental subsidies (HUD Section 8), financing guarantee requirements (HUD Section 232), federal income tax-exempt financing provisions (IRC Section 142 (d)), federal low income housing tax credit provisions (IRC Section 42), or Medicare or Medicaid "reimbursement" requirements. The federal government's involvement in seniors housing is a subject far beyond the scope of this overview, but it is quite important, particularly for ILFs built in reliance upon federal rent subsidies, and at the other end of the continuum for SNFs relying heavily upon Medicare and Medicaid reimbursements. ALFs are almost 100% private pay today, but Medicaid reimbursements have begun to occur under a so-called federal "waiver" option which a state may adopt.

C. Medicare and Medicaid

Medicare is the federal health insurance program for seniors (age 65 and older), using all federal money and administered by the Health Care Finance Agency (HCFA-"hic-fa") within the Department of Health and Human Services. Medicare reimburses providers of health care for their "costs," including fixed overhead costs (e.g., real estate), under a complex set of federal rules. In contrast, Medicaid is a shared federal/state health insurance program for indigents (including seniors who have "spent down" or otherwise suitably arranged their income and assets). The federal government provides about 50% of the money for Medicaid and sets some basic regulations. The states provide the other 50% of the money and have fairly broad discretion to choose various federal program options, to adopt unique statewide rules, and to administer and enforce Medicaid. Medicaid expenditures for SNFs have been growing rapidly, and totaled approximately $26 billion in federal fiscal year 1993 (U.S. GAO, 1994). Since 1987 the federal government has mandated that the states switch their method of paying providers of Medicaid healthcare from a retrospective Medicare-like cost-based reimbursement system to a prospective system based upon acuity levels. Some states have accomplished this switch to varying degrees and others have not. Understanding Medicaid is a state-by-state encounter.

D. State Regulation

The states regulate seniors housing in many other ways beyond the Medicaid system. States regulate ILFs in the same ways as other apartments, i.e., through building codes and other land use regulations at the development stage, and through various ongoing health and safety requirements. Some states add varying layers of regulation for CSHs. All states add layers of regulation for ALFs, SNFs, and CCRCs. Of the latter three, ALFs are the newest variety of seniors housing and to date the least regulated. SNFs have been regulated for a long time, and are highly regulated in all states for health and safety reasons, and in numerous states are only allowed to exist in the first place if they obtain a Certificate of Need (CON), thus creating a protected state market for their services. Some states have advanced their regulation of ALFs to the CON stage.

There is now a regulatory tension between ALF regulation and SNF regulation, because ALFs are "stealing" SNF customers. Where states draw the "line" between legally permissible ALF residents and SNF residents is a market share battle. The rationale for drawing a "line" is to protect those who need full SNF care from being placed in an ALF where such a level of care is not available, or at least not regulated to assure its availability. In some states, such as Virginia, the SNFs have prevailed in this regulatory battle and a "bright" line limiting permissible residents for ALFs has been established. In other states, such as Oregon, a blurred line has been established deliberately to allow unregulated market forces freer play (Bianculli, 1994). Most states add another layer of regulation to CCRCs. To the extent that many CCRCs "guarantee" a continuum of care for their residents, an insurance element is added, and CCRCs are regulated by the State Department of Insurance (as well as everybody else).

E. Resident Costs

The arrangement of the foregoing list of seniors housing varieties from ILF to CCRC also results in a listing by increasing order of resident cost, as would be expected from an increasing order of services and care. Resident costs within any single variety of seniors housing vary considerably depending upon location, age of facility, size of living quarters, and tack-on service fees. Typical monthly resident costs in late 1995 for 1980s construction one-bedroom units in comparable moderately-priced locations might be:

Table 4: Typical Monthly Resident Cost of 1 Bedroom Units

ILF	$1,000
CSH	$1,150
ALF	$1,650
SNF	$2,050
CCRC[3]	$1,350 (plus entrance fee)

Source: author's telephone survey

ALFs and SNFs are typically only rental facilities. ILFs and CSHs are usually rental facilities, but may also be structured as owned by residents as condominiums, cooperatives, or fee simple. CCRCs are usually rental facilities, with or without a refundable entrance fee.

---

[3] ILF accommodations only.

Entrance fees for a CCRC are usually a hefty amount, ranging from $50,000 to $150,000 or more. They may be anywhere from 100% to 50% refundable when the resident leaves the facility, whether voluntarily or upon death. CCRC residents must also pay monthly service fees, but the monthly service fees are marketed as less than they would be without the entrance fee. The entrance fees are used by the CCRC owner to retire all or most financing on the facilities, and the monthly fees are said to be reduced to the extent that there is no or little need for cash for debt service.

The marketing pitch for the CCRC entrance fee derived from new residents is a limited guarantee of continuing care for life and a tax angle. A CCRC is a campus containing an ILF, an ALF, and an SNF. Entrance-fee-paying residents, who begin in the ILF (which may be called an ILF, but more often than not is a CSH), are guaranteed a space in the ALF or SNF when required. If the ALF or SNF is full when needed, temporary space is guaranteed somewhere in the facility. Although monthly fee amounts in the facilities are not fixed at any guaranteed level, the operator agrees to use the entrance fee to cover monthly fees that the resident is unable to cover from the resident's income, and the operator usually further agrees to continue to subsidize monthly fees when the entrance fee is used up, provided that the resident has not deliberately dissipated his or her income producing assets. Sometimes the operator may guarantee the resident a certain number of days per year in the SNF—up to a lifetime maximum—without any increase in the resident's monthly fees. The key for the CCRC operator is to qualify residents both financially and physically. The key for the resident is to qualify the operator and to read the fine print in the CCRC contract.

The tax angle of the CCRC entrance fee is as follows. By "depositing" the entrance fee with the operator—who uses it to reduce debt service and then to cut monthly fees commensurately—the resident is in effect using the before-tax income from his or her asset to pay his or her monthly fees. For example, if a seniors housing resident had $100,000 and put it in a bank account earning 6% or $6,000 per year, and the resident were in an overall income tax bracket of 40%, then the resident would have only $3,600 of after-tax income to pay toward seniors housing rent. If, instead, the resident deposited the $100,000 as an entrance fee with the seniors housing landlord, and the seniors housing landlord put it in the same bank account earning 6% and used the $6,000 interest earned to pay $6,000 interest owed on debt service to the landlord's mortgage holder (thus offsetting the $6,000 interest earned with $6,000 interest paid and incurring no tax liability), then the landlord could reduce the resident's rent by $6,000. This tax angle has not been checked by your author with the IRS, but it is claimed to exist by at least some CCRC operators.

4. KEY FACTS AND TRENDS IN SENIORS HOUSING

A. Demographics.

This graph shows recent Census population projections (middle series) by age cohort:

Figure 1: U.S. Population Projections by Age Cohort

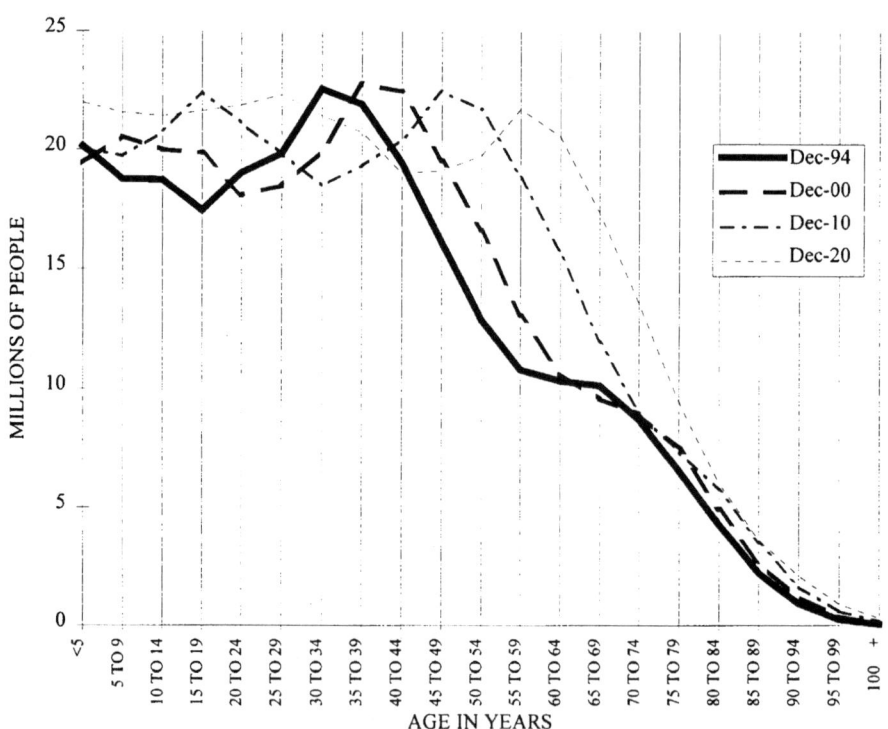

Source: DRI/McGraw Hill on-line database of Bureau of the Census data, 1994

Following is a list of seniors-related demographic trends gleaned from Figure 1 above, the Statistical Abstract of the United States 1995 (source of the table references below), and other sources, as noted:

1. The U.S. population is indeed "graying." The median age of the entire population has been increasing since it was first measured in the 1850 Census at 18.9 years. It was 32.8 years in 1990 and is projected to be 35.5 years by 2000 and 39 years by 2050 (table 13). Overall, the rate of increase in the seniors population is escalating. This rate of increase, through at least 2020, is higher than the rate of increase of any other age cohort except the leading edge of the baby boomers (now at 48 years old). The average annual compound rates of increase in members of the 65+ age cohort through 2020 are:

Table 5: Projected Increase Rates of the Seniors Population

Years	Average Annual Rate of Increase
1994-2000	1.05%
2000-2010	2.14%
2010-2020	4.87%

Sources: DRI/McGraw Hill on-line database of Bureau of the Census data, 1994; author's calculations

The first official baby boomer hits 65 and becomes a senior in 2011, and the boomer generation is generally considered to be 19 years wide—those born from 1946 to 1964. These facts bode quite well for increasing demand for seniors housing.

2. Within this rapidly growing seniors cohort, there is an anomaly. A subcohort, born between this century's two world wars from about 1925 to 1940 (now aged 56 to 71 in 1996), is relatively flat. It has approximately the same numbers in each year of the subcohort, so that as this subcohort ages, succeeding age subcohorts decline in numbers because of deaths. Thus, there is a declining subcohort moving through an overall rapidly increasing and larger seniors cohort. This anomaly is most easily seen in Figure 1 above by noting how the 65 to 69 age subcohort actually decreases from 1994 to 2000, whereas all other seniors subcohorts increase during this same time period, resulting in an overall seniors population increase of 1.05%.

Following is a table showing the dip periods from the year when various subcohorts of the overall 65+ seniors cohort begin to decline in numbers to the year when each subcohort has once again reached its previous high:

Table 6: Projected Dip Years of Seniors Subcohorts

Age Subcohort	Dip Years	Years Duration of Dip	Population at Start of Dip (in millions)	Year of Bottom of Dip	Population at Bottom of Dip (in millions)
65-69	1994-2006	12	10.14	2002	9.56
70-74	1996-2010	14	8.97	2007	8.55
75-79	2004-2015	11	7.66	2010	7.38
80-84	2012-2019	7	5.79	2015	5.62
85-89	2017-2023	6	3.72	2020	3.64
90-94	2022-2026	4	2.17	2024	2.15
95+	No Dip	0	N/A	N/A	N/A

Sources: DRI/McGraw Hill on-line database of Bureau of the Census data, 1994; author's calculations

The subcohort dips become shorter in duration and much less significant in numbers as the subcohorts get older.

To the extent that seniors housing owners or developers are marketing to certain seniors subcohorts, they may be rudely surprised if they are relying upon the rosy growing numbers of all seniors and not concentrating upon these subcohort anomalies. For example, ILF developers relying upon newly-minted 65-69 year old retirees are advised that these folks are decreasing in numbers right now and will continue to do so through 2002. Demographics alone will not carry their new projects to success, as much of the generalized hype might indicate. As noted, the opposite is true.

3. The older the residual subcohort within the overall 65+ seniors cohort, the higher the rate of increase through 2010, but the lower the absolute numbers. In other words, the older elderly are increasing at a faster rate, but in fewer absolute numbers, than the younger elderly. This pattern holds with only slight anomalies well beyond 2010. Here is a table:

Table 7: Projected Increases of Certain Residual Seniors Subcohorts

Residual Subcohort[4]	Overall Rate of Increase 1994 through 2010	Absolute Increase 1994 through 2010 (in millions)
65+	21%	6.94
75+	34%	4.82
85+	73%	2.51
95+	166%	.48

Sources: DRI/McGraw Hill on-line database of Bureau of the Census data, 1994; author's calculations.

Built into these numbers are increasing life expectancies. The current life expectancy from birth in 1995 for males and females combined was 76.3 years, and the Census projects that to increase to 77.9 years by 2010 (table 114). Life expectancies are increasing for older Americans, too. The life expectancy of a 65-year-old male was 14.2 years in 1980 and 15.4 years in 1992. For a 65-year-old female, life expectancy was 18.4 years in 1980 and 19.2 years in 1992 (table 116). Modest life expectancy increases are projected by the Census, and some private demographers are projecting dramatic life expectancy increases.

---

[4] Note that these sub-cohorts are not mutually exclusive ranges, but are overlapping; e.g., 65+ includes 75+, 85+ and 95+; 75+ includes 85+ and 95+; and 85+ includes 95+.

OVERVIEW OF SENIORS HOUSING 33

These numbers bode well for those portions of the seniors housing industry serving older seniors, but they also indicate that older seniors are still a relatively small market niche. In the real estate industry, great optimism about small market niches can lead quickly to oversupply.

4. Increased numbers of elderly seniors means increased numbers of people needing assistance with ADLs and IADLs. There were approximately 8 million seniors requiring ADL or IADL assistance in the mid-1980s (Taeuber, 1993). As the seniors population increases, and the older seniors cohort expands more than the younger seniors cohort, the need for ADL and IADL assistance will grow. The percentage of persons needing ADL assistance increases with age, as shown in this table:

Table 8: Percentage of Persons Needing ADL Assistance, by Age

Age:	16-64	65-69	70-74	75-79	80-84	85+
% Needing ADL Assistance:	2%	9%	11%	20%	31%	50%

Source: Bureau of the Census, 1995.

The increasing proportion of seniors needing ADL assistance as they age, combined with an aging population, means strong demand growth for ALFs. For example, if these ADL percentages in Table 8 and population projections in Figure 1 hold, then the following table shows the evolving potential ALF market:

Table 9: Potential ALF Market

Year	# Seniors (in millions)	# Needing ADL Assistance (in millions)	Absolute Annual Increase in # Needing ADL Assistance	Average Annual % Increase in # Needing ADL Assistance
1994	33.17	13.24		
2000	35.32	14.23	165,000	1.21%
2010	40.10	15.57	134,000	.90%
2020	53.35	21.17	559,000	3.12%

Sources: DRI/McGraw Hill on-line database of Bureau of the Census data, 1994; author's calculations.

Note that although this market is increasing rapidly now, its rate of increase stalls somewhat as the 70-79 year old sub-cohorts move through their dip years (see Table 6 above), but then takes off around 2010 as the first baby boomers become seniors.

5. In 1970, 38% of the total labor force was female. By 1994 that percentage had increased to 46%, and the Census projects an increase to 48% by 2005 (table 627). The participation rate of women in the labor force has increased from 43.3% in 1970 to 58.8% in 1994, and the Census projects an increase to 63.2% in 2005 (table 627). Traditionally, a high percentage of caregivers for non-institutionalized seniors has been unpaid women relatives (daughters or daughters-in-law). The increased female workforce and participation rate has reduced—and is projected to continue to reduce—the availability of home-based caregivers for seniors, thus increasing the need for non-home-based seniors care (i.e., seniors housing) at the same time as increasing numbers of seniors enter the care-needing years.

6. The percentage of seniors who live alone has increased from 25.4% in 1970 to 27.8% in 1994 (table 81). This trend—if it is one—is not easily interpreted. Single living requires more housing than group living, so on its face, this trend should bolster demand for seniors housing. This trend has been attributed to women outliving their husbands, however, it may indicate only a change in household composition, not the number of households. Increasing divorce rates have also been identified as a cause of more singles, but this may also mean only a shifting of household compositions, and not an increase in the number of households. Furthermore, these causes, whatever their import, may be ameliorating or even reversing, as women have begun to have the same stressful life-shortening careers as men, and as the economic penalties of divorce seem to escalate and militate against it.

7. The median retirement age has declined from 67 in 1950-55 to 63 in 1985-90 (Mergenhagen, 1994). This trend, if it continues, bodes well for seniors housing of the "retirement community" ILF type; however, this trend may be stalled or reversing for economic reasons. Medicare and Social Security are under rather severe financial pressure to cut back or postpone benefits for retirees, and the current savings of potential American retirees are notoriously inadequate (Karpel, 1995; Peterson, 1996). The Associated Press recently reported that the fifth annual Workplace Pulse survey conducted in November, 1996 by the Marketing Research Institute for the Employers Council on Flexible Compensation and Colonial Life & Accident Insurance Company found that "[w]orking Americans have improved their savings for retirement, but not nearly enough to achieve the income they want...the retirement savings of workers in every age group will fall far below their average annual retirement income expectations."

8. The average age of residents in all types of seniors housing, excluding ILFs, is about the same—today about 83 years. Three quarters of these residents are female. The seniors housing market segment today, again excluding ILFs, is generally considered to be age 75+. The 75+ age cohort numbered about 14.69 million people in December, 1995, and is projected by the Bureau of the Census (middle series) to increase 14% over the next 5 years to 16.77 million

people in the year 2000, then another 14% over the following 10 years to 19.13 million people in the year 2010, then another 17% over the following 10 years to 22.44 million people in the year 2020, and then another 44% over the following 10 years to 32.2 million people in the year 2030. The subcohort born from 1925 to 1940 will hit age 75 in 2000, causing a 15-year slow down in the growth rate of the age 75+ cohort (and even a moving dip not only in growth rate but in actual numbers in some age 75+ subcohorts), but the growth rate will pick up after 2015 and then really take off when the first boomer hits 75 in 2021. The point is that potential age 75+ seniors housing residents are increasing in numbers, and are projected to do so for at least the next 35 years, with the biggest jumps in numbers to come after 2020. Increasing demand is about as much of a given as a prognosticator could hope for. If there is to be a market problem in the future demand for seniors housing, it will take a new and unanticipated plague or cultural shift, which either kills large numbers of seniors or changes the cultural milieu such that the burgeoning numbers of seniors will not need seniors housing. Expanded home health care and adult day care are forces to be reckoned with in driving the latter result. Also, the temporary slowdown of the growth rate of the age 75+ sub-cohort from 2000 to 2015 does have the potential to discombobulate the demand side of the market. As for the supply side of seniors housing, overbuilding is always a risk—as it is with all real estate—but especially in a specialized market like seniors housing where there is very strong overall demand growth and industry optimism, but potential disruptions in age subcohorts and, as always, geographic segments.

B. Need Driven Market-More than Real Estate

The seniors housing industry learned from the 1980s CSH overbuilding and unsuccessful marketing to the newly retired that seniors housing is a needs-driven market, not a lifestyle choice. Seniors generally are not enticed from their homes or apartments into seniors housing by the prospect of a better life, but are generally pushed there by the death of a spouse or the need for assistance with ADLs or healthcare. Seniors housing has become much more than real estate. It has become a service and healthcare business.

C. Aging in Place

Seniors housing is often described as a continuum or progression which an aging person is expected to follow. CCRCs are built and marketed on this theory. Yet the average age of residents in CSHs, ALFs, SNFs, and CCRCs is essentially the same, and operators of each of these varieties of housing believe that for the most part their residents age in place and eventually die there; that there really is no progression of an individual from one facility to another. There is really a segmentation of the same population: some seniors are able to live and die in CSHs, whereas others live and die in SNFs. All of the CSH and ALF operators with whom I have spoken have stated emphatically that their goal is not to keep seniors until they are ready for an SNF or a hospice, but to provide a residential environment for them until they die. They claim to be largely successful, and also state that when they do fail and a resident must be moved to an SNF or hospice, that resident does not live much longer. An exception to this aging-in-place philosophy and practice may be noted in those operators who have different varieties of seniors housing on the same campus.

D. Congregate Housing

The foreclosure and reselling of CSH properties overbuilt during the 1980s has run much of its course. The CSHs have adapted to an older clientele than originally planned (75+ vs. 65+) and this property type is now well occupied and cash flowing, except for those properties where overextended debt remains. The median debt service coverage for congregate housing at the end of 1993, as reported by ASHA and Coopers & Lybrand (1994), was a still struggling 0.8.[5] Their year end 1994 number was considerably improved at 1.1 (ASHA and Coopers & Lybrand, 1996), indicating a widespread workout of debt service problems.

E. Healthcare Trends

Healthcare in the U.S. is now undergoing a significant transition, and this transition will impact particularly the ALF and SNF types of seniors housing, although all types of seniors housing will in some degree be affected because seniors themselves will be so affected. At least 3 significant healthcare trends are well underway and will continue with or without Congress:

1. **Consolidation.** The healthcare industry is consolidating, similar to the banking industry a few years ago. There are too many providers, payers, and suppliers. Mergers and acquisitions are rampant and will continue for years. One exception is the ALF segment, which is not yet substantial enough to consolidate.

2. **Capitation.** Payment for healthcare services is evolving from fee for services rendered to case rates (payment per diagnosis, or DRG—diagnosis related group) to per diem payment (a set payment per day of care rendered; e.g., as in

---

[5] Their survey states (p. 41) that "while it is possible that the severity of the problem may be overstated due to some owners incorrectly including non-cash items such as depreciation and amortization in operating costs, the survey indicates that despite high occupancies and increasing rents, the financial problems experienced by many congregate residences are still prevalent." Occasional foreclosure sales may still be occurring, however, as where HUD insured the mortgage and has taken an inordinate length of time to foreclose.

OVERVIEW OF SENIORS HOUSING   37

an ALF) to capitation. Capitation means a set payment per capita or per patient per time period, regardless of whether that patient needs any healthcare that period. This method is a similar system to insurance premiums. It is the payment system of "managed care" or HMOs (health maintenance organizations). The HMO is in many respects a melding of the healthcare insurer and provider. The HMO may have its own staff of medical personnel, or may contract with independent providers (physicians, ALFs, SNFs, *inter alia*) in the community to provide healthcare for its members, paying those providers through a system which is itself evolving.

The first stage of the evolution of payments from HMOs to providers is simply negotiated lower fees for services. The next stage is contracted fees per diagnosis, then per diem, and finally simply by enrollment or capitation—the same system by which the HMO's members pay it. These stages in the evolution of a capitation payment system by HMOs to providers recapitulate the overall evolution of healthcare payment from fee for services to capitation. HMOs are now paying their providers by all of these various payment methods in one place or another as transition occurs. The final stage of capitation—also called PMPM: per member per month—is not yet in use in the seniors housing industry to the author's knowledge, but it is surely coming. There are providers who are readying themselves for it in anticipation of profiting, because it carries the risk/return level of the healthcare business a notch higher.

Consider this diagram:

Figure 2: Risk/Return relationship of health care payment methods

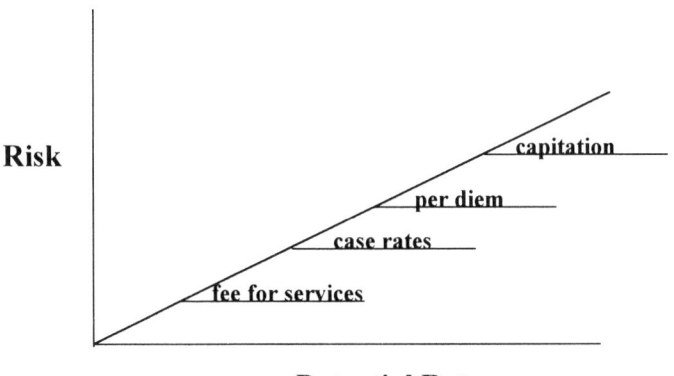

A fee for services is a very predictable payment—low risk, known return. The healthcare provider is paid for his or her time spent with the patient—like a lawyer's fee per hour. Case rates are riskier; the healthcare provider's pay is based on the classification of the patient's case or malady—not actual services rendered—so the provider can make more or less money depending upon how efficient the treatment and to some extent how severe the case within the classification. If all hospitals are paid the same amount for treating the same malady, then a more efficient hospital, or one which somehow manages to get the less acute cases within a classification of malady, or which can manage the classification process better, can make more money. By analogy, if all law firms were paid a set amount depending upon the case classification—for example, a hypothetical class 1 divorce—then a more efficient law firm, or one which somehow manages to get easier class 1 divorces, or to get more of its class 1 divorces classified as class 2 divorces (for which the hypothetical set fee is higher), can make more money than other law firms. There is an efficiency or management risk under a case rate payment system, and also an appropriate reward opportunity.

Per diem is more risky; per diem means the same pay per day for each patient, regardless of the malady being treated or level of care needed. If per diem rates are set the same for all healthcare providers, then a more cost-effective provider (or one lucky or managerially skillful enough to treat a less acute mix of patients or to keep "profitable" patients more days) can make more money. Continuing the law firm analogy, it would be as if all law firms were paid a set amount per day of services rendered to a client, regardless of the clients legal needs. Risk and potential reward escalate.

Capitation is the riskiest (and potentially most rewarding) payment method. For a set fee per member, the healthcare provider must care for all members who need healthcare. The provider receives a fee from every member, whether or not that member ever needs healthcare. A provider who can accurately assess the risk profile of the HMO membership and who can manage costs effectively while achieving acceptable outcomes has the potential to profit enormously from capitation payment. It would be as if a law firm served the legal needs of a membership group, received a standard fee from each member, and served all of the legal needs of the membership with no further compensation. The insurance analogy also springs forth. Risk and potential reward reach a higher level.

3. **Flattening the Pyramid**. Healthcare is being pushed down; from hospitals and physicians at the top to SNFs and nurses; from SNFs and nurses to ALFs and personal assistants; from ALFs and personal assistants to home health care. People are being discharged from hospitals sooner ("quicker and sicker"), or are receiving healthcare at a lower level in the first place than they would have a few years ago. If healthcare utilization is a pyramid with the highest level of care and cost at the top, then the pyramid is being flattened. Consider this diagram:

OVERVIEW OF SENIORS HOUSING 39

Figure 3: Flattening the pyramid of health care utilization

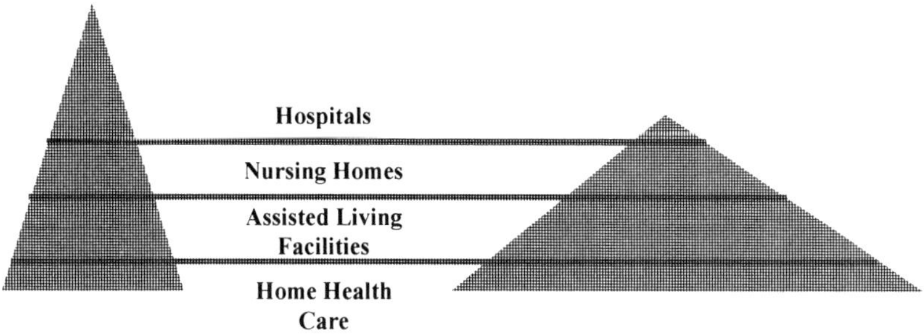

[Figure: Two triangles, one pointing up and one pointing down/flattened, with horizontal bands labeled from top to bottom: Hospitals, Nursing Homes, Assisted Living Facilities, Home Health Care]

Cost pressures are primarily causing this downward push, but another cause is the realization that our historic system of healthcare payment—fee for services (the more services, the more fees)—has caused overtreatment. "Less" care may be better for the patient as well as the wallet.

F. Sub-Acute Care

The pushdown of healthcare has created the current popularity of "subacute" care, sometimes described as "post-acute." Subacute care is care which has always been done in the medical and surgical wards of hospitals after treatment of an acute healthcare need. Now it is being pushed down to SNFs, which can do it less expensively than hospitals. The hospital will still be the site of the operation and the recovery room, but after that the SNF will take over the short-term care of the patient until discharge. The SNF may charge $350/day where the hospital would have been charging $650/day. The SNF is very glad to have this business to fill its $70/day beds which have been vacated by residents moving down to $55/day ALF rooms. Subacute care is now providing a significant lift to SNF bottom lines. The American Health Care Association quotes a study by investment analysts Cowen & Co. indicating that in 1992, on a daily basis, 66,000 to 132,000 hospital patients could have been adequately treated in subacute facilities. There were only about 15,000 subacute beds available at that time (American Health Care Association, 1994). As reported above, there are more than 1.5 million SNF beds in the U.S.. Conversion of nursing home beds to sub-acute beds is underway, but definitely has a limited potential, especially since new sub-acute facilities are also being built.

G. Nursing Homes

The SNF industry appears to be shifting its services rapidly to keep its business from being pulled away by ALFs and home health care. A panel consensus at the National Investment Conference for Seniors Housing in 1994 estimated that 40% of existing (and potential) SNF residents can be adequately served by ALFs. Lemov

(1994) has written that "most of the people in nursing homes do not need this level of service ... experts estimate that somewhere between 60 and as many as 75 percent of nursing home residents could be cared for in a more appropriate and less expensive way." Reinforcing the financial advantage of ALFs over SNFs is the consumer perception as stated by Kane and Wilson (1993): "Nursing homes are dreaded by almost all potential residents." Your author would add: "and families of potential residents too."

The SNFs are now compensating for the ALF competition by pulling subacute replacements down from hospitals, and branching into all kinds of specialties such as certain kinds of rehabilitation and Alzheimer's units, and even home health care and so-called assisted living units as well. Subacute care is giving a boost to SNF bottom lines now, as the so-called "long-term care" industry is turning to short-term care for its survival, but hospitals are beginning to respond with meaningful subacute competition to keep their medical and surgical wards open. Furthermore, as reported by Deane and Sherman (1994): "Many experts believe that HCFA[6] is unlikely to pursue aggressively the closing of hospitals, or even hospital wings, regardless of the potential savings of expanded SNF-base subacute care, because of the desire to maintain ready hospital access for U.S. citizens regardless of location."

Besides the risk of a shifting customer profile, SNFs face a significant payor source risk. Alan Plush (1994) of the Retirement & Healthcare Valuation Group states that "Medicaid/Medicare reimbursement is the key to understanding and forecasting the profitability" of an SNF. Dependence on this moving target as its major revenue source is a major risk for SNFs.

H. Assisted Living

ALFs are hot now. They are being built new and financed across the U.S.. A recent front-page article in the Triangle Business Journal (Raleigh, NC) proclaimed that assisted living centers are "going up at fever pace" (Harreld, 1996). The Wall Street Journal reported on February 26, 1996 that 6 assisted-living companies had gone public in the last year and have done very well for their investors (Baker, 1996). As noted above, the consensus from a number of different sources seems to be that a significant percentage of the existing residents of SNFs are receiving and paying for more intensive care than needed, and could be more appropriately cared for in ALFs. ALFs are generally homier, more comfortable-feeling places to live than SNFs, from the design of the facilities to the philosophy of operation to the lower cost. ALFs are powerful competitors to SNFs for all but the most infirm. Medicaid is beginning to realize the appropriateness and cost savings of ALFs as compared to SNFs, and will continue to move in this direction, with Oregon's system currently leading the way.

---

[6] The U.S. Health Care Financing Agency, which administers Medicare.

I. Legislation/Regulation

Seniors housing has been and continues to be a prolific generator of legislative involvement at both federal and state levels. Every month several newsletters outline the latest in federal and state legislative proposals. There is, of course, the continuing Congressional uproar over Medicare and Medicaid in connection with the budget-balancing debate. The current general state legislative focus is the effort to answer the question posed by Kane and Wilson for AARP (1993): "Can assisted living avoid the trap of substandard care resulting from underregulation and the trap of institutional care resulting from overregulation?"

J. Financing

The NIC—the National Investment Conference for Seniors Housing—held its 1995 annual meeting in Washington, D.C., where seniors housing lenders and borrowers met to consider the state of the financing market—and to make deals. This was its fifth meeting since its initiation in 1991. It has apparently grown exponentially in attendance over these last few years, as capital has returned to the seniors housing market.

Financing is now available for seniors housing from practically every source of commercial lending: commercial banks, insurance companies, pension funds, credit companies, REITs, and conduits for securitization. The niches vary tremendously. There is no standard lending format.

5. CONCLUSIONS

Overall, growing seniors housing demand is assured by compelling demographics, albeit modified by the curious anomaly of a declining subcohort within the overall seniors cohort. Currently, there is a new version and vigor for the old concept of assisted living. Unfortunately, this uprising is counteracted by turbulence in our healthcare delivery system.

The seniors housing industry has recovered strongly from the late 1980s and early 1990s real estate debacle, and there is now plenty of flowing capital. The supply of seniors housing is neither uniformly categorized nor well measured, and overbuilding in certain demographic and geographic markets is likely.

APPENDIX A

Selected Data on the Seniors Housing Industry

	ILF	CSH	ALF	SNF	CCRC
# properties 1991[1]	not available	2,500	40,000-65,000	15,600	800
# units/beds 1991[1]	not available	375,000	1,000,000	1,650,000	200,000
# residents 1991[1]	not available	281,000	900,000	1,580,000	186,000
Annual revenues 1991[1]	not available	$3.7 billion	$10.3 billion	$42.8 billion	$3.6 billion
1993 occupancy %	not available	93%[2]	91%[2]	96%	94%[2]
Avg. resident age 1993	75	82[2]	83[2]	83	85%[2]
% female 1993	72%	77%[2]	81%[2]	74%	76%[2]
Annual resident turnover	not available	23%[2]	44%[2]	100%	38%[2]
Payor sources:					
Private (self-pay)	100%	100%	95%	25%	95%
Insurance ?					
Medicaid			5%	64%	
Medicare				6%	
Other				5%	5%
Operating ratios 1994:[3]					
Profit margin	not available	42%	37%	18%	not available
NOI per resident day	not available	$24	$42	$22	not available
Cap rate 1995[4]	10.1%	11.1%	12.0%	13.1%	12.1%

[1] Feinberg (1993)
[2] ASHA & Coopers & Lybrand (1994)
[3] Capital Valuation Group (1994)
[4] Senior Living Valuation Services, Inc. (Spring 1994)

APPENDIX B: INDUSTRY ASSOCIATIONS

American Health Care Association
1201 L Street NW, Washington, DC 20005-4014
(202) 842-4444
Publication: Provider—a monthly magazine

American Seniors Housing Association (ASHA)
1850 M Street, NW, Suite 540
Washington, DC 20036
(202) 659-3381

Assisted Living Facilities Association of America (ALFAA)
10300 Eaton Place, Suite 400
Fairfax, VA 22030
(703) 691-8100
Publication: Assisted Living Today—a quarterly magazine

National Association Of Senior Living Industries (NASLI)
184 Duke of Gloucester Street
Annapolis, MD 21401-2523
(410) 263-0991
Publication: Spectrum—a bimonthly magazine

National Council of the Multifamily Housing Industry
1201 15th Street, NW
Washington, DC 20005-2800
(202) 822-0215

National Investment Conference (NIC)
705 Melvin Ave., Suite 201
Annapolis, MD 21401
(410) 267-0504

REFERENCES

American Health Care Association, Background, Subacute Care, Handout at NIC, 1994.
American Seniors Housing Association and Coopers & Lybrand, *The State of Seniors Housing 1994*, Washington, DC: American Seniors Housing Association, 1995.
American Seniors Housing Association and Coopers & Lybrand, *The State of Seniors Housing 1995*, Washington, DC: American Seniors Housing Association, 1996.
American Seniors Housing Association, *Selected Seniors Housing Transactions 1985-1993*, Washington, DC: American Seniors Housing Association, 1994.
Associated Press, Savings Up, but Still Falling Short of Retirement Plans, Survey Finds, *Portland Press Herald*, December 4, 1996, 4A.
Baker, M., Assisted Living Health Care Centers are Making Investors Feel Better, *The Wall Street Journal*, February 26, 1996, C1.
Bergsman, S., Senior Housing is an Old Story: A Market Revives, but Gives Off Warnings of Overheating, *Barron's*, October 16, 1995, 38.
Bianculli, J. L., What's Your Threshold?, *Provider*, September 1994, 67-68.
Bureau of the Census, *Nursing Home Population Increases in Every State* (CB93-117), Washington, DC: U.S. Government Printing Office, 1993.
Bureau of the Census, *Statistical Abstract of the United States 1995*, Washington, DC: U.S. Government Printing Office, 1995.
Bureau of the Census, Statistical Brief (SB/95-8), Washington, DC: U.S. Government Printing Office, May 1995.
Capital Valuation Group, *Operating Profit Margins and Net Operating Income (PRD basis) Compared Among Modalities.* Newark, DE: [publisher], 1994.
Feinberg, P., Senior Housing: Investments Coming, *Real Estate Forum*, September 1993, 84-95.
Harreld, H., Assisted Living Centers Going Up at Fever Pace, *Triangle Business Journal*, March 1, 1996, 1.
Kane, R. A., & Wilson K. B., *Assisted Living in the United States: A New Paradigm for Residential Care for Frail Older Persons?*, Washington, DC: American Association of Retired Persons, 1993.
Karpel, C., *The Retirement Myth*, New York: Harper Perennial, 1995.
Lemov, P., Nursing Homes and Common Sense, *Governing*, July 1994, 44-49.
Mergenhagen, P., Rethinking Retirement, *American Demographics*, June 1994, 28-34.
Peterson, P., *Will America Grow Up Before It Grows Old?*, New York: Random House, 1996.
Plush, A. C., Nursing Homes, *Retirement & Healthcare Valuation Group Quarterly Industry Review*, November 1994, 2.
Real Estate Research Corporation, *Rental Retirement Housing: New Opportunities*, Washington, DC: The National Housing Partnership, 1985.
Senior Living Valuation Services, Inc., *Senior Housing Investment Survey*, San Francisco, CA: [publisher], Spring 1995.
Taeuber, C. M., *Sixty-Five Plus in America* (Current Population Reports P23-178RV), Washington, DC: U.S. Government Printing Office, 1993. U.S. Department of Commerce & U.S. Department of Housing and Urban Development, *American Housing Survey for the United States in 1993* (Current Housing Reports H150/93), Washington, DC: U.S. Government Printing Office, 1995.
U.S. General Accounting Office, *Medicaid Long-Term Care* (GAO/HEHS-94-167), Washington, DC: U.S. General Accounting Office, 1994.

3

VALUE INFLUENCES PAST, PRESENT AND FUTURE

Mark D. Roth
Capital Valuation Group, Newark, DE

Charles J. Herman, Jr.
Capital Valuation Group, Newark, DE

Christopher Urban
Capital Valuation Group, Atlanta, GA

ABSTRACT

This paper examines value influences of four care modalities of the long-term care industry: independent or congregate, assisted living, nursing, and subacute care. Six influences that affect asset values are identified and examined. They comprise the evolution of managed care, financing, buyer motivations, seller motivations, opportunities, and threats. Their effect is examined through per-unit sale prices and capitalization rates over the past six years. While their effect on value differs, they are unified by several underlying themes that indicate that the market will ultimately reward and align with the lowest cost quality providers.

1. INTRODUCTION

The early 1990s was a turbulent period for the healthcare industry. Changes that occurred during this five-year span have altered the industry. These changes include the creation and consolidation of regional health networks in an effort to gain market share, therefore providing leverage in negotiating with HMOs. During the past year, the seniors housing and long-term care industries have strengthened and stabilized. Many underperforming assets have stabilized, a significant number of construction projects are underway, and new capital has entered the market. Most investors and lenders believe that there has been a restoration of sanity in the acquisition markets and the industry has developed sound fundamentals. While healthy skepticism remains due to current healthcare reform proposals, many feel that the senior services industry stands on a firm footing.

This paper will examine six factors that affect asset values of independent living or congregate care, assisted living, skilled nursing, and subacute nursing facilities. The six value influencers studied are investors' perceptions of managed care, financing opportunities, buyer motivations for buying assets, seller motivations for selling assets, new opportunities for growth, and threats to the value of the assets. The three time periods studied in our analysis are the time periods between 1990 and 1993 (the past), between 1994 and 1996 (the present) and from 1997 to 2000 (the future).

To gain insight into the value influencers, many key industry players were interviewed, providing further understanding of what drives the seniors housing and long-term care industries. These industry leaders include directors of development for major seniors housing providers, lending directors for financial institutions that lend to seniors development projects, and directors of major industry associations. Additionally, for each modality studied, national averages of per-unit/bed values and capitalization rate trends over the past six years were examined. These averages are based on data collected on sales of facilities over this time span. The data provide support for the strategic trends indicated by the value influencers.

2. INDEPENDENT LIVING OR CONGREGATE HOUSING

Independent living facilities house residents who are independent and ambulatory but desire companionship with members of their own age group. These residents also desire services such as cooked meals, housekeeping, linen service, planned activities, and transportation. Congregate housing residences cater to a similar clientele, but increasingly utilize a home healthcare service provided by in-house staff or an outside agency.

After several years in the doldrums, many industry leaders believe that the independent living/ congregate housing market is back and performing well. Rising occupancies have occurred in many markets, and with little new construction over the past few years, demand has surged back to meet supply. Currently, four factors point an optimistic finger toward the future for independent living and congregate housing. The factors are:

- Demand equals supply

- New projects are beginning to be constructed

- The care modality is back in favor with lenders and investors

- Acceptance of product type by seniors

Over the past several years, the role of independent living/congregate housing in the continuum of care has become clearer, with acceptance of many different service models. This industry is expected to continue its evolution as traditional apartment facilities offer services specifically for seniors in an attempt to retain residents.

The following table outlines the six factors that influence asset value for independent living and congregate housing assets. All six factors are examined over the three major time periods.

A. Independent Living and Congregate Housing Acquisition Markets

As shown in the following chart, over the past six years the average price per unit of independent living/congregate housing projects has been increasing. Averages were calculated using data collected from congregate housing sales across the United States over the past six years. During 1991, the average sale price was $37,800 per unit, which increased 86 percent over six years to $70,400 per unit during 1996. During 1995 alone, the purchase prices for 30 independent living/congregate care assets ranged from $14,000 per unit to $116,000 per unit. This range is indicative of the differences in project quality in the market.

Values of independent living facilities have stabilized after several years of increases. Purchasers are paying full value for projects without significant discounting for risk. Risks can include maintaining occupancy and rate growth. Several industry sources see capitalization rates declining for independent living properties.

As the price per unit has been increasing, capitalization rates have been steadily decreasing, as buyers are willing to pay a higher cash flow multiple for the available facilities. Since it is very difficult to isolate retirement sales, we often see capitalization rates that vary over a wide range. However, it is widely acknowledged that stabilized independent living facilities sell for capitalization rates between 10.0 to 11.5 percent based on forecasted cash flow. Cash flow is defined as earnings before interest, depreciation, taxes, and amortization (EBIDTA), but after a management fee (typically between four and six percent of total revenues).

The consensus among the market makers is that the universe of sellers has rapidly diminished. Values, after increasing significantly over the past few years, will begin to increase more moderately. Capitalization rates will continue to trend down slowly, as buyers continue to pay more for existing cash flow.

Independent Living and Congregate Housing: Value Influencers

	PAST 1990-1993	PRESENT 1994-1996	FUTURE 1997-2000
MANAGED CARE	• Very little value influence.	• Very little value influence.	• Little value influence. • May encourage independent living operators to explore models that allow aging in place.
FINANCING	• Inexperienced lenders. • Little involvement by Wall Street and major healthcare lenders. • Viewed as a multi-family play.	• Capital hitting the market for acquisitions. • Funding for development projects.	• Overbuilding in some markets hurts some lenders. • Cautious lenders fund only established operators.
BUYER MOTIVATIONS	• Few development dollars available, growth through acquisitions.	• As prices have been bid up, buyers analyze potential purchases more carefully than the past. • Little available product on market.	• After development spree ends, many projects suffer from poor occupancy due to overbuilding. • Many acquisition targets for well-capitalized and experienced providers.
SELLER MOTIVATIONS	• Lack of development financing drove up per unit prices for existing projects.	• Per unit prices may peak, few sellers and many buyers. • Bidding wars.	• Continued market consolidation as smaller, less well-capitalized chains sell to larger industry players.
OPPORTUNITIES	• Strong demographics, growing elderly market.	• Strong demographics, aging baby boomers. • Acceptance of product type by seniors.	• Continued strong demographics, people live longer and are healthier. • Increasing consumer sophistication leads to wider acceptance of this housing option.
THREATS	• Lack of market sophistication. • Inexperienced operators and developers. • Overbuilt projects.	• Overbuilding in some markets. • Lack of clear product definition. • Few barriers to entry for new competitors.	• Suffering occupancy due to overbuilding. • Lack of opportunity to keep residents who want to age in place. • Increased regulation due to larger frail elderly population.

3. ASSISTED LIVING

Assisted living can be defined as housing and care for frail seniors who need significant assistance with activities of daily living (i.e., bathing, dressing, and supervision of medications) but do not require continuous skilled nursing care. Assisted living is also known as personal care, board and care, residential care, or sheltered care.

Undoubtedly, assisted living is the hottest area in the senior living and long-term care industries. Several providers have gone public over the past year and the market continues to grow. Assisted living is attractive to operators, given the largely private-pay population and relatively high operating profit margins (around 40 percent). Developers like the relatively quick absorption of new facilities and relative lack of regulation, and lenders feel that assisted living is the lowest cost provider of care for those residents needing assistance with one to two activities of daily living (ADLs).

Investors are still somewhat cautious about assisted living since it is a relatively new product type. Quality of care issues are still being defined by this fledging industry. Other concerns include the lack of funding for financially-challenged residents and the prospect of future government regulation. According to Diana Gaines, Director of Senior Living and Healthcare Lending for G.E. Capital, "it is critical for operators of assisted living facilities to be prepared to handle regulation and Federal reimbursement." The management information systems (MIS) need to be developed in order to track costs for Federal reimbursement programs. Additionally, human resources must be allocated and trained to interact with government offices and ensure that providers capture Federal dollars earned.

The following table outlines the six factors that influence asset value for assisted living assets. All six factors are examined over the three major time periods.

A. Assisted Living Acquisition Markets

The acquisition market for assisted living facilities has been slow. This may be due to the lack of available product on the market over the past few years and the inability of small operators to raise both debt and equity dollars. With the rapid development of new facilities and the relatively recent (over the last 12 to 24 months) availability of development capital, several operators are beginning to reach critical mass. Look for several major acquisitions within the assisted living modality in the near future.

Assisted Living: Value Influencers

	PAST 1990-1993	PRESENT 1994-1996	FUTURE 1997-2000
MANAGED CARE	• Very little value influence.	• Increasing presence of regulation and government reimbursement programs.	• Strong influence as providers need to develop information systems and reimbursement staff.
FINANCING	• Inexperienced lenders. • Little involvement by Wall Street and major lenders. • Infancy of care type. • REITs have a significant influence on development	• Capital hitting the market for development. • Significant involvement by several Wall Street firms.	• Overbuilding in some markets hurts some lenders. • Cautious lenders fund only established operators. • Acquisition financing available for successful operators.
BUYER MOTIVATIONS	• New industry forming, tough to get financing for development, looking to grow anyway possible. • Less expensive to buy underperforming assets than to build new ones.	• As prices have been bid up, analyze potential purchases carefully. • Little available product on market. • Purchasing convertible facilities. • New development activity.	• After development spree ends, some projects suffer from poor occupancy due to over-aggressive development. • Many acquisition targets for well-capitalized providers.
SELLER MOTIVATIONS	• Lack of development financing drove of per unit prices for existing projects.	• Per bed prices continue to rise, few sellers and many buyers. • Bidding war.	• Industry consolidation begins, as smaller, less well-capitalized chains sell to larger industry forces.
OPPORTUNITIES	• Strong demographics, growing elderly market. • Relatively untapped penetration for assisted living providers.	• Strong demographics, growing elderly market. • Continued penetration available in care modality mix. • Larger market acceptance of product type. • Few barriers to entry.	• Strong demographics, growing elderly market. • Acceptance of assisted living as a custodial care provider. • Availability of funding for financially insecure. • Increasing presence of traditional nursing providers offering assisted living. • Increased presence of private long-term care insurance as a payor source.

VALUE INFLUENCES PAST, PRESENT AND FUTURE

Assisted Living: Value Influencers *(continued)*

THREATS	• Lack of market sophistication. • Lack of product definition.	• Beginning oversupply in some markets. • State regulation. • Some states fail to recognize ability to care for higher acuity residents. • Retaliation by some nursing providers. • Limited growth because of only being able to provide services to a private pay population.	• Suffering occupancy due to overbuilding in some markets. • Lack of opportunity to keep residents who want to age in place. • Increased regulation.

As shown in the following chart, over the past five years, the average price per bed for assisted living has increased sharply, from $27,500 per bed during 1991 to $60,400 per bed during 1996, a total increase in value of 120 percent. These averages are based on sales information gathered on facilities across the United States. During 1995, the sale prices of 26 facilities ranged from $39,000 per bed to $100,000 per bed. This range is indicative of the differences in project quality on the market. Given the relative few open market sales of assisted living facilities outlying values may skew the range.

As the price per bed has been increasing, the capitalization rates have fluctuated, reflecting several sales at above market capitalization rates, thus skewing the average. Both 1994 and 1996 have been consistent, around the 12 percent benchmark recognized by industry sources.

4. NURSING

This care modality is often divided into two acuity tiers: skilled care and intermediate or custodial care. Skilled nursing is increasingly becoming synonymous with Medicare-certified nursing care, since many residents are higher acuity and require therapies and ancillary services in addition to nursing care. Intermediate care is increasingly becoming obsolete, since healthier, more ambulatory residents can be cared for by assisted living facilities. This shift of intermediate care residents is slowed, however, by state regulation and lack of financial assistance for assisted living care.

While custodial care providers are still an endangered species (especially with many recent Medicaid program spending cuts), many nursing providers have improved their earnings by offering an array of enhanced services, many of which are reimbursed by Medicare Part B payments. Additionally, the future is bright for construction given the pressing need for redevelopment of nursing homes in many states.

However, new development is stalled in many states, with certificate of need (CON) regulations still a significant barrier. Strong demographics and increasing occupancies may help break the moratoriums in many states.

Future success of the nursing home industry (or any senior living industry) is dependent upon the people involved. As Renee DuBois, Director of Acquisitions for Meditrust—the largest healthcare REIT in the United States—states

> nursing home lending is still a people business; (this includes) quality facility-level people, quality management and quality ownership. We lend to quality providers only, as evidenced in maintained physical structures, high quality of care and effective marketing programs.

However, even the best managed facilities are not immune from the governmental posturing by reducing entitlement programs, notably Medicare and Medicaid.

The following table outlines the six factors that influence asset value for nursing home assets. All six factors are examined over the three major time periods.

Nursing: Value Influencers

	PAST 1990-1993	PRESENT 1994-1996	FUTURE 1997-2000
MANAGED CARE	• Regulation and reimbursement issues provide the impetus for growth rates and development activities.	• Entitlement programs under scrutiny. • Medicaid block grants may be eliminated.	• Shift to managed care providers to manage Medicaid reimbursement programs. • Capitated programs impact skilled nursing programs. • Continued heavy-handed regulation.
FINANCING	• Established lenders and well-capitalized operators.	• Product is understood and market is sophisticated. • Wall Street is fearful of entitlement programs shrinking.	• Strong financing markets as new funding sources (conduits) establish presence in nursing home lending.
BUYER MOTIVATIONS	• Looking for established facilities in states with favorable reimbursement systems and high private pay population.	• Purchasing facilities with higher acuity residents. • Purchasing facilities at a premium that are convertible to subacute.	• Strong regional providers formed. • Target facilities that can offer a mixture of Medicare reimbursable and subacute services.

VALUE INFLUENCES PAST, PRESENT AND FUTURE 53

Nursing: Value Influencers *(continued)*

SELLER MOTIVATIONS	• Tired of dealing with regulation and reimbursement headaches.	• Per bed prices continue to rise, especially for projects that can be converted to subacute. • Active acquisition markets in certain states. • Many operators aging, selling facilities to well-capitalized, sophisticated providers.	• Smaller, less well-capitalized chains sell to larger industry forces.
OPPORTUNITIES	• Strong demographics, growing elderly market. • Certain states offer capital reimbursement incentives.	• Strong demographics, growing elderly market. • Opportunity to increase revenue via expanded services and ancillaries.	• Strong demographics, growing elderly market. • Availability of managed care as a payor source. • Higher acuity residents treated in facilities. • Increasing presence of private long-term care insurance as a payor source.
THREATS	• Over-regulated.	• Overbuilding in some markets. • State regulation. • Lack of support in some states to recognize care for higher acuity residents. • Private pay population is dwindling as residents shift to assisted living residences. • High degree of Medicaid dependency.	• Increased regulation. • Aging physical plants. • Competition with assisted living for custodial care private pay residents. • Increasing strength of home health programs.

A. Nursing Home Acquisition Markets

After several years of price increases in per bed values for nursing homes and strong activity, prices appear to be stabilizing. Information on nursing home sales from various states was used to determine the average price per bed. As shown in the following chart, over the past six years the average price per bed has slowly increased, from $29,000 per bed during 1991 to $43,700 per bed during 1996, a total increase in value of 50 percent. During 1995, the sale prices of 118 facilities ranged from $15,000 per bed to $73,000 per bed. This range is indicative of the regional differences and type of services offered, in addition to many other factors.

Following the increasing price per bed trends over the past four years, capitalization rates have been steady. Capitalization rates are expected to stabilize around the 14 percent benchmark, based on conversations with those in the industry.

The acquisition markets appear to be strong throughout the continental United States, with little regional difference in activity. While the acquisition markets have been steady, several major acquisitions have begun to unravel. These aborted transactions include Mariner's acquisition of Convalescent Services, Inc. (CSI) and Living Centers of America's acquisition of Brian Center Corporation. Wall Street has not embraced aggressive acquisition strategies of several major publicly-traded companies and the stock prices have dropped for many of the major players.

Some experts have indicated that some deals may be amended after the parties involved realized that even with increased competition among lenders, they are still holding firm on certain terms and concessions. The purchasers can no longer get "more money with fewer strings attached." While the finance markets are still very competitive, most lenders appear to be sticking to their underwriting criteria.

5. SUBACUTE NURSING

The definition of subacute care is one that has been evolving over the past year as the industry forms. Subacute, or "post acute" as some providers have labeled it, can be defined as short-term, intensive transitional care. Subacute nursing care can be provided in a dedicated nursing facility or in a wing of a long-term care facility or acute care hospital. The majority of subacute nursing beds result when an operating nursing facility converts beds or an area into a dedicated subacute wing.

Subacute is helping turn skilled nursing providers into "mini-hospitals" that provide post-acute services to medically-complex residents as well as those needing extensive rehabilitation. Subacute care has gained popularity in recent years because it costs less than an average hospital stay. Formerly, post-acute residents were treated first in hospitals, then in dedicated rehabilitation hospitals, and now in the subacute setting. The implementation of the Diagnosis Related Group (DRG) payment system for Medicare reimbursement forced acute care hospitals to shorten the length of stay for patients, creating the need for subacute services.

Traditional acute care hospitals are reacting to this patient loss and are converting acute care beds and wings into subacute care. Many states allow hospitals to convert beds without a certificate of need (CON). Nursing home provider lobbies are fighting this exemption, most notably in the states of Maryland and New Jersey.

Currently, the subacute setting of choice is most likely within a skilled nursing home located near a major hospital with a dedicated subacute wing or section of a facility. This concept places subacute residents with sicker custodial care residents and traditional skilled nursing residents.

The following table outlines the six factors that influence asset value for subacute nursing assets. All six factors are examined over the three major time periods.

VALUE INFLUENCES PAST, PRESENT AND FUTURE

Subacute Nursing: Value Influencers

	PAST 1990-1993	PRESENT 1994-1996	FUTURE 1997-2000
MANAGED CARE	• Some influence.	• Industry moving toward serving capitated programs.	• Strong influence as managed care and capitated programs influence patient referral. • Increase penetration by managed care.
FINANCING	• Inexperienced lenders. • Some involvement by Wall Street and major healthcare lenders. • High REIT involvement with development and acquisition financing. • Infancy of care type.	• Significant capital hitting the market for acquisition. • Wall Street bullish on subacute.	• Wall Street involvement with expansion of successful chains. • More involvement by traditional lenders, e.g. commercial banks.
BUYER MOTIVATIONS	• Build or buy dedicated subacute hospitals. • Lack of Certificate of Need (CON) restrictions make it difficult to develop new subacute programs.	• Nursing homes converted, subacute facility within a facility. • Pay premium for suitable facilities. • Form regional provider network and obtain critical mass in selected markets.	• Pursue opportunities in non-traditional areas such as within hospitals. • Purchase ancillary service and equipment providers, vertical integration.
SELLER MOTIVATIONS	• Watch subacute providers pay premium prices per bed.	• Per bed prices, especially for convertible properties, continue to rise. • Active acquisition markets in certain states.	• Capitated payor programs force some providers to sell.
OPPORTUNITIES	• Lower cost alternative to hospital care. • Embraced by Wall Street. • Existence of lucrative Medicare payment streams.	• Lower cost alternative to hospital care. • Acceptance as a care alternative by managed care providers.	• Vertical integration by providers allows care costs to be lowered. • Penetration is a fraction of current demand.
THREATS	• Lack of product understanding. • Providers look for contracts before facilities. • Rehabilitation hospitals provide majority of care. • Freestanding rehabilitation hospitals still did not provide the lowest cost structure.	• State regulation. • Lack of support in some states to recognize care for higher acuity residents. • Retaliation by hospitals. • Development of subacute units within hospitals that are not subject to CON regulations. • Reliance on Medicare as a major payor source.	• Increased regulation. • Uncertainty about continued growth of entitlement programs. • Stark legislation regarding referral for ancillary services to owned providers. • Increased competition from hospitals as they control patient flow.

A. Subacute Acquisition Markets

As shown in the following chart, over the past two years the average price per bed has dipped, after peaking during 1994. Per-bed prices had increased from $41,500 per bed during 1991 to $62,400 per bed during 1994, only to drop slightly to $58,600 per bed. Transactions identified as subacute have all or part of their operation dedicated to serving medical needs of subacute residents. These subacute average bed prices are the result of analysis of data on sales from across the United States.

Contrary to conventional wisdom, the acquisition markets for subacute facilities have exhibited abnormally low capitalization rates. Those within the industry feel that subacute capitalization rates should stabilize around 15 to 16 percent. It appears that acquirers are paying cash flow premiums based on future revenue growth. Subacute facilities typically consume cash early on during the operation, with heavy outflows for operating expenses during the establishment of the subacute unit. After stabilization, subacute facilities produce significantly higher cash flow on a per bed basis than typical nursing homes.

6. VALUE INFLUENCERS

A. Managed Care

For those involved with the acute care industries, managed care has been the impetus for change. Capitated programs, risk sharing, and referral networks have become commonplace phrases. Government involvement and regulation has also increased. Thus far, both independent and assisted living facilities have been relatively free of the managed care tidal wave. That will change in the coming years. Subacute care is already being exposed to capitated systems. It is expected that skilled nursing will also come under the influence of managed care.

Another major influence of managed care is on quality mix (or payor mix). The quality mix of the future, especially for assisted living and nursing providers, will likely include private long-term care insurance as a major payor class. For nursing and subacute providers, Medicaid and Medicare beneficiaries are most likely to be enrolled within a managed care program for their entitlement benefits. That program is most likely to be within a health maintenance organization (HMO) with provider contracts and a capitated fee structure.

These changes are precipitated by the effectiveness of managed care in controlling healthcare costs. Additionally, the universe of private-pay residents is shrinking, forcing some providers to seek alternatives to fill beds. As alluring as capitation and entitlement program dollars are, they carry increased regulatory presence.

Increased regulations are already influencing the growth of the assisted living industry, as many states are enacting or debating licensure and reimbursement laws. Some nursing home operators are using regulatory influence to stem the outflow of intermediate care residents to assisted living providers. Additionally, subacute facilities are lobbying for recognition as a distinct and unique care modality for entitlement reimbursement purposes. Only independent living/congregate housing (with the exception of CCRCs) has been relatively free of governmental involvement.

B. Financing

Suddenly, it seems that many lenders have become comfortable with healthcare lending and development. Financiers of seniors housing properties have only recently become comfortable with the product and operators of both assisted and independent living facilities. An industry source mentioned that the lenders are competing with higher loan to value ratios and lower cost capital. Diana Gaines, among others, expects capital for new development to increase significantly over the next 12 to 18 months.

The increased availability of development funding benefits the financing of independent and assisted living projects. The market's operators and lenders are becoming more sophisticated. For instance, several lenders are instituting 20 mile noncompete clauses for assisted living projects. The inflow of capital into assisted living has not come from traditional sources solely, with recent deals having been completed through the United States Department of Housing and Urban Development (HUD), using the 232 program and tax-exempt bond financing.

Nursing home financing was once relegated to a few traditional commercial lenders, in addition to healthcare-oriented REITs. Recently, many new entrants are creating healthcare lending groups and actively pursuing new deals. Conduit financing has also enjoyed a strong two-year run, with healthcare debt securitized by Wall Street. These new lenders are raising the stakes and increasing pressure on traditional lenders. Subacute care has also benefited from the new influx of capital, as Wall Street is rewarding public companies that boast subacute holdings and operations.

While the gates are open for healthcare lenders, those gates may be floodgates. In unregulated industries such as independent and assisted living, too much capital may lead to overbuilding and oversaturation of some geographic markets. It is widely viewed that the market will take at least five years to shake out, which may lead to sell-offs in the selected overbuilt markets.

C. Buyer Motivations

The best way to uncover buyer motivations is to attempt to get inside the collective minds of active acquirers within the long-term care and senior living industries. We queried many operators as to what they look for in a successful acquisition.

Thilo Best of Holiday Retirement Corporation looks for retirement projects in markets that have solid demographics and no signs of overbuilding. James Hands, with The Hampstead Group, agrees with this assessment and adds that the key to a successful acquisition is to fully evaluate any long-term sustainable competitive advantages (or lack thereof) of a potential acquisition.

Paul Hannon, Director of Development for The Kapson Group, looks for facilities that have stabilized occupancy or show upside potential for increased occupancy based on market fundamentals. Additionally, some projects show upside potential if the current owners are not pricing what the market will bear or what the competition is charging. Unfortunately, all acquisitions do not have such upside potential. The Kapson Group, like several other assisted living providers, is pursuing a three-pronged growth strategy:

1. Acquisition of existing facilities

2. Acquisition and conversion of non-healthcare facilities (e.g., hotels)

3. New development

Nursing home buyers are looking for facilities that have the opportunity to increase value through improvements or changes. Improvements or changes can include addition of Medicare services, cosmetic rehabilitation to the physical structure, or implementation of marketing programs to improve overall census or quality mix. Savvy acquirers need to quantify upside potential to justify an acquisition price.

Acquisitions that are deemed subacute are typically nursing homes that currently offer those services or are purchased by a subacute operator who plans to add subacute services. The subacute portion of the facility should account for a substantial portion of the revenue, census, and profitability. Those facilities that are convertible to subacute will continue to garner a premium price from the market.

Subacute providers are interested in establishing a critical mass in selected markets, where they can implement all phases of subacute care services, including therapy, ancillary, and other medical services through wholly-owned or partner providers. Additionally, the presence of a strong geographical network gives subacute providers critical mass to bargain with managed care insurers. Strong regional providers are also more attractive as joint venture partners with acute care medical systems.

D. Seller Motivations

David Schless, Executive Director of the American Seniors Housing Association (ASHA) sums up the demand for independent and assisted living properties as "a tremendous amount of interest in senior housing acquisitions ... not a day goes by without a call from somebody looking for senior housing properties to acquire." Given the acquisition fever, it is hard not to be a motivated seller.

The consensus in most industries is that the universe of sellers is greatly reduced. There are few individual owners of seniors housing and long-term care facilities remaining. It is widely acknowledged that acquisitions have slowed down due to lack of available product for purchase. Most of the remaining suitable product for acquisitions is coming to the market one facility at a time. A notable exception has been the portfolio reduction of underperforming and nonperforming independent living properties with mortgages guaranteed by the United States Department of Housing and Urban Development (HUD). Nobody really knows how many troubled properties are left in the HUD portfolio, but it is estimated to be between 50 and 80 properties.

E. Opportunities

Clearly, one of the biggest opportunities for those involved with senior living and long-term care industries is the burgeoning United States elderly population. The over-75 population has exhibited strong growth, increasing 12.6 percent over the past five years, and is expected to continue its rise unabated. During 1995, it is estimated that the over-75 population totals 14,791,673 people, or 5.6 percent of the total U.S. population. Projected forward to year 2000, the over-75 population is expected to increase 12.6 percent to 16,658,016 people, or 6 percent of the total population.

The current senior housing supply currently does not meet demand. While some states and areas are overbedded in certain care modalities, there still is room for savvy operators to increase their market penetration. All markets need to have a mixture of care modalities. According to industry experts, the care modality mix within any given market should be broken down as follows:

Care Modality Index

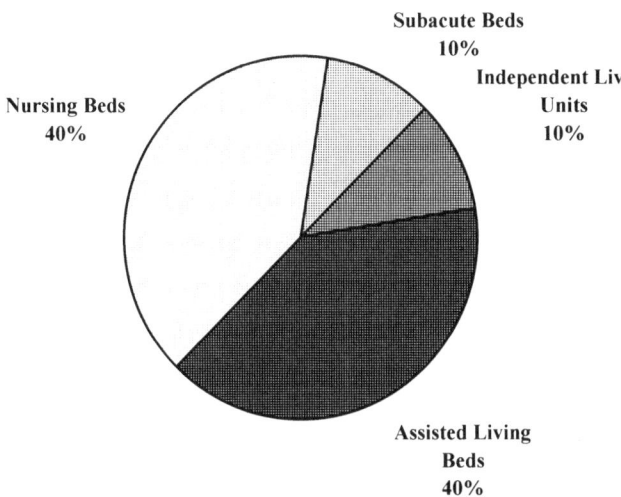

The opportunity to increase penetration for certain modalities may come at the expense of other industries. For example, assisted living in many markets has an opportunity to increase its penetration rate up to 40 percent of the overall senior services. However, many of the occupancy gains by assisted living providers may come at the expense of nursing homes with custodial care residents. Likewise, subacute providers often fill beds with former residents of rehabilitation and acute care hospitals.

For operators, especially nursing and subacute, who establish themselves as strong regional providers the opportunity to create critical mass is present. The primary means by which a provider can establish critical mass is through vertical integration. Many major nursing chains have recently purchased therapy, pharmacy, managed care, and durable medical equipment providers. The addition of these ancillary providers can increase cash flow significantly, thus adding value.

F. Threats

In one sense, overregulation in some care modalities, especially subacute and nursing, serves as a threats to the seniors housing and long-term care industries. However, regulation also serves as a deterrent to growth, which can be construed as both a threat and an opportunity. Additionally, independent living and assisted living, while benefiting from less regulation, may suffer in the future due to overbuilding in certain markets.

With today's aggressive capital markets, it is easier to obtain the funds necessary to build new seniors housing projects than it has been during the last several years. Therefore, many assisted and independent living projects that have been on hold may soon be under construction. This may lead to future occupancy problems as supply again outpaces demand. "You cannot dig deep enough when researching the probability of new competition and its potential impact on absorption, effective rental rates and stabilized occupancies," James Hands cautions.

Given the relative maturity of nursing within the long-term care spectrum, many acquirers are searching for stabilized projects located within states and areas that do not have severe overbedding problems. According to Daren Cortese, Director of Development for Community Care of America, nursing occupancies below 80 to 85 percent betray an overbedded market. Texas and Indiana, for example, are often mentioned as overbedded states for nursing providers. Mr. Cortese cautions that examining nursing values are on a per bed basis across state lines can be misleading, as profitability varies from state to state based on the reimbursement systems.

Threats to subacute nursing include retaliation by hospitals who are losing patients to subacute providers. Maintaining a positive relationship with referring hospitals is critical for the success of any subacute provider. However, even with cordial relations, hospitals may not continue to outsource subacute services.

7. CONCLUSION

While each care modality can be considered separately, all have consistent value influencers. While the effect on value by the evolution of managed care, financing, buyer motivations, seller motivations, opportunities, and threats differs, they are tied together by several underlying themes.

Managed care is increasing its presence within the long-term care industry and will have a stronger effect on providers. Financing sources are embracing all care modalities to an extent never before seen. Buyers are motivated to establish a strong regional presence, with critical mass in defined geographic areas to offer an array of services and negotiate with managed care. Owners are motivated to sell, given the impression that value for their facility has never been higher. The strongest opportunity is primarily a result of demographics, as the sheer number of service users grows rapidly. Future threats may be the cumulation of all positive forces, as developers overexploit penetration opportunities and operators fight over private-pay residents.

The bottom line is that the market at large will eventually reward and align with the lowest cost quality providers. The healthcare industry has been, and will continue to be, in a state of flux. However, it is the consensus that the senior living and long-term care industries have stabilized and are fundamentally sound.

4

1996 ACQUISITION MARKETS SENIORS HOUSING AND LONG-TERM CARE INDUSTRIES

American Seniors Housing Association
Washington, DC

Capital Research Group
Newark, DE

The findings in this report depict market trends and identify some of the driving forces behind these trends. Although every effort was made to ensure the accuracy of the information, the lack of industry-standard reporting procedures is an impediment when grouping such data.

ABSTRACT

This study explores transactions in the seniors housing and long term care industries. The sales statistics were collected from a variety of sources, including press releases from various public companies, leads from industry magazines confirmed by participants in each sale, and a number of state agencies across the country. The level of care examined includes congregate seniors housing, assisted living facilities, and skilled nursing facilities. Regardless of the type of facility and care, transactions are compared using several financial indicators, including price per bed, gross income multiplier, capitalization rate, and price per square foot. An extensive amount of the sales and development activity is bolstered by consolidation efforts to form integrated health networks.

1. INTRODUCTION: OVERVIEW OF THE SENIORS HOUSING AND LONG-TERM CARE INDUSTRIES

Congregate seniors housing, assisted living, and skilled nursing are the three major care modalities within the continuum of senior living services. Acuity levels, services, and regulation distinguish these modalities from one another. The three market segments appear to be at disparate levels in the business cycle. The following table illustrates the differences:

Industry	Stage in Business Cycle	Characteristics
Congregate Seniors Housing	Rebound/ Expansion	• New development in certain markets • Diminished sell-off of under-performing assets • Declining risk rates
Assisted Living	Expansion	• Rash of Initial Public Offerings (IPOs) to raise equity • Substantial development activity • Recent IPO struggles to reach projected offering prices
Skilled Nursing	Maturity/ Consolidation	• Merger and acquisition markets strengthening • Stock prices volatile, as investors closely watch earnings and growth estimates • Growth through vertical integration • Increasing influence of managed care

Although these three sectors have different measures of success and market characteristics, their fundamentals are very similar. All three have strong real estate components within the business enterprise. The business component enhances the value of the assets, but the real estate component represents the value base. While assisted living firms rely primarily on development for growth, skilled nursing providers typically rely on acquisition for growth.

The long-term-care continuum has gained greater access to capital and is using this money in myriad ways. The congregate seniors housing field has seen mass acquisition of previously non-performing assets, as well as an expansion of service options within existing communities. The assisted living industry has funded aggressive development.

1996 ACQUISITION MARKETS 65

And the nursing industry has seen continued consolidation through both single facility and multifacility acquisitions.

2. SCOPE OF THE STUDY

This study is an update and expansion of two previous ASHA/Capital Valuation Group studies: *Seniors Housing Acquisitions and Construction 1995*[1] and *Selected Seniors Housing Transactions 1987–1993*.[2] These previous studies considered only seniors housing transactions and excluded skilled nursing. As the lines distinguishing the various care modalities continue to blur, however, it is increasingly important to consider all three, collectively labeled as the seniors housing and long-term care industries.

Regardless of the level of care, all transactions are compared using several financial denominators, adjusted on a common basis. The major value indicators include:

- Sale price per bed

- Gross income (revenue) multiplier (GIM)

- Capitalization rate or cash flow multiple

- Price per square foot

Sale price per bed is calculated by dividing sale price by the total number of beds in the facility. Costs for required or anticipated renovations and additions are added to the purchase price. Assisted living and skilled nursing facility providers typically use licensed beds, while congregate seniors housing providers use rentable units as the common size base.

The **gross income multiplier** is derived by dividing the sale price by annual gross revenue. Annual gross revenue is defined as total revenue, net of contractual allowances and bad debt.

Capitalization rates are a market-driven measure of risk and growth. The capitalization rate measures both risk and expectations for future growth. The capitalization rate represents earnings before interest, taxes, depreciation, and amortization (EBITDA), divided by the sale price (including expected renovation and construction costs). The capitalization rate can also be represented as the inverse of the cash flow multiple.

Price per square foot represents the overall sale price, including renovations and other costs, divided by the building's square footage, including common and service areas. This calculation provides a common basis to compare the subject with other real estate assets, including apartment and multifamily assets.

---

[1] Capital Valuation Group and American Seniors Housing Association, *Seniors Housing Acquisitions and Construction 1995*, (1996).
[2] Capital Valuation Group, Selected Seniors Housing Transactions 1987-1993, (1996).

In keeping with industry standard practices, revenues, cash flows, and profitability are based on forecasted performance—typically the first stabilized year. Buyers typically consider stabilized revenues and cash flows given improvements, changes in operations, and performance expected to be affected by the new management team. Asset values and purchase price decisions—while affected by historic multiples—typically are based on forecasted and stabilized operations.

3. CONGREGATE SENIORS HOUSING MARKET ACTIVITY

The overall market for congregate seniors housing has been strong during the last 12 to 18 months. Capital inflow, coupled with heightened interest in this asset type from assisted living providers, has driven acquisition prices up and capitalization rates down. Additionally, several new entrants have been aggressively purchasing congregate care residences. Major industry forces Holiday Retirement Corp. and Marriott International, Inc. (through its Senior Living division) have grown through a combination of acquisition and development, as have ARV Assisted Living, Emeritus Corp., Sunrise Assisted Living, Karrington Health, Kapson Senior Quarters, Sterling House Corporation, Assisted Living Concepts, and others.

Along the care continuum, congregate housing assets occupy the lower acuity echelon of the continuum and are typically generically classified as seniors housing. Congregate seniors housing facilities generally offer retirement living in apartment suites with some basic services provided, which may include meals, housekeeping, linen service, planned activities, and transportation. These residences often cater to clientele utilizing home health care services provided by in-house staff or an outside agency.

A. Deals

A deal that attracted much interest during mid-1996 had yet to close at press time. Aetna Insurance, through its Aetna Realty Investors subsidiary, is selling four stabilized, upscale congregate communities in the Northeast and Southeast. The bid winners are expected to be announced in late 1996. Preliminary indications show successful bids matched or exceeded asking prices, with a price range of $90,000 to $125,000 per unit, coupled with aggressive capitalization rates.

Manor Care's purchase of six campus-style communities from Beverly Enterprises in October 1995 was another major congregate transaction. The properties are located throughout the United States with a total of approximately 1,515 units and were purchased for approximately $74.3 million ($49,000 per unit). The United States Department of Housing and Urban Development (HUD) has also been an active seller, auctioning off congregate seniors housing properties at a rate of two to three a month, as it continues to purge its portfolio of underperforming assets.

The Prime Group has been building its portfolio of retirement projects to achieve critical mass. During October 1996, Prime Group registered and priced a public offering through Brookdale Living Communities, Inc.. It will own around 40 percent of Brookdale after the offering. American Retirement Corp. has been active in the acquisition markets as well, purchasing three facilities divested from the Living Environment For An Aging America Fund (a pension fund), as well as several other properties.

Reflecting the increasing competitiveness of the market, several long-term care companies are *decreasing* their investment in the seniors housing industry. These moves reflect the strong sellers' market and need for management to focus on core business strengths. Integrated Health Services (IHS), for example, has been shedding retirement assets, selling six retirement properties to Emeritus Corporation, as well as spinning off its assisted living business (Integrated Living Communities went public in early fall).

Throughout the last year, equity market investors poured millions of dollars into the seniors housing business. The current crop of seniors housing initial public offerings (IPOs), although dominated by assisted living providers, includes several hybrid congregate/assisted living companies. Grand Court Lifestyles (formerly known as Leisure Centers and J&B Management) has filed for a public offering, and Retirement Care Associates plans to do the same with its assisted living/seniors housing business. Atria Communities, Inc. was spun off by Vencor and went public during mid-August 1996. Atria has approximately 2,400 independent living and 650 assisted living units. Its offering went to market at a lower share price than expected, but over $50 million was raised nevertheless.

B. Buyer Motivations

Purchasers are paying a premium for residences that offer—or have the potential to offer—assisted living services. Many former congregate properties are being purchased by assisted living providers and converted to offer support services. Additionally, multiple properties that can add to a provider's regional network are commanding higher prices.

The following table summarizes some key statistics and averages for sales examined by Capital Valuation Group and ASHA between 1993 and October 1996. These 98 transactions are believed to be at arms' length and indicative of the market.

Congregate Seniors Housing Transactions

Year/ Number of Transactions	Average Number of Units	Average Price per Unit	Average Price per Square Foot	Average Net Operating Income	Average Gross Income Multiplier	Average Capitalization Rate
1993 n = 30	186	$46,700	$68.10	34.5%	3.0	11.9%
1994 n = 15	155	$52,000	$62.90	32.8%	2.9	11.7%
1995 n = 30	162	$53,100	$67.20	29.6%	2.8	10.7%
1996 n = 23	170	$70,400	$81.80	36.4%	3.4	11.0%

The preceding grid portrays continued strength in per-unit and per-square-foot prices during the periods observed. Capitalization rates, however, appear to be edging slightly upward. This reversal in capitalization rate trends may be tied to several factors, including:

1. Change in asset profile for purchased residences, reflecting the addition of assisted living care within the traditional congregate settings.

2. Reflection of higher per-unit prices carrying higher risk premium in maintaining cash flow and debt service coverage.

3. Impact of slightly higher interest rates, with inflation worries slightly pushing rates up.

4. Increased risk perception in light of aggressive development in some markets, which may cause pressure on occupancy and rates.

Many believe that the prices paid per unit may be moderating after a protracted period of rapid increases. Most of the buyers seeking to increase their portfolios in preparation for an initial public offering completed their offerings during the last 18 months. At the same time, as capitalization rates have decreased and prices have increased, several well-established operators have curtailed acquisition activity and turned to development. Purchase prices average $70,000 per unit, while retirement and assisted living development costs average $82,700 per unit and $71,200 per bed (includes assisted living and mixed modality retirement projects).[3]

---

[3] Capital Valuation Group, Assisted Living Development Cost Survey, 1996 Midyear Update.

4. ASSISTED LIVING MARKET

The assisted living market in 1996 experienced a surge in acquisition activity, as well as a rash of assisted living companies going public. Many buyers are chasing a limited supply of stabilized, performing projects. Given the scarcity of available product, some companies have elected to expand through development. Others are seeking assets such as hotels, apartments, and nursing homes that can be converted to assisted living. Rural areas are also receiving more attention.

A. Initial Public Offerings

The market for assisted living IPOs has been uneven, following a lull earlier in the year. There are approximately 15 publicly-traded assisted living companies, with several joining the ranks in the past few months. As recently as one year ago, there were only a handful of public assisted living companies. New issues include Sunrise Assisted Living, Alternative Living Services (ALS), and Karrington Communities (trading as Karrington Health). The demand for assisted living IPOs has softened. The ALS and Atria Assisted Living offerings in August 1996, as well as the Kapson Senior Quarters and Integrated Living Communities offerings in September, came to market at lower share prices than expected.

Several firms have filed registration statements to go public, including Grand Court Lifestyles and Brookdale Living Communities. Two other firms that recently joined the public ranks are spinoffs from nursing home chains: Integrated Health Services' (IHS) spinoff of Integrated Living Communities (ILC) and Vencor's spinoff of Atria Assisted Living. Retirement Care Associates also recently announced plans to spin off its assisted living and retirement business.

Entering the public markets compels these companies to add sites—either through development or acquisition—in order to meet growth expectations. Publicly-traded assisted living companies have a market capitalization estimated between $700 million to $1 billion, which is ample capitalization for significant growth activity. The increasing number of publicly-traded chains has increased competition for assets. This appetite for growth, as well as greater financing availability, are driving the merger and acquisitions markets.

B. Deals

In October 1996, Sunrise Assisted Living, Inc. purchased—for approximately $34 million in cash with no assumption of debt—five assisted living and congregate seniors housing residences located in Georgia, Florida, and South Carolina, with a total capacity of 511 residents. Sunrise also entered into a contract to purchase two assisted living and congregate seniors housing residences in California with a total capacity of 258 residents. The purchase price is anticipated to be approximately $30.8 million in cash.

This transaction is expected to close during the first quarter of 1997 after a due diligence period.

Greenbriar Corporation recently signed an agreement to merge with American Care Communities, a major assisted living provider in the Southeast. American Care Communities presently owns or leases and manages 15 assisted living facilities with approximately 1,350 units. The merger is expected to be completed before the end of 1996. Greenbriar will purchase all the shares of American Care Communities with 1.3 million shares of Greenbriar common stock, which is valued at approximately $20 million.

The following table summarizes some key statistics and averages for sales between 1993 and October 1996. These 70 transactions are considered to be at arms' length and indicative of the market examined by Capital Valuation Group and ASHA.

Assisted Living Transactions

Year/ Number of Transactions	Average Number of Beds	Average Price per Bed	Average Price per Square Foot	Average Net Operating Income	Average Gross Income Multiplier	Average Capitalization Rate
1993 n = 6	57	$47,000	$124.00	31.1%	2.6	12.2%
1994 n = 19	75	$45,300	$92.90	27.6%	2.3	12.2%
1995 n = 26	95	$64,000	$132.30	31.1%	2.8	11.3%
1996 n = 23	100	$60,400	$134.30	31.1%	2.5	12.4%

The preceding grid indicates per-bed and per-square-foot prices moderated during the periods observed. However, capitalization rates appear to be edging slightly upward.

5. NURSING HOME MARKET ACTIVITY

After a slowdown during the last year in the megadeal market among nursing and subacute companies, consolidation and merger activity is increasing again. Strategic initiatives aimed at developing regional networks, coupled with an increased availability of capital, have energized the acquisition markets. While 1995 was the year of megadeals for the nursing home industry, 1996 is shaping up to be the year of medium-sized transactions, as rapidly growing public companies acquire mid-sized chains.

A. Deals

During January 1996 alone, two major acquisitions took place. Mariner Health Group (New London, Connecticut-based) announced the acquisition of Convalescent Services, Inc. (CSI). Under the terms of the acquisition, Mariner issued 5,853,658 shares of common stock, paid $6 million in cash, and assumed debt obligations of $36 million. Mariner had been managing the 27 skilled nursing facilities owned by Convalescent Services in Florida, Georgia, and Texas since mid-1995.

The second major acquisition during January 1996 was Multicare's purchase of Concord Health Group. Concord Health Group owned and operated 15 long-term care facilities (assisted living as well as nursing) in Pennsylvania, an institutional pharmacy, a home health care company, and a rehabilitation business. The actual sale price has been estimated at $114 million.

During February 1996, Regency Health announced that it acquired Liberty Healthcare for $41.5 million. Liberty owned and operated 18 nursing homes in Tennessee and North Carolina. Another large acquisition took place in June 1996 when the Multicare Companies signed a definitive agreement to acquire The ADS Group, a privately-held long-term care company located in Newton, Massachusetts. By mid-year 1996, Genesis Health Ventures had announced its intent to buy Geriatric & Medical Centers. The deal was valued at approximately $223 million and closed during mid-fall. On August 1, 1996, Mariner Health Group announced plans to purchase Maryland-based Allegis Health for approximately $110 million and closed the deal on September 30.

Although the large nursing home chains are growing, these multifacility providers by no means dominate the long-term care market. The largest 20 chains, for example, constituted only 18 percent of the industry during 1994, whereas all nursing home chains accounted for only about one-third of all facilities. During the past two years, the national chain penetration has increased significantly.

B. Buyer Motivations

Purchasers are willing to pay a premium for skilled nursing facilities that offer, or have the opportunity to offer, subacute services. Additionally, facilities and chains that enhance or add to a provider's regional network will command higher prices. The creation of networks, which provide the full care continuum along with ancillary services, has heightened consolidation and acquisition activity. The ability to offer a wide range of services over a broad geographic area with competitive pricing will help the industry grow during the era of managed care and capitation.

The following table summarizes some key statistics and averages for sales from 1993 to October 1996. These 362 transactions are considered to be at arms' length and indicative of the market examined by Capital Valuation Group and ASHA.

Nursing Home Transactions

Year/ Number of Transactions	Average Number of Beds	Average Price per Bed	Average Price per Square Foot	Average Net Operating Income	Average Gross Income Multiplier	Average Capitalization Rate
1993 n = 101	116	$32,800	$106.30	16.1%	1.1	14.5%
1994 n = 124	125	$35,900	$123.60	15.4%	1.1	14.4%
1995 n = 118	122	$39,700	$120.30	15.5%	1.1	14.8%
1996 n = 19	96	$43,700	$135.80	15.9%	1.1	15.1%

The preceding grid indicates continued strength in per-bed and per-square-foot prices during the periods observed. Capitalization rates have been moving slightly upward over the past few years, as acuity levels have increased. Long-term care providers have been delivering an increasing array of services, including home health care, pharmacy, and therapies.

6. SUMMARY AND CONCLUSION

The seniors housing and long-term care industries are currently undergoing significant change. The congregate seniors housing segment is experiencing a resurgence with significant development and acquisition activity. The assisted living segment, fueled by public equity dollars and demand, is in the midst of a development boom. The nursing home industry, facing increasing managed care influence and decreasing entitlement funding, continues to consolidate.

All of this activity is partially in response to the increased availability of debt and equity dollars. Much of the consolidation and development activity is due to the need to form integrated health care networks. These networks offer direct care along the care continuum, in addition to a wide range of ancillary services over a broad geographic area.

While the seniors housing and long-term care industries remain highly fragmented, several key industry players will continue to build critical mass through consolidation, acquisition, and development. In the corporate acquisition market, smaller regional players are expected to continue to merge into increasingly larger networks. These health networks, with integrated delivery systems, will stress the cost and service advantages necessary to succeed in the era of managed care.

5

THE EVOLUTION AND STATUS OF SENIORS HOUSING TERMINOLOGY:
A REVIEW AND ANALYSIS BY SERVICES, PRODUCT TYPES, AND POLITICAL JURISDICTIONS

David Scribner, Jr.
Scribner & Partners

John A. Dalkowski, III
Managing Director
Phoenix Real Estate Counselors

ABSTRACT

Considerable confusion has developed over the past twenty-five years about the types of seniors housing that exist and the terms by which they are known. From such simple origins as "mother-in-law" units in individual homes and "Old Age Homes" of the past, seniors housing alternatives have multiplied and diversified into several different property types that attempt to address in real estate terms the medical, personal, and social services required. The data suggest that the proliferation of terminology surrounding these alternatives can be traced to legislative initiatives at the state level and confusion between the medical or real estate aspects of the product. The industry is far from achieving any meaningful standardization of terminology, and no government agency, medical group, or professional organization has been able to successfully standardize the terminology. A further segmentation of product types is likely to occur as states impose new regulations on seniors living alternatives, especially on the assisted living segment of the market. Professional organizations are expanding the terminology independently in their attempts to control the industry, but their lack of coordination further exacerbates the confusion.

"People make values and determine prices (Ratcliff, 1972)."

1. INTRODUCTION

The population of the United States has been undergoing a number of major social and demographic changes, the significance of which we are only beginning to comprehend. The U.S. Bureau of the Census forecasts that the population aged 65 and over will increase by 37.2 percent by the year 2000 and jump another 46.7 percent by the year 2020. The 75-and-over population—which comprises the largest segment of retirement community and assisted living residents—will increase 35 percent by the year 2000 to 17.5 million people. By 2030, the over-75 population is expected to almost double again in size to 30 million. In this decade alone, the population aged 85 and above is projected to increase by 42 percent. Between 2000 and 2010, this age group is expected to increase again by an additional 32 percent.

The preceding figures refer to "seniors" as people over the age of 64. Yet many figures that refer to "seniors" relate to those over the age of 54. For example, Health Care Investment Analysts, in its Directory of Retirement Facilities (1995), states that currently, there are more than 24,000 assisted living, congregate care facilities, independent living, and continuing care communities serving the needs of senior citizens over the age of 55.

In defining the term "senior" even statisticians differ, emphasizing different medical needs and treatments, treatment levels, and age ranges. Generally speaking, seniors housing participants can be anyone over 55; though in most cases, over 65 marks the starting point, because it is the usual retirement age and because Social Security and Medicare benefits become fully available to people of that age.

With an increase in the overall population and its extending longevity, senior citizens constitute one of the fastest growing population segments in the nation. Benefits for seniors have grown to command an increasingly greater share of federal and state budgets, stressing the budgets for other programs and creating a major health care dilemma for our society that will continue to grow as the first wave of baby boomers joins the senior citizen ranks in the year 2005.

In recent years, real estate developers, working with seniors and their families, have created an alternative long-term care option—seniors housing—that combines residential multifamily housing with direct access to needed social support services and health care. They developed various configurations of seniors housing, congregate care, assisted living, and continuing care retirement communities to accommodate the needs of older adults and their families. Grounded in basic human needs and featuring community-based settings, alternative forms of seniors housing provide direct access to social supportive services and health care, security, opportunities for social interaction, individualized care, economic efficiency, personal choice, wellness and preventive health programs, and independence-enhancing living environments.

Lifecare, or continuing care retirement, communities have evolved over the past thirty years in response to the need for long-term care. The "nursing home" had been the institutional source for this care, and retirement communities added or converted beds into nursing home beds. Only in recent decades have sophisticated medical diagnostic and treatment methods permitted more short-term hospital, nursing home, or outpatient treatment resulting in less need for long-term health care systems and increased need for various forms of assisted living.

Many Lifecare communities offer services on a fee-for-service basis, which calls for payment of a specific up-front entrance fee and ongoing monthly rental fees for a living unit. In essence, the early arrangement was a self-insured health care program that often guaranteed care until death, with no increase in cost. Problems arose with this approach due to shortcomings in the structuring of fees related to unit size (a real estate basis) rather than to a resident's age or physical condition (an actuarial basis). The real estate-based thinking persists in the minds of the public and legislatures. At the same time, most proprietary seniors housing continues to receive an entrance fee in addition to a monthly service fee. Fixed endowments made no provision for increased longevity or increases in the cost of healthcare. As both of these conditions occurred, communities were increasingly unable to cope with the rapidly-escalating costs, and fee-for-service options replaced the concept of unlimited health benefits.

Outsiders, such as real estate developers, tend to consider the needs of senior citizens in real estate terms to which they can relate; geriatric professionals think of needs in terms of services based on a patient's condition. Those who rely on both segments and on others for expertise, such as federal and state legislatures, have created their own terminology (see Table 1). These terminology discrepancies extend to all levels within the continuum of care, including continuing care retirement communities (CCRCs), congregate care, and skilled nursing. Without a common dialogue, as seniors housing alternatives expand, the multiplicity of terms to describe them will continue to grow without standardization.

Other outsiders such as lenders and appraisers are attempting to serve seniors and their housing on a regional and national basis, but must learn different terms and methods of public financing in each state. For example, in its national seminar, Appraisal of Nursing Homes, the Appraisal Institute (1996) teaches ways of valuing a type of facility that has existed for many years—the nursing home—and on which there is general accord as to its characteristics. However, more than half of the seminar is devoted to ways of analyzing the different forms of public finance because of the lack of consistency among the states. Comment is made in the seminar about the other forms of seniors housing as representing a wide range of housing alternatives (e.g., "Licensing of assisted living facilities varies greatly from state to state, and thus physical facilities and scope of services vary, too.").

Table 1. Licensing Terminology, by States

State	Licensing Terminology
Alabama	• Assisted living facility
Alaska	• Adult residential care facility
Arizona	• Unclassified residential care institution
Arkansas	• Residential care facility
California	• Residential care facility for the elderly
Colorado	• Personal care boarding home
Connecticut	• Assisted living services agency
Delaware	• Rest (residential) home
District of Columbia	• Community residence facility
Florida	• Adult congregate living facility
Georgia	• Personal care home
Hawaii	• Adult residential care home
Idaho	• Residential care facility
Illinois	• Sheltered care facility
Indiana	• Residential care facility
Iowa	• Residential care facility
Kansas	• Residential care facility • Intermediate personal care home
Kentucky	• Personal care home
Louisiana	• Adult residential care home
Maine	• Boarding home (boarding care facility)
Maryland	• Domiciliary care home
Massachusetts	• Assisted living residence
Michigan	• Home for the aged
Minnesota	• Board & lodging home with special services • Residential care home
Mississippi	• Personal care home
Missouri	• Residential care facility
Montana	• Personal care facility
Nebraska	• Residential care facility
Nevada	• Residential care for groups
New Hampshire	• Residential care home
New Jersey	• Assisted living residence • Comprehensive personal care home • Residential health care facility • Class "C" boarding home
New Mexico	• Adult residential shelter care home
New York	• Adult home • Enriched housing • Assisted living program

Table 1. Licensing Terminology, by States *(continued)*

North Carolina	• Adult care home
	• Assisted living residence*
North Dakota	• Basic care facility
Ohio	• Rest home
	• Assisted living facility*
Oklahoma	• Residential care home
Oregon	• Assisted living facility
Pennsylvania	• Personal care home
Rhode Island	• Residential care facility
	• Assisted living facility
South Carolina	• Community residential care facility
South Dakota	• Assisted living center
Tennessee	• Home for the aged
Texas	• Personal care facility
Utah	• Residential care facility
	• Assisted living facility*
Vermont	• Residential care home
Virginia	• Home for adults
	• Assisted living facility
Washington	• Boarding home
West Virginia	• Personal care home
Wisconsin	• Community based residential facility
	• Assisted living facility
Wyoming	• Boarding home
	• Assisted living facility*

*A new name for assisted living facilities either adopted recently by the state or pending with approval anticipated in the near future.

Source: The Kaplan Group, Presented at the Fall 1995 NASLI EXPO, Palm Springs, California, December 5, 1995.

2. LITERATURE REVIEW

Several professional organizations have attempted to either codify (AAHSA, 1995 and Kane, AARP, 1993) or suggest a common nomenclature (ALFAA, 1994). Some have included the different terminology headings referred to in state regulations but without annotation as to meaning or lists of state licensing terminology (Kaplan, 1995; Mollica, 1995). These sources treat all types of seniors housing products as discrete when hybrid facilities exist, and they include no comparison of terminology in terms of services needed by end users (the elderly clients) of the housing.

3. HISTORICAL PERSPECTIVE AND THE GROWTH OF SENIORS HOUSING

The origins of today's retirement housing industry predate the creation of Social Security. They can be found in the communities developed by various church groups to care for elderly clergy and parishioners. Gradually, these church-based facilities began to extend their services to members of the church, and then to the community. The residents of these facilities were provided housing, medical care, and assistance in daily living, and were required either (1) to forfeit all or a majority of their assets and monthly income to the sponsor facility or (2) to pay an endowment fee and a monthly service fee. In return, residents received lifetime care, including medical care; a nursing home was usually included in the facilities (Brecht, 1991). Other than these, few alternatives for housing the elderly outside the family existed. Often, families would add apartments or "mother-in law units" to their homes. Thus, primary care responsibilities and burdens still rested with the family. As family values have changed, elderly care alternatives have increased.

Increased longevity and the resulting medical care needs of the elderly have coincided with a sociological change in the American family: increased mobility and relocation, the overall need for double incomes, the increase in college-educated women working in the marketplace, the decline in the birth rate, the increasing divorce rate, and the increase in single parenthood. These structural changes have contributed to the marked decline of the historic practice of caring for one's elderly family members within the family setting. Concomitantly, housing design has changed and no longer provides separate space such as "mother-in-law units."

In 1966, approximately 28.5 percent of American citizens aged 65 and older had incomes at or below the poverty level (Congressional Research Service, 1985, 1986). Consequently, the Social Security Act of 1965 created Medicare—"the national health insurance program for people age 65 and over" (NASLI, 1996)—and Medicaid—"a federally-aided, state-operated and administered program providing medical benefits to certain low-income individuals" (NASLI, 1996).

While Medicaid pays for the vast majority of public funding for long-term care, Medicare, the universal insurance program for all persons aged 65 and older, primarily provides acute-care coverage for hospital and surgical care and accompanying rehabilitation. Consumer misperceptions notwithstanding, Medicare covers neither long-term nor custodial care, encouraging even the wealthiest individuals to shelter their assets in order to qualify for Medicaid nursing home benefits.

Since 1970, costs for nursing home care have increased by an average of 12.6 percent per year—far above the rate experienced in other health care sectors including hospital care, drugs, and physician services (Scanlon, 1992). Many senior citizens of all economic levels have availed themselves of Medicaid by transferring assets to family members to assure that their funds would not be depleted by medical expenses. This form of asset liquidation is legal when carefully planned, and when not planned, requires patients to exhaust their assets before Medicaid takes over.[1]

---

[1] *Compiler's Note:* Recent legislation has cast doubt on the ability of an individual to seek legal assistance in planning the acceleration of Medicaid eligibility. The passing of the Kennedy-Kassebaum

Due to the increasing profitability of retirement facilities, many developers began constructing alternative configurations of retirement facilities in the 1980s. Purely rental retirement communities started to become popular. As rental-only retirement facilities, they targeted the middle income group, and emphasized that they charged no annual or entrance fee in keeping with the strictures of the Department of Housing and Urban Development's (HUD) 221(d)(4) mortgage insurance program, the Retirement Service Center program, which supported the development of continuing care retirement communities and Lifecare communities, but did not offer nursing care. They also initiated assisted living, otherwise known as personal care units. Skilled care was not available, but residents could receive qualified help in the performance of daily living functions.

4. BASIC CONCEPTS IN THE SENIOR LIVING INDUSTRY

Concepts and related terminology are couched in fundamental social premises that drive the industry. These premises reflect normal emotions and the realities of advancing age. Bodies and minds age at different speeds. For some the body deteriorates faster; for others, the mind. The configurations of seniors housing should reflect the various occupants' attitudes, their forms, and stages of aging.

Most people dislike moving, especially elderly people who want to "age in place;" i.e., remain in a familiar, comfortable residential setting surrounded by the people, possessions, and memories that are dear to them. This is evidenced by the recent reverse-migration trend from the Sunbelt to the colder areas that were the migrants' lifelong homes. Overwhelmingly, these people cite the need to stay close to their children, friends, and familiar surroundings as the reasons for their moves. More than that, they want to avoid the institutionalization (regimented schedule, food, space, etc.) and the inability to select their own companions. This institutionalization signified the reality of mortality; going to a final home—moreover, an unfamiliar place—to die.

The problem with remaining in the home occurs when the realities of medical conditions—sometimes exaggerated by overburdened family members—cause the elderly to move, particularly when coupled with the recent loss of a spouse. Various levels of healthcare services have been defined to describe the extent of the assistance required by people as they age. The one notable exception is independent living communities like Heritage Village, Leisure World, and similar active-adult, or "active seniors" over-55 communities. The primary market for these independent living, active-adult communities is married, 55-to 64-year old couples, who want to lead active social lives within a community of similarly-aged, active people who have no medical problems or needs for assistance.

Act and subsequent opposing lobbying efforts have muddled the issue to the extent that it is not clear whether an attorney or other planner can help an individual to accelerate Medicaid eligibility.

Few people other than the "active seniors" segment voluntarily choose to avail themselves of seniors housing alternatives. Instead they are usually persuaded to move, or are physically placed in a facility by hospitals, physicians, family, or other caregivers who can no longer provide for their needs. While the marketing of seniors housing is addressed to all levels of seniors, the primary focus is on those who move. Those who are fully dependent are moved into specially-equipped facilities. Often, these moves are the result of an unfortunate incident; an accident or a stroke. Alzheimer's disease—now the fourth-largest cause of death of dependent patients in the U.S.—is becoming common. Many assisted living facilities have begun recently to include rooms or wings for the treatment of Alzheimer's disease and other forms of dementia at different stages.

Consequently, the mission of long-term care for these medically—and physically-impaired people is the provision of programs that enhance the quality of life and life-satisfaction for older adults, through a continuum of geriatric health care services and assistance with daily-living activities within caring communities. Geriatric service facilities continue to pioneer new health care programs and housing opportunities for older persons. Instead of viewing aging as a disease requiring treatment, many facilities institute programs that stress health, wellness, and a sense of self-worth to help residents of their communities maximize their independence and sense of well-being.

5. DEMOGRAPHIC CHARACTERISTICS OF THE SENIORS HOUSING MARKET

Forty-three percent of all older households in 1989 were single-person households, the majority of which (79 percent) were maintained by women (AARP, 1993). In 1990, the average age of assisted living facility residents was 82 years old, and approximately 80 percent were widowed females. Many operators have begun focusing their marketing efforts toward the elderly female, designing and decorating residences with these consumers in mind.

Socially, most older men are married and live in family settings, but most older women are widowed and live alone. Most older persons are adequately housed. However, lower income households find affordable housing scarce. Older women have lower incomes than older men: married older women have a median income of $5,253, while married older men earn $12,265, and widowed older women have a median income of $6,993, while widowed older men earn $9,258. Most elderly depend on Social Security and asset income as employment declines with age. Most older women retire earlier than age 65, but part-time employment is increasing for all workers aged 65 and over.

Seniors housing officials consider the "affluent market" to comprise households with pretax incomes of $25,000 and more. This market represents approximately 17 to 20 percent of all households aged 65+ and 20 to 25 percent of those aged 55 to 64, for a combined total market of 33.3 percent of all households aged 55 and over. The "moderately-affluent market" is represented by those households with pretax incomes of $15,000 to $25,000 upon retirement. This market makes up 17 to 20 percent of the total 65-and-over households, and 30 to 35 percent of the 55 to 64 age group.

Households with at least one spouse over 55 fall into a wide range of characteristics. Many are active and employed "empty nesters" whose children have grown. Other retired actives have returned to school or travel. The education gap between older and younger persons is closing. As these active people age, their physical limitations increase and they may seek the support of nearby congregations or Lifecare communities. Those who become frail require more personal care or skilled nursing. They may need to move to an assisted living facility or skilled nursing facility depending upon the extent of their needs.

6. THE CURRENT CONTINUUM OF CARE AND SENIORS HOUSING

The levels of health care range from minimal or no care for independent, live-at-home people to acute skilled care for those who are fully dependent. No list can fully describe all the variations available throughout the United States today. Table 1 illustrates the seemingly scattershot proliferation of seniors housing terminology. NASLI (pp. 21-22) describes seven levels:

1. First and Second Level Intensities of Care: Independent Living and Home Care

Generally, independent living encompasses the range of options available to senior citizens, and includes remaining in the home, moving in with a child, and moving into seniors housing. Some of the terms for the housing available to those who move from their homes are:

- Empty-nester homes
- Retirement communities
- Active adult communities
- Single-room occupancies
- Rest homes

Services used by these "independent oldsters" include adult day care and adult day (outpatient) health programs. The "social" model—sometimes referred to as Adult Day Care—offers treatment of the emotional, psychological, and social needs of older people and usually involves structured activities as well as a noon meal. The "medical" model—Adult Day Health Programs—primarily addresses the health needs of the participants. Depending upon the model of care, participants often receive counseling, personal care, help in taking medication, and many other services. It is common for Adult Day Programs to feature some combination of both models.

Some of the elderly need minor assistance and are able to receive home health care services. These services are provided to aged, disabled, sick, or convalescent individuals who are not in need of institutional care. Services may be specialized or comprehensive and may include nursing services, speech, physical, rehabilitation or occupational therapy, homemaker services, and social services. For medical reimbursement, such services must be provided by a home health agency. Under Medicaid, states may, but do not have to, restrict coverage of home health care to services provided by home health agencies.

Additional services used include homemaker services, such as non-medical support services like food preparation and bathing, given to homebound individuals unable to perform these tasks themselves. Such services not covered under the Medicare program may be covered by Medicaid under home and community-based waivers. These services also may be included in the Social Security Block Grant programs developed by individual states. Homemaker services are intended to preserve independent living and normal family life for the aged, disabled, sick, or convalescent. Adult foster care is used to provide the senior citizen moderate independence, but under the watchful eye of a caregiver.

2. Third, Fourth, and Fifth Level Intensities of Health Care

These levels comprise the broadest range of care alternatives, and are found in a variety of seniors housing configurations, including board and care homes, congregate care, assisted living residences, and some nursing homes. The third level of care includes custodial care, which involves temporary 24-hour companionship to recover from an illness or injury, and congregate care, which provides services similar to those found in a hotel, including meal service, housekeeping, and linen service (Gimmy, 1988). Intermediate care—defined as "bed care under the overall supervision of a registered nurse but generally under the immediate care of a practical nurse or attendant with some nursing training" (NASLI, 1996)—is found at the fifth level of intensity.

Assisted living is a general term that is used synonymously to denote both a seniors housing option and the intensity of care. It refers to a broad category of housing types and terms (see Table 1). Generally, assisted living facilities provide care below the level provided in skilled nursing facilities, but above the level of care provided in independent living and congregate care facilities. A primary distinguishing feature between assisted living facilities and skilled nursing facilities is a license to administer drugs. Skilled nursing facilities require this license; assisted living facilities are not licensed to administer drugs, but often provide medication supervision.

Assisted living programs purposefully combine elements of residential surroundings and outcome-based clinical services to help residents maintain their independence and state of health. Supportive services are available, 24 hours a day, to meet scheduled and unscheduled needs, in a way that promotes maximum independence and dignity for each resident and encourages the involvement of a resident's family, neighbors, and friends (ALFAA definition, revised in 1994).

Most recently, assisted living has witnessed dramatic growth, although it is believed to be a Scandinavian concept that is over 25 years old. This growth is evidenced by strong investor interest in assisted living facilities, demonstrated by the number of providers who have recently gone public. In 1995, six assisted living corporations successfully completed their initial public offerings (IPO). The industry is approaching $14 billion in business according to NatWest Securities of New York. This growth is being fueled by the public's desire for homelike settings for an increasingly-aged population. Furthermore, assisted living is cost-effective; its services and amenities cost approximately two thirds the price of a comparable stay at a skilled nursing facility (Provider, 1995).

To date, assisted living residences have been modeled on residential structures, usually with less than 100 units. Situated in both urban and suburban areas with good transportation access, they may replicate large single-family dwellings, housing 30 to 60 residents in private or semiprivate rooms with kitchenettes and common living and dining areas. Assisted living residences can be free standing, operated independently from other types of housing or health care facilities. They can also be sections of other residences such as congregate housing (ASHA, 1993).

Many healthcare experts anticipate that assisted living facilities will become the largest healthcare growth market during the next decade. The Assisted Living Facilities Association of America (ALFAA) was formed in 1990 to assist and guide this growing health care market. According to ALFAA, approximately 1.5 million people currently live in 40,000 assisted living facilities in the U.S.. Approximately 16,000 of current assisted living facilities provide services exclusively to the elderly, while the remaining facilities are used to house those who suffer from mental illness or retardation, and for the developmentally disabled.

To date, there has been little reimbursement from Medicare and Medicaid for services provided in assisted living facilities. Individuals who use these facilities have to pay for services with personal funds. In addition, many residences have the capacity either directly or indirectly (through third-party providers) to allow residents to purchase needed services in the most cost-effective and appropriate time increments. For example, since many seniors only require short-duration personal care assistance (such as assistance with dressing or eating), supportive care can often be purchased in 15-or 30-minute increments (ASHA, 1993).

Because assisted living facilities have traditionally been private-pay options, most developers have targeted only the affluent population—which is the smallest population segment. A vast market exists for this housing option; a market which cannot afford to pay the costs without federal or state entitlements. In an attempt to improve this situation, and recognizing that assisted living is a less-costly alternative to skilled nursing care, several states have legislated Medicaid waivers to increase the availability of home-and community-based services. In addition, a growing number of states are considering some form of waiver for "people who need long-term care services ... [to] enable states to help individuals who would otherwise require institutional care to remain in the community" (Snow, 1995).

Several developers have skirted the Medicaid reimbursement regulations by creating independent living communities, converting former apartment complexes to senior citizen communities, and contracting for the provision of home health care services to the residents. Where Medicaid pays for home health care through waivers, these developers have created communities that, in essence, provide services similar to assisted living.

3. Sixth and Seventh Level Intensities of Health Care

At the sixth level of the continuum of care spectrum are skilled nursing facilities, or nursing homes, both with 24-hour registered nursing and physicians on full-time call. Traditionally, nursing homes have provided formal long-term care services. Nursing homes are full-care facilities, with dining both in room and in common areas. These properties provide total assistance by on-site staff in private or semiprivate rooms. Many nursing homes have recently become licensed to perform subacute care and rehabilitation services. With the advent of managed care, these facilities are more cost effective than full skilled nursing facilities. They provide recovery services and a full array of physical, speech, occupational, and recreational therapies for adults of all ages, to help restore optimum levels of functioning for residents and patients in the system. They are usually located in low and midrise buildings in urban and suburban locations. Occasionally these properties may be highrise buildings when associated with other medical facilities or in urban centers.

Although home health care has made great strides in recent years, only five percent of the Medicaid budget in 1992 was spent on these services, compared with 21 percent for nursing home care. While nursing facilities provide a full range of health, social, nutrition, and housing services for one payment, the cost averages $38,000 per year for private-paying residents. Many people enter nursing homes as private-pay residents, and then spend down their resources to Medicaid eligibility levels. Currently, there are approximately 16,000 nursing homes nationally, with more than 1.6 million beds (Lee, 1992). Finally, the seventh and highest level intensity of health care is hospitalization, or acute care under 24-hour physician supervision.

In contrast to the foregoing NASLI levels of health care are the activities of daily living (ADLs), which are used in evaluating residents for determining a level of care. These are demonstrated in Table 2.

7. IMPACTS OF FEDERAL AND STATE REGULATIONS

As outlined above, the segmentation of the seniors housing market is a subject of considerable debate, which varies depending upon the view of each special interest group. The already tenuous distinctions are further blurred by a proliferation of terminology based largely on disagreements between groups.

Table 2. Functional Limitations of Persons—65 Years and Older: 1984

Functional Limitation	Persons 65 Years and Older
Total civilian noninstitutional population (000)	26,433
Percent with difficulty due to a health or physical problem	
Walking	18.7%
Getting Outside	9.6
Bathing or showering	9.8
Getting in or out of bed	8.0
Dressing	6.2
Using toilet	4.3
Eating	1.8
Preparing meals	7.1
Shopping for personal items	11.3
Managing money	5.1
Using the telephone	4.8
Doing heavy housework	23.8
Doing light housework	7.1

Source: U.S. Bureau of the Census, Sixty-Five Plus in America, Washington, DC: U.S. Government Printing Office (August 1992).

Much of the confusion occurs because of basic similarities in all seniors housing options: the medical needs of the patient or occupant, the costs of the care (including housing), and the patient's or occupant's ability to pay. To date, each of the described major levels of care is secular. Independent living is an option primarily paid for by the elderly homeowner. Assisted living, because it is largely unregulated and differently defined by the states (see Table 1), is also primarily a private-pay option. Skilled nursing, however, is largely funded by Federal and state entitlements, supplemented by private long-term care insurance, and some private-pay clients.

As a condition of governmental reimbursements, skilled nursing facilities function under considerable regulatory pressures. Many states require a certificate of need (CON) before approving the construction and licensing of nursing homes. This CON process is an attempt by government to control its Medicare and Medicaid funding responsibilities, and to limit competition—which some facility owners support. Therefore, although the shortage of skilled nursing beds continues to increase, it often takes several years to obtain approval to build a skilled nursing facility, so the process serves to restrict competition to existing facilities.

States are beginning to realize that assisted living is a cost-effective alternative to warehousing the elderly without severe health problems in nursing facilities. Allowing the development of an assisted living industry to proceed unchecked would undoubtedly open seniors housing alternatives to millions of consumers who currently cannot take advantage of the alternatives. If Medicare and Medicaid reimbursements were required for these new assisted living patients, the results on a system that is already faced with bankruptcy in five years would be disastrous. Therefore, the government is now further regulating the assisted living industry in an attempt to limit the access of lower income people.

Managed care is also the result of attempts by insurance companies and governments to limit the double-digit growth in healthcare expenditures. Prior to managed care, medical care was rendered on a fee-for-service basis; patients selected physicians and paid for office visits, which were reimbursed by health insurance. Further care, specialists, hospital stays, and other services were also handled on a fee-for-service basis.

The idea behind managed care is that people will belong to a health maintenance organization (HMO), with the primary care physician as a "gatekeeper." In order to profit, the physician must keep medical visits and services below a certain level, because there is no additional reimbursement past the predetermined service levels. Understanding the reimbursement system is a central issue that casts a new light on the topic of seniors housing.

8. SUMMARY AND GENERAL OBSERVATIONS

The changing social makeup of the American family has helped the demand for retirement community units. Due to the decentralization of families and the increase in dual-income families, the social acceptance of alternative housing for the elderly has increased. The rise in single-parent homes has also aided acceptance. National organizations, such as the American Association of Retired Persons (AARP) and the National Association for Senior Living Industries (NASLI), and other state and local organizations, have initiated educational efforts to increase the awareness and acceptance of alternative housing for seniors. Individual facilities are also beginning to publicize themselves through advertising and community outreach programs. These factors should all help to increase the demand for quality retirement communities.

As numerous gerontological researchers have noted, seniors housing incorporates a range of design features to address the physical, informational, perceptual, cognitive, and social needs of the elderly. Recognizing the unique needs of older persons, seniors housing has developed a host of design techniques that result in supportive environments that maximize an individual's ability to function. In addition, unlike other institutional long-term care settings that are developed and operated much like acute care medical facilities, seniors housing maintains the residential qualities that seniors and their families overwhelmingly prefer.

Today's political environment is changing the relationship of the federal and state governments toward an increase in jurisdiction for the latter. One outcome of this shift will be a significant increase in varying terminology. Much of this increase will result from the fact that the industry is relatively young and still emerging. With the increased involvement of state legislatures, local gerontologists, social workers, and professional organizations, industry maturity is unlikely to bring a commonality of terms. The only hope may lie with the efforts of managed care firms, who each operate in many states and require a commonality of terms, but their focus so far has been on specific reimbursable treatments, not on real estate.

SELECTED REFERENCES

Appraisal Institute, Appraisal of Nursing Homes. Chicago: Appraisal Institute, 1996.
American Association of Retired Persons (AARP), Briefings on Long-Term Care Regulations, Washington, DC: AARP, November 1995.
AARP, Progress in Elderly Housing, 1993.
American Seniors Housing Association (ASHA), The State of Seniors Housing 1993, Washington, DC: ASHA, 1993.
ASHA, Seniors Housing: The Market-Driven Solution To Long-Term Care, Washington, DC: ASHA, August 1994.
Bowe, J., Long-Term Care Wields Growing Clout, 1994.
Brecht, S.B., Retirement Housing Markets: Project Planning and Feasibility Analysis, New York: John Wiley & Sons, Inc., 1991.
CD Publications, "Assisted Living: State-by-State Report," Housing the Elderly Report, Silver Spring, MD: CD Publications, May 1995.
Congressional Research Service, Aging America, 1985, 1986.
Health Care Investment Analysts (HCIA), The Directory of Retirement Facilities—1995 edition, Baltimore, MD: HCIA, 1995.
Gimmy, A.E. and M.G. Boehm, Elderly Housing: A Guide to Appraisal, Market Analysis, Development, and Financing, Chicago: American Institute of Real Estate Appraisers, 1988.
Gordon, P., Developing Retirement Communities, 2d ed., New York: John Wiley & Sons, Inc., 1993.
Hoeflich, M.H., "Housing the Elderly in a Changing America: Innovation Through Private Sector Initiative," University of Illinois Law Review, Volume No. 1, 1985.
Hospitals & Health Networks Provider, November 1995.
Hospitals & Health Networks Provider, December 1995.
Kane, R.A., and K.B. Wilson, Assisted Living in the United States: A New Paradigm for Residential Care for Frail Older Persons?, Washington, DC: Public Policy Institute, AARP, 1993.
Kaplan Group, The List of Assisted Housing Terms by States, 1995.
Lee, State Long Term Care Systems: Region I Profile, Washington, DC: AARP, 1992.
Medicare Managed Care Program Update, 1995.
Minnesota Association of Homes for the Aging, "Common Seniors Housing Definitions," Contemporary Long Term Care Magazine [n.d.].
Mollica, Robert L., K.B. Wilson, B.S. Ryther, and H.J. Lamarche, Guide to Assisted Living State Policy, Portland, ME: National Academy for State Health Policy, May 1995.
National Association for Seniors Living Industries (NASLI), Dictionary of Terms for Senior Citizens and the Industries that Serve Them, Annapolis, MD.
NASLI News, February 1996.
Provider Magazine, Annual Survey of the Top 25 Assisted Living Providers, 1995.
"Pursuing the Frail Elderly Population," Assisted Living Today, Summer 1995.
Ratcliff, R.U., Valuation for Real Estate Decisions, Santa Cruz, CA: Democrat Press, 1972.
Redfoot, D., "Long Term Care Reform and the Role of Housing Finance," Housing Policy Debate, 1993.
"States Seek Medicaid Waivers For Assisted Living," Currents, ASHA, May 1995.
Scanlon, W.J., "Possible Reforms for Financing Long-Term Care," Journal of Economic Perspectives, 1992.
Snow, K.I., State Long Term Care Programs At A Glance, The Center for Vulnerable Populations, December 1995.

U.S. Bureau of the Census, Sixty-Five Plus in America, Washington, DC: U.S. Government Printing Office, 1992.
U.S. Department of Commerce, Economics and Statistics Administration, Bureau of the Census, "Population Projections of the United States by Age, Sex, Race and Hispanic origin: 1992-2050," Current Population Reports P-25, No. 1092, 1992.
U.S. Senate Special Committee on Aging, Aging America: Trends and Projections, 1991.
U.S. Special Committee on Aging, Developments in Aging, 1991.
U.S. Special Committee on Aging, Developments in Aging, 1992.
Winklevoss, H. and A. Powell, Continuing Care Retirement Communities: An Empirical, Financial and Legal Analysis, Homewood, IL: Richard D. Irwin, Inc., 1984. Published for the Pension Research Council, Wharton School, University of Pennsylvania.

6

TOWARD STANDARDIZING SENIORS HOUSING INDUSTRY DEFINITIONS BY PROJECT TYPE

Michael A. Anikeeff
The Berman Real Estate Institute
Johns Hopkins University

Glenn R. Mueller
Legg Mason and The Berman Real Estate Institute
Johns Hopkins University

ABSTRACT

Standardizing seniors housing industry definitions by project type would improve decision making in the industry. The problem is not a lack of definitions; rather, there is minimal agreement on precise definitions. This poses an immediate practical problem for seniors housing institutional investment. Inability to define the business prevents measurement of performance. If they cannot measure performance, investors will not be able to measure the risk and the return. Finally, owners and managers will not have the means to benchmark their performance with industry norms, therefore, standardized data is needed to enhance performance.

This paper points out the difficulty with current seniors housing definitions and provides a potential solution. By defining the categories operationally, seniors housing candidates—as well as project types—may be categorized objectively rather than subjectively or arbitrarily. Under the current definitional regime, terms such as "nursing home" can mean very different things in terms of an individual's ability to function, considering the varying uses of the term in the states of Washington and Oregon, for example.

The choice of categories is currently qualitative and discontinuous in the seniors housing industry. It could be continuous and numerical. Research suggests that industry-standard definitions can be developed by linking a Gutman-type functional disability scale with projects by the types of services they deliver. This would allow analysts to more precisely calculate the most effective and efficient way to deliver a level of care.

1. INTRODUCTION

The seniors housing industry is in a state of evolution, rising from a heritage of nursing homes in the 1960s and 1970s to an overbuilding boom of congregate-care facilities in the 1980s. The industry has now identified a number of different care needs for seniors citizens that require different levels of service and therefore different types of real estate. Unlike other property types in real estate, seniors housing can not be separated easily from the operating business of providing care, much like hotel properties rely heavily on the service they provide for consistent revenue generation in the real estate.

As with most growing and evolving industries, a major impediment to expansion is the lack of standard definitions. This paper attempts to define industry standards for seniors housing real estate products so that future study and investment can take place in a more orderly fashion. The major types of seniors-focused real estate are often placed on a continuum ranging from unassisted living through independent living, assisted living, and skilled nursing care. A description of the business as well as the real estate is undertaken to help define the reasons for certain building design requirements. The seniors living industry provides not only shelter for people, but also different levels of care service.

These defined levels of care-service provision help to differentiate the business of care provision as well as determine the design criteria for the shelter being provided. At the level where no care or assistance is provided (unassisted living), seniors housing looks like any other form of residential housing including single family and multifamily units. At this level of "no care provided" the only design criteria difference between seniors and non-seniors housing is in the recreational amenities provided. Most seniors do not work, and adult-only communities (apartment or single family) usually provide expanded recreational and meeting room facilities for seniors to use at all times of the day. Many communities also provide organized activities, recreation, and even travel opportunities.

At the beginning level, unassisted seniors living is identical to apartment investment with management requirements on a monthly basis. With independent living, the management intensity increases to a daily level similar to that found in a hotel. With the assisted living and skilled nursing care areas, management intensity increases from daily to hourly depending upon the circumstances. Therefore, the physical facility requirements can change dramatically with services provided.

2. NEED FOR STANDARDIZATION

Standardizing seniors-housing industry definitions by project type would improve decision making in the industry. The problem is not a lack of definitions; rather, there is minimal agreement on precise definitions. This problem could be relegated to an interesting academic issue of research methods of description, classification, and measurement if it were not for the immediate practical problem of fostering institutional investment. Inability to define the business prevents measurement of performance. If they cannot measure performance, investors will not be able to measure the risk and the return. Owners and managers will not have the means to benchmark their performance with industry norms—data needed to enhance performance.

DuBrin (1995) examines institutional reluctance to invest in seniors housing and points to several fundamental concerns. How is the investment product type evaluated and the risk quantified? Is seniors housing real estate or is it a business? Thus, there is a need for clearly-defined categories so that performance by product type can be measured. This will permit the growth of the seniors housing industry that can result from increased institutional investment.

The lack of definitions is troublesome to other stakeholders in the seniors housing industry. The long-term care industry lacks standardized definitions for the continuum of real estate, hospitality, and health-care services marketed primarily to the senior adult, according to Sherman and Logan (1996). They say that the growing variety of seniors living and long-term care developments has created fragmentation within the health care delivery system, leading to confusion for consumers seeking appropriate living arrangements. Significant operating differences within the same product lines make it difficult to discuss development and operating statistics for long-term care products in general terms.

3. ECOLOGICAL MODEL

If aging is a problem of decreasing function and seniors housing is a means of helping to maintain function, then there should be a relationship between individual function and the need for certain types of housing; i.e., the form of the seniors-living facility should follow the function it is meant to support.

Lawton developed an ecological model of the person-environment fit. The model describes the everyday environmental choices and tradeoffs that elderly people make in their effort to maintain their independence in their community. Lawton and Nahemow (1973) conceptualized the relationship between the person and his environment. Figure 1 illustrates the model.

The vertical axis of the graph represents the ability of a person to function independently. The health care community uses the terms "activities of daily living" (ADLs) and "instrumental activities of daily living" (IADLs). Competence is a measure of personal ability or weakness and includes physical, mental, and emotional qualities. Moving up the axis, the overall competence of the individual increases. An older individual with heart problems, arthritis, trouble walking, and poor vision would be classified as a person with low competency. A former athlete who runs to work and is socially active would have a high level of competency.

The horizontal axis represents the level of difficulty associated with the built environment. This factor is labeled environmental press. Press is a measure of the environment's supportive or adverse qualities. Moving from the left to the right along the axis demonstrates an increase in environmental press. A nursing home environment complete with health and meal preparation services, hand rails, grab bars, and elevators between floors would be an environment with low press. An isolated farm house, several miles from city services, without access to emergency health would be a high press environment.

At any point each individual has a given level of competency and lives with a given level of press. The match between the support of the environment and the person's ability to cope is the primary purpose of the model. A person of high compe-

Figure 1. Ecological model

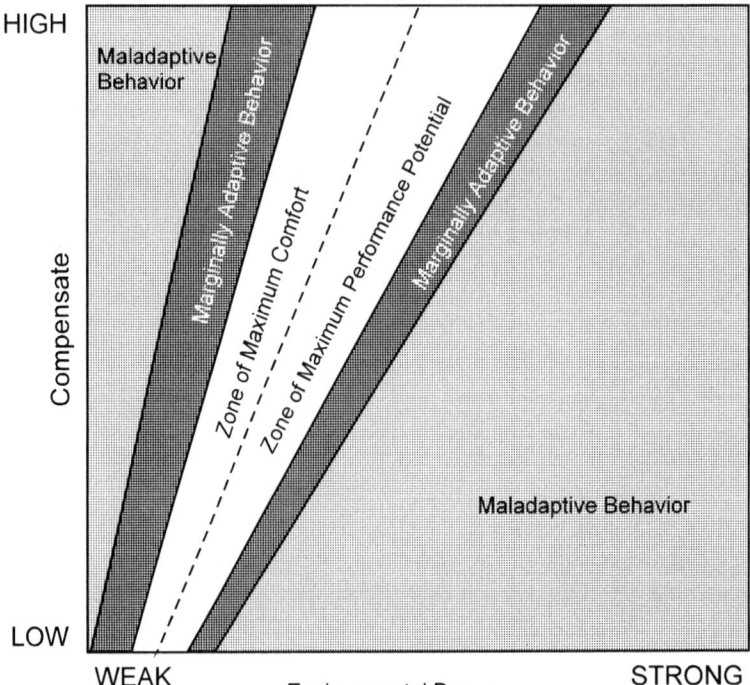

Source: Adapted from M.P. Lawton, 1980.

tency living in a high press environment is likely to feel comfortable with the match of his environmental situation and his ability, just as a person with low competency in a low press environment would. Problems in adaptation occur when an individual's competence (ability to function) is mismatched with the environmental press (type of seniors housing). The problem of misplacing individuals in nursing homes who could be supported in a lower level of care is an example of lack of fit. The individual is unhappy with the overly-institutionalized environment as well as the expense. In the next section we will explore how health care professionals define the appropriate levels of function.

4. ASSESSING PHYSICAL FUNCTION

Guralnik and Lacroix (1992) discuss health status and the quality of life. Functional independence is an important component of the quality of life. They point out that the magnitude of loss of independence increases significantly with age after 65. Among those age 85 and older, 46 percent of men and 62 percent of women either are in nursing homes or need help at home. Guralnik and Lacroix examine the domain of physical functioning and disability. Their study describes the theoretical framework for assessing functioning, the process of selecting appropriate measures of physical function, general issues of functional assessment, and specific assessment instruments.

The general approaches to measuring physical function have been used in research and in clinical settings for years. Katz et al. (1963) introduced a formal instrument for the assessment of activities of daily living. The number of instruments has increased significantly since. Guralnik and Lacroix point out that in evaluating seniors, it is important to understand that measuring physical functioning is only one of many domains of functioning that is important to consider in measuring overall health and the impairment of disease. Other domains include cognitive, psychological, and social functions as well as sensory function, including vision and hearing. These domains are interrelated, they say, and that fact must be considered when attempting to make measurements in these areas.

A large number of instruments have been developed for the assessment of physical functioning in older populations. Guralnik and Lacroix classify them into five categories: 1) self-care; activities of daily living, 2) maintenance of independence in the community; instruments of daily living, 3) other measures of usual functioning, 4) physical activity/exercise/recreation, and 5) performance measures of functioning.

The most commonly-known measures are the activities of daily living (ADLs). These measures were originally developed to assess older persons in long-term care or rehabilitation settings, and reflect a substantial degree of disability. The ADLs have been used in measuring community dwelling populations where the prevalence of difficulty or the need for help is low, but these measures do identify the most severely disabled individuals. For most uses of ADLs, there are five basic activities that are always assessed. In increasing order of severity of disability, these are bathing, dressing, transferring from bed to chair, using the toilet, and eating. The original scale developed by Katz et al. also included continence. Continence is generally not included in population estimates of ADL impairment because it may occur in persons who are otherwise in very good health.

The prevalence of disabilities in ADLs has been assessed in several U.S. national surveys. Overall, these surveys found that between 5.0 percent and 8.1 percent of people 65 and older need help from another person in performing one or more ADLs. Most surveys have found an increase with age and a higher prevalence among women compared to men of the same age group.

The instrumental activities of daily living (IADLs) are activities that are required for independence in the community. They are more difficult and more complex than the ADLs. Lawton and Brody (1969) first described a scale with a number of activities including shopping, food preparation, housekeeping, doing laundry, using transportation, taking medicine, handling finances, and using the telephone. The IADLs incorporate more than the physical domain of functioning and may be difficult to interpret as direct measures of physical functioning and disability. Cognitive functioning plays a significant role in performing these tasks. IADLs can serve in a valuable role as indicators of need to perform tasks that are necessary if the individual is to continue to live in the community.

In addition to ADLs and IADLs there are other activities that have been used to assess physical functioning in older populations. The tasks are less complex, but more vigorous than ADLs or IADLs, according to Guralnik and LaCroix. They evaluate a particular function of the body, rather than a task that has multiple components.

Beyond ADLs, IADLs, and the other measures of usual functioning, physical activity, exercise, and vigorous recreational activities may serve as a measure of physical functioning. The assessment of physical activity in the community-dwelling segment of the older population with no serious disability may be of value in placing them along a continuum of the full spectrum of physical functioning (Guralnik and Lacroix, 1992). Examples of these activities include gardening, taking walks, jogging, bike riding, swimming, fishing, camping, and boating. These activities do not have to be performed for the individual to be independent in the community. However, they do indicate high levels of functioning in individuals that perform the activities.

The final category of physical functioning addressed by Guralnik and Lacroix is performance measures of functioning. In this evaluation the individual is asked to perform a specific task and is evaluated in an objective, standardized manner using predetermined criteria. The technique measures functioning rather than the kind of function; i.e., testing the individual's ability to walk rather than asking how well the individual walks.

5. PRODUCT/MARKET DEFINITION

The way in which ADLs are often reported is an example of summarizing multiple items in gerontological research. Individuals are classified according to their relative need for help in performing various ADLs.

This issue is important to market analysis because ADLs and IADLs are used to determine eligibility for different products, such as placing an individual in a nursing home or in an assisted-living facility. Long-term care insurance policies often use ability to perform ADLs as a trigger for benefits. It is important for real estate analysts to understand that in the future a more comprehensive scaling will allow functional status to be classified across a continuum instead of simply dichotomized into disabled versus not disabled (Guralnik and Lacroix, 1992). The construction of a scale or an index by aggregating a number of items is a common activity in the social sciences. The two most commonly-used types of scales are the summative and the cumulative scales. In the summative scale, also called an index, individual items are scored and then summed to arrive at an aggregate score. Before adding items, certain summated scores apply weights—obtained through analytical techniques—to each item. Cumulative scaling, also called Gutman scaling (Gutman, 1944), is appropriate when rank ordering hierarchical items. Items are rank ordered by difficulty. When the subjects select an item, it can be assumed that they can complete all easier items. This rank order feature differentiates cumulative scales from summative scales.

An example of a modified summated scale of physical functioning is the Health Assessment Questionnaire Disability Index, developed to assess the impact of arthritis on functional status (Fries et al., 1982). The scale includes eight different domains: dressing, grooming, hygiene, arising, eating, walking, conducting IADL-type activities, reaching, and gripping. Each domain includes two or three items, with each item scored as a 0 for no difficulty, 1 for some difficulty, 2 for much difficulty, and 3 for unable to do. The score for the domain is the individual's poorest score in that domain. The scores for the eight domains are summated and then averaged; the total score ranges from 0 to 3.

An example of a cumulative or Gutman scale of functioning is the scale used by Pinsky et al. (1987). They found a strong hierarchical pattern for three sets of questionnaire items: the ADLs, mobility items (Rosow-Breslau, 1966), and strength and flexibility items (Nagi, 1976). In the cumulative scale, 0 indicates no disability in any of the three subscales, 1 indicates disability in Nagi items only, 2 indicates disability in Nagi and Rosow-Breslau items, and 3 indicates disability in all three scales. Guralnik and Lacroix point out that aggregate scales of functioning have a number of advantages as summary measures, but their reliability and validity need to be tested further.

A scale will allow measurement of function or competency in the ecological model described earlier. In other words, a single number can define the individual's functional needs. Each seniors housing environment should correspond to a discrete level of individual need along the continuum. The next section describes the definitions of different seniors housing environments.

6. CURRENT DEFINITIONS OF SENIORS HOUSING ENVIRONMENTS

This section summarizes contemporary definitions from various stakeholders in the seniors housing industry.

The American Seniors Housing Association (ASHA) categorizes property units and beds, combines these categories into project types, and then gives operational and performance data by project type. These types include:

Congregate/independent living units. Designed for seniors who pay for some congregate service—i.e., housekeeping, transportation, meals, etc.—as part of a monthly fee or rental rate and who require little, if any, assistance with activities of daily living. Residents of congregate/independent living units may have some home health care services provided to them by in-house staff or an outside agency. Congregate units may be part of a congregate residence, a property that provides congregate and assisted-living services, or a continuing care retirement community (CCRC), but not a free-standing assisted-living residence.

Assisted living beds. Designed for frail seniors who need assistance with the activities of daily living—i.e., bathing, dressing, eating, etc.—but do not require continuous skilled nursing care. These beds are typically offered in a separate wing, separate floor, or separate building and usually have more stringent licensing requirements than congregate/independent living units. Assisted living may also be referred to as personal care, residential care, or sheltered care. Included in this category are Alzheimer's/dementia care beds and other specialty care beds that are not licensed as nursing beds. Assisted living beds may be part of a congregate residence or CCRC, or may be contained in a residence that includes assisted living and nursing beds, or may be contained in a free standing assisted living residence. The final project type is *nursing beds*, which includes all licensed nursing beds.

Using the unit and bed type categories described above, ASHA then defines three property types. The *congregate* property type category includes properties with congregate units only, and properties with both congregate units and assisted living beds. The *assisted living* property type comprises free-standing residences that feature only assisted living units and properties that combine assisted living with skilled nursing, Alzheimer's/dementia care beds, or other specialty care beds. *Continuing care retirement communities* (CCRC) property types are those properties that feature a combination of congregate units, assisted living beds, and nursing beds, as well as properties that combine congregate units and nursing beds.

The ASHA annual seniors housing survey is currently the most widely used in the industry. The survey provides a great deal of information by project type for occupancy, age, size, development costs, revenues and expenses, key cost items, and measures of performance. The problem is that the survey includes different unit/bed mixes in the different property types. Congregate comprises 87.4% independent living and 12.6% assisted living. Assisted living is 99.1% assisted living and .9% skilled nursing, and CCRC is 67% independent living, 22.8% assisted living and 10.2% skilled nursing. If the survey authors would eliminate the assisted living units from congregate care and the few nursing units from assisted living, the categories would be exclusive and the information more meaningful. If it were possible to have the CCRC results reported by separate categories—e.g., congregate care, assisted living, and nursing—industry analysts and owners/managers could make meaningful comparisons, such as whether independent living and assisted living units are more efficient in separate facilities or in CCRCs.

The Appraisal Institute (Gimmy and Boehm, 1988) has developed its own definitions of seniors housing facilities. This is important because these are the analysts who appraise property purchase and financing decisions. The definitions they use include:

Independent living. Housing that allows the resident to live in a totally independent manner and does not provide care or services designed for those with physical or mental limitations. Units include houses, cottages, townhouses, condominiums, apartments, or retirement residences. Congregate care facilities (see below) are not included in this category.

Retirement community. A large, privately-built development which focuses on young retirees by emphasizing outdoor recreation amenities such as golf courses, swimming pools, tennis courts, and club complexes. Housing options are usually offered for purchase and include single-family homes, duplexes, townhouses, and condominium units. These units are also called retirement resorts or retirement new towns. Examples include Rossmore Leisure World in Laguna Hills, California and Sun City, Arizona.

Retirement villages and subdivisions. Large, planned retirement developments. Retirement villages house from 1,000 to 5,000 people, while subdivisions average 500 residents. The variety of this category of housing is enormous, ranging from single-family homes and low- and high-rise apartments to mobile home parks. Villages frequently offer recreational activities and security, while subdivisions depend more on the surrounding community and offer amenities that may be limited to a recreation room. Examples include Orange Gardens in Kissimmee, Florida and Leisure Village West, Manchester, New Jersey.

Congregate housing. This type is characterized by multiunit, usually rental, housing for the elderly that features an array of services designed to aid the residents' independence. Common services including housekeeping, transportation, organized activities, security, and grounds maintenance. Although most units have kitchens, congregate facilities usually serve at least one meal a day in a central dining area to ease the resident's workload and encourage socialization. Most congregate facilities do not provide health care; they are targeted to the fully ambulatory and healthy. Residents are usually between 75 and 85 years old and tend to be female and widowed.

Residential Care Facility (RCF). A facility commonly known as a board and care facility, offering more care than a congregate center but less than an ICF or SNF. The resident receives daily assistance with meals, dressing, personal hygiene, transportation, housekeeping, and mobility as necessary, in a private or shared room. Facilities are licensed and may offer health care.

Intermediate Care Facility (ICF). A licensed facility which stands between residential care and skilled care in the level of health care provided. It is aimed at persons not capable of fully-independent living who need noncontinuous medical, nursing, and rehabilitative services in addition to room and board, and may offer limited health care.

Skilled Nursing Facility (SNF). A state-licensed facility commonly known as a nursing home, which provides around-the-clock nursing care for convalescent patients. This form of care is one level below acute hospital care, and includes restorative, physical, occupational, and other therapy.

Lifecare Facilities. A campus-type elderly project offering degrees of care ranging from independent living through intermediate or skilled nursing care. Lifecare centers offer the same services as congregate centers—housekeeping, meals, transportation, security—with the addition of living assistance and medical care. Traditional Lifecare facilities require an endowment fee that guarantees the resident lifetime residence and medical care as well as a monthly maintenance fee. Because of several bankruptcies in this industry in the 1970s, many facilities have curtailed guaranteed services in favor of a fee-for-service approach.

Continuing Care Retirement Center (CCRC). A newer, modified version of the Lifecare center that is distinguished by its method of financing, which emphasizes either a monthly maintenance fee and a partially- or fully-refundable entrance fee, or services on a fee-for-service basis. CCRCs are licensed in many states. Like Lifecare centers, the CCRC includes a residential complex, with possible units ranging from cottages to high-rise apartments, a commons area including administrative, dining, and activities areas, and the health center, usually composed of nursing beds and an infirmary or clinic. The growth of CCRCs was a response to the financial troubles in the Lifecare industry that surfaced in the 1970s.

The US Department of Health and Human Services, National Center for Health Statistics, produces the most comprehensive data on long term care facilities (Sirocco, 1995). The information comes from the National Health Provider Inventory database, a survey conducted by the Bureau of the Census. The classification system is important because it is a comprehensive source of data and it has official government status. Data is provided on the supply of different facilities and beds. Vacancy rates, facility size, profit and nonprofit, free standing and hospital-based information is provided by state. Definitions used by this survey include:

Home Health Care Agency. An agency providing health services to individuals in their homes for the purpose of (a) promoting, maintaining, or restoring health; or (b) maximizing the level of independence, while minimizing the effects of disability and illness (including terminal illness).

Hospice. An agency providing specialized services for terminally-ill people and their families, including medical services, social and emotional support for patients and families, volunteer support, and bereavement services for families following the death of the patient.

Nursing Homes. A nursing home is a facility with three beds or more that is either licensed as a nursing home, certified as a nursing facility under Medicare or Medicaid, identified as a nursing care unit of a retirement center, or otherwise determined to provide nursing or medical care. These are broken down into freestanding and hospital based facilities.

Board and Care Homes. This generic term describes a residential setting that provides either routine general protective oversight or assistance with activities necessary for independent living to physically-limited persons (excludes those for the mentally retarded).

U.S. Government Standard Industrial Code (SIC) definitions are important, because sources of financial performance such as Dun and Bradstreet, Robert Morris, and Frank Russell collect their data in this format. Sheflin (1994) provides financial information for nursing homes and other personal care facilities. Dun and Bradstreet (1996) provides information on skilled nursing, intermediate care, and general hospitals. Ratios are given for solvency, efficiency, and profitability for firms in the upper, middle, and lower ranks. The firm data can be compared with performance data of firms in other industries, making the information particularly useful to investors and analysts. The problem is that "nursing homes" provide different services in different states. Therefore, the performance data may not be comparable. For example, Oregon provides care for only the most-disabled residents in nursing homes. Therefore, nursing home costs in Oregon would be higher than those in Washington, where nursing homes have a patient mix of severely- and less-severely-disabled patients. Also, the assisted living facilities (intermediate care) in Oregon would have higher costs since they also care for more severely-disabled residents than those in Washington.

7. REAL ESTATE OR PHYSICAL PROPERTY TYPES DEFINED

Real estate professionals know that the facilities reflect the business strategy and the services provided by an organization. This is certainly the case in the seniors living industry. In this section, we describe the impact of the different seniors housing businesses described above on the design of facilities.

Unassisted living units are similar to apartment units or housing developments. The main additional functions found in these facilities are recreational in nature. Because senior citizens are typically retired, the recreational and social amenities become an important part of their everyday living. Enhanced security is typically another concern of senior residents. In addition, many seniors prefer to live in complexes that are exclusively dedicated to their age group to avoid the disturbances and offensive activities of younger residents.

Independent Living units is a product similar to unassisted living in appearance. However, it differs in that a certain level of services is provided in the area of transportation, housekeeping, meals, etc.

Congregate care is seniors housing where some level of additional care is provided. Industry stakeholders today suggest that a person is appropriate for an assisted living facility when he needs help with IADLs on a daily basis. IADL help is considered to be low or unskilled work that requires little or no training and therefore has a fairly low cost and low frequency of contact. Congregate/independent facilities are typically multiunit dwellings that have common recreational facilities, a common cafeteria with an institutional-quality kitchen to offer daily meals, handicapped-accessible or wheelchair-equipped bath facilities, emergency buzzer system, and local community transportation access. Transportation may be either public transportation such as city bus stops or a subway station, or private transportation such as shuttle bus service for residents. If the buildings are multifloored, elevator systems are necessary. HVAC systems that can maintain constant temperatures with few "drafts" are also a necessity for temperature-sensitive seniors. Hallways and common areas are usually equipped with railings and other walking aids. Buildings are usually located near the resident's former neighborhood so that the residents can continue to maintain their social and civic contacts. Units vary in size from under 20 to over 200, but unit sizes around 100 provide the most efficient and profitable service capabilities while still providing a residential instead of an institutional atmosphere. One of the problems experienced with these facilities was the fact that operators had not planned for the "aging in place" process whereby active, independent seniors eventually deteriorated and required more services and support than those for which the existing facility was designed and the existing staff trained.

Assisted Living. The Assisted Living Facilities Association of America (ALFAA) defines assisted living as "a special combination of housing, personalized supportive services, and health care designed to respond to individuals who need help with daily living activities, but do not need the skilled medical care of a nursing home" (Fitzgerald, 1995). The additional services provided in assisted living facilities require different building design components to provide for these additional services. Offices for the additional service providers are necessary, common areas need to be designed to handle residents with additional support needs, and the increased use of wheelchairs in all areas must be considered in building design. The use of intercom systems and room monitoring systems is usually necessary to provide additional safety and improved reaction time in emergency situations. The staff in these facilities usually require a higher level of training to provide more complex care and they must also be able to identify and correct more complex problems that residents may have.

In recent years, the amount of care given in assisted living facilities has increased because the costs of an assisted living facility are lower than those of a skilled nursing home. Thus, assisted living facilities are now moving to care for more physical disabilities, some non-ambulatory situations, and even early stages of specific diseases where intensive medical care is not required. Residents in these situations are "not quite" in need of the full services found in the intense hospital bed environment of a nursing home.

Historically, *skilled nursing care* facilities used to house many seniors in all levels of care need when they were not able to remain in their own homes or within the care of their families. The high expense of nursing homes made these facilities inaccessible to a large portion of the population. Today, skilled nursing homes handle seniors with intensive medical care needs, usually keeping these patients bed ridden or in a state where any ambulatory movement requires assistance or monitoring. Many facilities now specialize in specific disease care such as Alzheimer's or dementia.

The skilled nursing facilities require the same physical characteristics of all previous seniors facilities with the additional requirements of medical care that bring them up to a hospital standard. Typically, an on-site emergency room exists with all the medical equipment to treat major problems, sometimes including minor emergency surgery. Most rooms may be equipped with patient monitoring devices and emergency call systems. Oxygen systems may also be present. Immediate response staff stations are also part of the design scheme. By their nature, these facilities tend to take on a more institutional atmosphere that allows for efficient cleaning and sterilization. Both multiple-floor and single-floor designs are common. These facilities historically have been located near hospitals to allow doctors the ease of visiting patients in an efficient manner. Today, the location seems to be less critical as rotational visiting systems allow doctors to share the work and higher skilled nursing staff take care of more functions formerly handled by the doctors.

8. DEFINING SENIORS HOUSING INDUSTRY PROJECT TYPES BY HEALTH CARE FUNCTION

The nursing home problem illustrates the difficulty in creating standardized definitions in the industry. Nursing homes are subject to state licensing and regulations as well as federal regulations prescribed by Medicare and Medicaid. Surveys counting the number of nursing homes are conducted by the Census for the Department of Health and Human Services. The long-term-care continuum is anchored by the nursing home. The need for the other health-oriented parts of the continuum results from nursing home residents not having the medical needs or not being sufficiently-disabled to require the services of nursing homes. Yet, estimates of misplacement in nursing homes have ranged from 10 to 40 percent (Williams et al., 1973; Congressional Budget Office, 1977).

As perspective, in 1990, there were 1.6 million seniors in nursing homes, 900,000 in assisted living units, 186,000 in continuing care retirement communities, and 281,000 in congregate care (see Sexton, Chapter 2). The remainder was in rented or owned housing units.

Even though there have been changes since 1970 in the types of long term care available—adult day care, home care, assisted living—and there is greater use of pre-admission screening and periodic inspections of care in nursing homes, and stricter regulatory requirements for nursing homes, clinically-inappropriate residents are still placed in nursing homes. Spector et al. (1996) demonstrate by example that the number of nursing home residents that might be served by lower levels of care can vary significantly using clinical measures and definitions in use currently in two states. The point is that market share for nursing homes is difficult to define using empirical, clinical measures because state regulations define what services must be performed in the nursing home. As a result, because the market for the nursing home—anchor of the long-term-care continuum—is difficult to define, the other product types are also difficult to define.

With all of the changes in the long-term-care market, the perception remains that a large number of residents in nursing homes could be placed in lower levels of care. Spector et al. (1996) first identified the size of the population using clinical criteria. Since there is no standard for nursing home placement, the authors provided three estimates using the most recent nationally-representative data. The data are from the

Institutional Population Component of the National Medical Expenditure Survey (NMES-IPC) of 1987. The survey represents 21,643 nursing and personal care homes nationally, which contain in the aggregate 1,510,869 residents. The researchers chose to make estimates based on criteria being used in the states of Oregon and Washington to target persons for assisted living. The Oregon and Washington criteria were chosen to represent the extremes of practices across the states. The Oregon criteria make high estimates of the number of clinically-inappropriate nursing home residents, while the Washington state criteria make low estimates. The study also provided an intermediate estimate. This study reminds us that these clinical criteria are one set of many that must be considered when making decisions; consumer preference, availability of alternatives, and cost are other factors.

The three sets of criteria are summarized in Table 1. The Oregon (High) criteria identify the most residents as clinically appropriate for lower levels of care; i.e., assisted living. Oregon is least restrictive regarding who is appropriate for assisted living. It accepts residents who have no severe medical conditions or rehabilitation needs and can function socially, and allows for some behavioral problems. Acceptable residents may need personal care but are not bed or chair bound.

Table 1. Criteria for clinically appropriate placement in nursing homes (NH) or lower levels of care (LCC)[a]

Patient Characteristic	Oregon High	Middle	Washington State Low
Substantial medical/rehab. needs[b]	NH	NH	NH
Comatose	NH	NH	NH
Bed/chair fast	NH	NH	NH
Hurts self/others	NH	NH	NH
Can't communicate	NH	NH	NH
Can't understand conversation	NH	NH	NH
Has bedsores	NH	NH	NH
Fecal incontinent	LLC	NH	NH
Urinary incontinent	LLC	LLC	NH
Requires ADL help beyond bathing and dressing	LLC	LLC	NH
Unable to avoid dangers	LLC	LLC	NH
Wanders	LLC	LLC	NH
Has hallucinations/delusions	LLC	LLC	NH
None of the above characteristics.	LLC	LLC	LLC

[a]To be classified as appropriate for lower levels of care (or clinically inapproprite for nursing home care), residents can not have any characteristics marked NH.
[b]Indicated by Medicare payment for basic charges.

Source: Spector et al (1996).

TOWARD STANDARDIZING SENIORS HOUSING

The Middle criteria include a single additional element to the High or Oregon criteria: those fecally-incontinent are no longer classified as appropriate for assisted living. This is very prevalent in nursing home populations.

The Low or Washington state criteria are more restrictive. In addition to the previous criteria, Washington restricts from being designated as appropriate for lower levels of care residents who are urinary-incontinent, receive ADL help beyond bathing and dressing, are unable to avoid dangers, wander, or have hallucinations or delusions.

The first two rows of Table 2 present the number and percentage of current nursing home residents who would be classified as transferable under alternative criteria. The table shows that 70% of the nation's current nursing home residents would be candidates for lower-level care under the Oregon criteria. This proportion would be reduced to 47% under the Middle criteria, and only 15% under the Washington state criteria.

Table 2. Number of nursing home residents appropriate for lower levels of care under alternative clinical criteria.

	Clinical Criteria		
	Oregon		Washington State
Patient Characteristic	High[a]	Middle	Low
	970,360 (70.3)[b,c]	655,956 (47.5)	214,042 (15.5)
Additional Criterion:			
Doesn't wander/avoids dangers	810,969 (58.7)	534,615 (40.5)	N/A
No hallucinations/delusions	736,098 (53.3)	493,666 (35.7)	N/A
Fecal continent	655,956 (47.5)	N/A	N/A
Urinary continent	593,388 (43.0)	516,786 (37.4)	N/A
Bathing or dressing disabilities only	346,651 (25.1)	321,869 (23.3)	N/A

[a]For definition of High, Middle, and Low, see Table 1.
[b]Percent of total nursing residents in parentheses. Total nursing home residents=1,381,075.
[c]For Medicaid residents the proportions are 70.0 for the High criteria, 45.9 for the Middle criteria, and 14.3 for the Low criteria.

Spector et al (1996).

The other rows in Table 2 show the effect on the number of persons classified as appropriate for lower levels of care when single additional elements are added to the criteria, making them more restrictive. If having no hallucinations or delusions were added to the Oregon criteria the percentage of nursing home residents appropriate for assisted living would fall from 70% to 53%.

The results also show the impact of ADL criteria. If persons were included based on not have more than bathing or dressing limitations, only one quarter of current nursing home residents would qualify for a lower level of care. Also note the impact of incontinence criteria if ADL restrictions are not included. If urinary incontinence were added to the restrictive criteria, the number of the nation's current nursing home residents who would qualify for lower levels of care would be reduced by about 280,000—a reduction from 70% to 43% of nursing home residents.

In the last example, assume that nursing home care costs $40 thousand a year and assisted living can be provided for $30 thousand a year. A change in the regulations allowing continence assistance to be a service provided in assisted living would bring a cost savings of about $2.8 billion—certainly a motivation for change for cash-strapped governments. The transfer of 280,000 residents of nursing homes to assisted living would bring about a decrease of $11.2 billion in the nursing care sector (at a loss of $40 thousand per resident) and an increase of $8.4 billion (at a gain of $30 thousand per resident) in the assisted living sector. A swing of $19.6 billion in market share based on the inclusion of one functional disability demonstrates the impact of these definitions. Thus, physical function criteria play a significant role in defining the business of seniors housing.

9. STANDARDIZING SENIORS HOUSING INDUSTRY DEFINITIONS BY PROJECT TYPE

In the initial section of the paper we described the ecological model, which was based on the idea that aging is a problem of decreasing function. In this model, seniors housing is a means of helping to maintain function and independence in the community.

In the next section we examined the functions that decrease as people age and the ways in which these are defined and measured. We have seen that a unique vocabulary is necessary to understand the seniors living industry—just as with any specialty industry. Definitions related to functions are particularly important. The two major indices of needs analysis for seniors are Activities of Daily Living (ADLs) and Instrumental Activities of Daily Living (IADLs). The ADL index describes the physical activities that an elderly person may need help with, such as walking, dressing, bathing, eating, bathroom use, and medication administering. A study by the Assisted Living Facilities Association of America found that walking, going outdoors, and bathing were the most common ADL limitations for the elderly population over the age of 85, while bathing, dressing, and medication reminder or dispensing are the most common ADL limitations for assisted living residents. The IADL index describes more complex mental/physical functions that usually indicate some level of cognitive impairment. The major areas of IADL help include meal preparation, shopping, telephone use, doing housework, and money management. These activities rely heavily on memory or mental function alertness, in addition to physical function.

Further, we identified other measures of functioning—Nagi and Rosow-Breslau. The research suggests that the measures of function fit the criteria for a Gutman scale. This means that we can potentially summarize the level of need—or competency, to use the ecological model—with one number on an interval scale; e.g., no assistance required = 0, assistance with Nagi items = 1, assistance with Nagi and Rosow-Breslau items = 2, assistance with IADLs = 3, assistance with ADLs = 4, and intensive medical care = 5. This interval is presented on Figure 2.

The next section of the paper examined the second concept of the model—the environment—and gave a summary of the different seniors housing real estate project types used in the industry and of the design elements in the project types. Figure 3 provides a summary of the definitions used in this paper and shows how they relate to one another. We attempt to translate all of this complex information into a simple "Rosetta Stone"-type graph that will allow analysts to compare various definitions currently in use. This figure points out the difficulty with current definitions of seniors housing and provides a potential solution.

The basic criterion for a definition is that it should allow classification of people into meaningful categories that have different names. The names are a convenience, and should have little significance. When you categorize, you assert that everyone in that category will be treated in a similar fashion and that people in different categories will be treated differently. We have shown in this paper that the basic category "nursing home" used in the seniors housing industry means very different things in terms of an individual's ability to function depending upon the individual's location in either Washington and Oregon.

In classifying, the choice of categories should suit the purpose of the study. In this instance, the definition should be helpful in understanding the business aspects of the seniors housing industry—potential market, effective projects, administrative structures, technological advantages, and investment opportunities. In defining the categories operationally, most observations/people should fit into one category or another with minimal arbitrary influence.

The choice of categories is currently qualitative and discontinuous in the seniors housing industry. It could be continuous and numerical. The Gutman scale in Figure 2 suggests that an industry-standard definition can be developed by linking the Gutman functional disability scale with project types by the types of services they deliver. This would allow analysts to more precisely calculate the most effective and efficient way to deliver a level of care. In addition, a scale grounded in empirical measures of physical functions can make the need for facilities easier to estimate with a degree of accuracy.

In future research, definitions of seniors housing industry project types could be done in terms of level of service provided. For example, Level 1 would be residential with no service, Level 2 provides a facility that enables mobility, Level 3 would be a facility that enables IADLs, Level 4 assists with ADLs, and Level 5 provides full medical assistance.

Figure 2. Functional index similar to a Gutman or Rossman measure of physical function

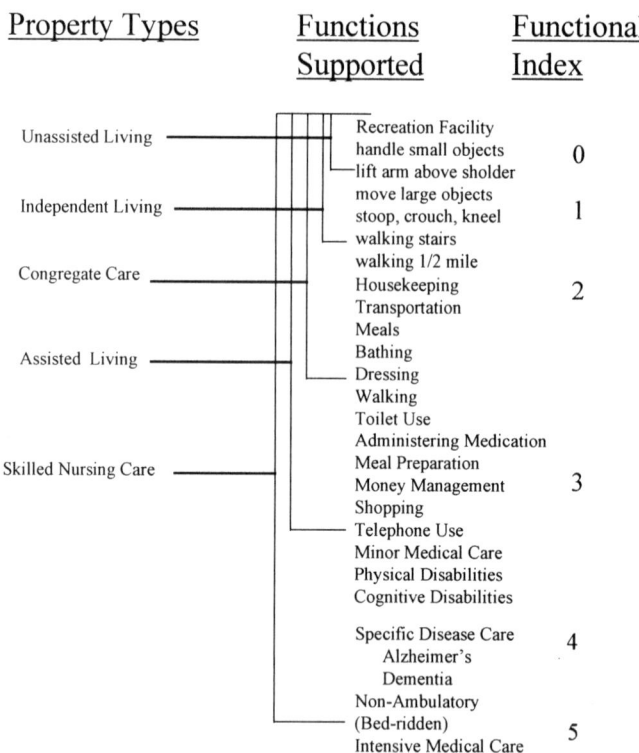

10. CONCLUSION

Industry vocabulary sometimes confuses rather than clarifies analysis. In real estate, the terms "vacancy rate" and "rent per square foot" come to mind as terms defined differently by different groups. The best solution is to develop an industry standard. The next-best solution is to provide a means of understanding, using operational definitions. This paper is a first step in establishing standard definitions by operationalizing definitions with empirical functional measures. Health providers have developed measures of function that define the market for services to the elderly. The real estate and seniors housing industries can develop product types to effectively serve these markets for services.

Figure 3. ARES scale, appropriate real estate or services

Gutman Scale Definition	Functions Supported	Appraisal Definition	Government Definition	ASHA Definition	Washington State Definition	Oregon State Definition
0	Recreation	Independent		Independent		
1	Handle small objects; Raise arm; Move large objects; Stoop, crouch, kneel	Independent		Independent		
2	Walk up stairs; Walk 1/2 mile					
3	Shopping; Meal preparation; Housekeeping; Laundry; Transportation; Taking medications; Handling finances; Using telephone	Congregate	Board and care	Congregate or independent		
	Bathing; Dressing; Transferring; Toilet use; Eating			Assisted	Nursing	
4	Continent; Minor medical care; Physical disabilities; Cognitive disabilities	Intermediate	Nursing			Nursing
	Specific disease care; Non-ambulatory; Intensive medical care	Nursing		Nursing		

REFERENCES

DuBrin, L.R., Seniors Housing Investment, *NIC 95 Review*, Annapolis: National Investment Conference, 1995, 1-11.

Congressional Budget Office, *Long-Term Care for the Elderly and Disabled*, Budget Issue Paper, Washington, DC: Government Printing Office, 1977.

Dun and Bradstreet Information Services, *Industry Norms and Key Business Ratios*, One Year, Desktop Edition, New York: Dun and Bradstreet Corporation, 1996.

Edwards, W. and B. Edwards, Questionnaire and Data for Institutional Population Component (DHHS Publication Number (PHS) 89-3440) *National Medical Expenditure Survey Methods 1*, National Center for Health Services Research and Health Technologies Assessment, Rockville, MD: Public Health Service, 1989.

Fries, J.F., P.W. Spitz and D.Y. Young, The Dimensions of Health Outcomes: The Health Assessment Questionnaire, Disability and Pain Scales, *Journal Rheumatol*, 1982, 9:789-793.

Gimmy, A.E. and M.G. Boehm, Elderly Housing: A Guide to Appraisal, Market Analysis, Development and Financing, Chicago: American Institute of Real Estate Appraisers, 1988.

Guralnik, J.M. and A.Z. LaCroix, Assessing Physical Function in Older Populations, in R.B. Wallace and R.F.Woolson, editors, *The Epidemiological Study of the Elderly*, 159-181, New York: Oxford University Press, 1992.

Gutman, L. A., Basis for Scaling Qualitative Data, *American Sociological Review*, 1944, 9:139-150.

Katz, S.C., A.B. Ford and R.W. Moskowitz et al., Studies of Illness in the Aged The Index of ADL, A Standardized Measure of Biological and Psychological Function, *Journal of the American Medical Association*, 1963, 185: 914-919.

Lawton, M.P. and E.M. Brody, Assessment of Older People: Self-Maintaining and Instrumental Activities of Daily Living, Gerontologist, 1969, 9:179-186.

Lawton, M.P. and L.N. Nahemow, Ecology and the Aging Process, in C. Eisdorfer and M.P. Lawton, editors, *Psychology of Adult Development and Aging*, American Psychological Association, 1973.

Nagi, S.Z., An Epidemiology of Disability Among Adults in the United States, *Milbank Memorial Fund Quarterly*, 1976, 6:493-508.

Pinsky, J.L., P.E. Leaverton and J. Stokes III, Predictors of Good Function: The Framingham Study, *Journal of Chronic Disease*, 1987, 40:159S-167S.

RMA, *Annual Statement Studies*, Robert Morris Associates, Philadelphia: The Association of Lending and Risk Professionals, 1995.

Rosow, I. and N. Breslau, A Gutman Health Scale for the Aged, *Journal of Gerontology*, 1966, 21:556-559.

Sheflin, N., Tax and Financial Statement Benchmarks, New York: John Wiley, 1994.

Sherman, J.F. and P.A. Logan, Financing Alternatives for Long-Term Care and Senior Living Developments in R.E. Mills, editor, *Long-Term Care Investment Strategies*, Chicago: Irwin, 1996.

Spector, W.D., J.D. Reschovsky, and J.W. Cohen, Appropriate Placement of Nursing Home Residents in Lower Levels of Care, Milbank Quarterly, 1996, 74 (1).

Stewart, A.L., J.E.Ware, Jr., and R.H. Brook, Advances in the Measurement of Functional Status: Construction of Aggregate Indexes, Medical Care, 1981, 19:473-488.

Williams, T.F., J.G. Hill, M.E. Fairbanks, and K.G. Knox, Appropriate Placement of Chronically Ill and Aged: A Successful Approach to Evaluation, Journal of the American Medical Association, 1973, 226 (11):1332-1335.

7

RETIREMENT HOUSING AND LONG-TERM HEALTH CARE:
ATTITUDES OF THE ELDERLY

Karen Martin Gibler
Stetson School of Business and Economics
Mercer University

James R. Lumpkin
Dean, Foster College of Business Administration
Bradley University

George P. Moschis
Center for Mature Consumer Studies
Georgia State University

ABSTRACT

Focus groups and a national survey explored the awareness, attitudes, and preferences of elderly consumers to assist in planning retirement housing and long-term care services. The study found many elderly consumers are uninformed about housing and care options. Aging in their single-family home in a mixed-age neighborhood is preferred while living with children or in a nursing home are least desirable. Retirement housing that offers cheerful facilities, understanding staff, high quality food, and reasonable monthly charges for a range of personal and medical services that allow the residents to age in place is attractive.

1. INTRODUCTION

The U.S. elderly population will continue to grow as people live longer and the large number of baby boomers reaches retirement age. Because elderly residents experience greater incidence of chronic illnesses, disability, and mental and physical frailty, the demand for long-term healthcare services and supportive living environments will also increase. Meanwhile, gains in private retirement plans and Social Security support ensure an elderly population with more income to contribute to their housing and health care in the future.

The financial problems of many congregate care housing facilities built in the 1980s point to the need for investors and developers to have a better understanding of their customers. Housing providers need to know these consumers' level of awareness and understanding of housing alternatives and their perceptions of different types of living facilities. They also must understand consumer needs and preferences for supportive services. This requirement for supportive services introduces a major non-real estate management component into seniors housing which developers and operators must address.

Many studies cite the demographic trends indicating a growing number of senior citizens in the coming decades. Much previous seniors housing research has focused almost exclusively on consumption behavior rather than the decision processes that lead to selection, purchase, and consumption of retirement housing and long-term care. This current research focused on consumer awareness, understanding, and perceptions of retirement housing and long-term care alternatives. Knowledge about factors affecting the consumer's retirement housing decision will assist housing providers in developing products and services that will better satisfy older consumer needs. Industry interest in consumer awareness of housing and care options is exemplified by the more recent Harvard School of Public Health and Louis Harris and Associates (1996) Long-Term Care Awareness Survey sponsored by the American Health Care Association and the National Investment Conference for the Senior Living and Long-Term Care Industries, which has provided additional support for several of the conclusions reached by these researchers.

Relatively few real estate firms have experience developing and managing housing for seniors that blends aspects of residential, hotel, and medical facilities (Porter, 1995), yet industry analysts are predicting growth, especially in the assisted housing market (Gamzon, 1996). To help housing market participants, this study examines elderly consumers' awareness, attitudes, concerns, and behavior concerning retirement housing and long-term care facilities. Differences between mixed-age housing residents and those already residing in retirement housing are examined and the attributes both groups want in a housing facility are identified to help policy makers, developers, and operators better serve the elderly housing market.

This paper first presents the current housing arrangements of older Americans, along with research relevant to consumer awareness and interest in retirement housing and long-term care alternatives. Next, the methodology and results of this study are presented. A discussion of the findings and their implications follows.

2. HOUSING AND SUPPORTIVE SERVICES

Older Americans who live in mixed-age neighborhoods of single-family detached houses often receive no formal supportive services. Others live in housing specifically planned for older residents—either single-family or multifamily units—which provides no personal services. Still others choose age-segregated housing that incorporates supportive services. Group or congregate housing allows residents to occupy private rooms but share meals, transportation, and activities. Assisted living facilities provide meals and assistance in performing activities of daily living (ADLs).[1] Continuing care retirement communities (CCRCs) offer a full range of housing alternatives ranging from independent living units to skilled nursing units. Custodial care provides unskilled nursing care 24-hours-a-day in a private unit. Skilled nursing facilities provide various levels of nursing and medical care to residents 24-hours-a-day.

Many Americans are not familiar with the variety of long-term care options available to them. A survey by Harvard and Louis Harris and Associates (1996) found that 61% of respondents age 70 and older had never heard of continuing care retirement communities, 48% had never heard of assisted living, 49% had never heard of congregate living, 39% had never heard of paid in-home care services, and 32% had never heard of home health care. The figures are similar for those age 50 to 69. Two-thirds of those age 70 and older have visited a nursing home, but only 23% visited an assisted living facility, 32% visited a congregate care facility, and 18% visited a continuing care retirement community.

According to the U.S. Bureau of the Census (1993), more than three fourths of householders age 65 and older are homeowners and approximately 6% are renters; the rest live with other homeowners or renters, or are institutionalized. Seven in ten homes occupied by elderly householders are single-family homes.

The majority of older residents prefer to live in the homes they purchased during middle age. In a 1992 national survey by the American Association of Retired Persons (AARP), 84% of respondents age 55 or older said they never wanted to move. Just over 5% of those age 65 or older move each year—over one half within the same county, but one quarter to a different state (U.S. Bureau of the Census, 1994). A survey of Madison, Wisconsin elderly (Hunt, 1991; Hunt and Gunter-Hunt, 1986; Merrill and Hunt, 1990) found that those most interested in moving were older, single, and living alone. Failing health, lack of social support groups, and inability to maintain the home tend to trigger such moves.

Problems with ADLs can make living in a traditional single-family home difficult, especially for the 30% of the elderly who live alone (U.S. Bureau of the Census, 1994). Older residents with the fewest limitations are more likely to live alone while

---

[1] Two widely used scales to measure the ability to perform physical tasks are called the Activities of Daily Living (ADLs) and Instrumental Activities of Daily Living (IADLs). ADLs include bathing, dressing, eating, getting out of bed, using the toilet, and walking. IADLs include more complex tasks such as managing money, preparing meals, shopping, using the telephone, and doing housework (Cohen, Van Nostrand, and Furner, 1993).

older women with higher numbers of ADL and IADL limitations are more likely to live with nonrelatives (Cohen, Van Nostrand, and Furner, 1993).

In general, most older persons who require only periodic assistance with shopping and other activities rely on family and friends, whereas those with more complex and continual needs often depend on a mix of formal and informal support services (Doty, 1986; Soldo, 1985). Over 90% of functionally-limited elderly persons receive personal care assistance from informal support networks, usually their family (Crystal et al., 1987).

In an AARP (1990) survey, 17% of the elderly respondents said they would consider moving in with a family member, with only 3% seriously considering that option. Elderly who live with their children tend to be older (Hess and Markson, 1980), with lower morale, more physical and psychological impairments, and more negative self-image (Mindel and Wright, 1985) than elderly living alone or with a spouse.

The majority of the elderly prefers to remain independent and receive help in their own homes rather than move to a relative's home or enter an assisted living community (McAuley and Blieszner, 1985). The number of home health agencies providing such services in the U.S. has grown to more than 10,000 (Strahan, 1996). Over 1.4 million Americans age 65 and older receive home health care services. They are predominately women (71%), age 75 to 84 (42%), white (68%), widowed (47%), living in a private residence (93%), and living with family members (51%). More than one half are receiving help with at least one ADL and one IADL; however, skilled nursing services are the most frequently-used home health care services (Dey, 1996). Among noninstitutionalized persons age 60 and older in northern California, Kushman and Freeman (1986) found that those most likely to be aware of services to help them remain independent were urban females who were younger, better educated, and had more frequent contact with friends and relatives.

An Assisted Living Facilities Association of America and Coopers & Lybrand report (1993) estimated that there may be at least 60,000 assisted living facilities in the U.S., housing between 100,000 and one million residents, depending on how assisted living is defined. Residents of assisted living facilities tend to be widowed females with an average age in the 80s (Coopers & Lybrand, 1993; Kane and Wilson, 1993; Newcomer and Preston, 1994). Among those interviewed in 1995 by Harvard and Louis Harris and Associates (1996), 26% think of congregate living as a place for sick people, not a place for retirement.

The typical person moving into an independent unit in a CCRC is a white, better educated, higher income, widowed female in her 70s without children nearby and with few disabilities (Cohen, Tell, Bishop, Wallack, and Branch, 1989; Kichen and Roche, 1990; Newcomer, Preston, and Roderick, 1995; Sherwood et al., 1990). Again, 26% of those surveyed in the Harvard/Louis Harris (1996) study thought a continuing care retirement community was a place for sick people, not a place to retire.

About 5% of the U.S. population age 65 and older resides in nursing or personal care homes (National Center for Health Statistics, 1995). Those most likely to enter a nursing home are females at least 80 years old who live alone, use ambulation aids, are mentally disoriented, and need assistance in performing ADLs and IADLs (Branch and Jette, 1982; Cohen, Tell, and Wallack, 1986).

Recent study of consumer preferences among retirement and long-term care alternatives is limited. Festervand and Lumpkin (1990) found two-thirds of residents age 65 to 75 surveyed in a southeastern city were not familiar with the 10 local retirement facilities that were available. Madison, Wisconsin older residents want a garage, two bedrooms, health care, transportation options, emergency call system, same age residents, one meal per day, a 24-hour staff, on-site laundry, health clinic, planned activities, and housekeeping services in a retirement facility (Merrill and Hunt, 1990). Parr et al. (1988) found in five market studies that the features and services most important to potential retirement center residents are emergency services, ability to stay in the facility for the rest of their lives, private kitchens, a group dining room, building security, maid service, transportation service, and an on-site nursing center. Major barriers to considering retirement centers include non-refundable entrance fees and concern about the financial security of projects.

The most important factors in residents' decisions to enter a CCRC are availability of long-term care, desire to remain independent, and availability of health maintenance and other services (Kichen and Roche, 1990). Tell et al. (1987) found the same factors important along with protection against the cost of long-term care, availability of staff, and desire not to become a burden to family members. Almost one-half of those considering a move to a CCRC were concerned about the cost of such a facility. Regnier and Gelwicks (1981) found that security, convenient retail services, public transportation, and emergency health services were the most preferred services among middle- and upper-income Southern elderly residents. Mandatory services and physical activities were the least preferred.

Examination of the elderly's current housing situation and previous research indicates a desire by most older Americans to age in a single-family house in a mixed-age neighborhood. Many of these older residents are unaware of support services which would make this alternative practical. A substantial minority—either voluntarily or involuntarily—is considering retirement housing options that may include support services such as long-term care. As long as most elderly consumers remain uninformed about housing and care options and the industry is unable to distinguish among the options it offers, these consumers will have a difficult time obtaining the housing and service combination that best satisfies their needs.

3. METHODOLOGY

A two-stage study was undertaken to explore the behavior, attitudes, and concerns of elderly consumers regarding long-term care and retirement housing. In the first stage, focus groups of elderly consumers were gathered in early 1990 to explore attitudes and opinions about retirement housing and long-term care. The results of the first stage were used to develop the questionnaire which was distributed to a national sample by mail in the second stage.

The survey identified elderly consumer awareness of retirement housing and long-term care alternatives, attitudes toward long-term care facilities and living situations, and important attributes in choosing a retirement home or long-term care facility. Cross tabulations, factor analysis, and differences among group means were used to identify relationships and provide explanations for differences in attitudes among the respondents.

A. Focus Groups

In the first stage of the research, two focus groups with 12 participants each were conducted with members of the Retired Senior Volunteers Program (RSVP) who reside in retirement communities in Tampa, Florida, and two focus groups of RSVP members who do not reside in a retirement facility were conducted in Chicago, Illinois. The focus groups explored attitudes and opinions about retirement housing and long-term care. The results of the focus group discussions were used to develop the mail questionnaire. Additionally, quotes from these discussions are used in the paper to amplify survey results.

B. Mail Survey

Questionnaires were mailed to a national sample of 4,800 householders age 60 and older who are members of the Market Facts Consumer Mail Panel, a group of consumers who had already agreed to participate in research studies. The sample included elderly residents of both mixed-age and retirement housing. The sample was intentionally disproportionately representative of the elderly age 70 to 79 (50% of the sample) and the elderly age 80 and older (15%) compared to the U.S. population because the first group is expected to be most involved in the retirement housing and long-term care decision and the second group is the most likely to have made a housing change during recent years. In an attempt to reach households already residing in retirement communities, the sample was disproportionately representative of those geographic areas (as defined by zip codes) that have a high concentration of retirement communities. Because of the nature of the sample and the study objectives, the focus is on describing market behavior and profiling older consumer behavior rather than developing estimates of national consumer responses and demand.

A total of 3,327 usable mail responses was received, a usable response rate of 69.3%. A demographic and socioeconomic profile of these respondents is shown in Table 1. Based on the sample profile, the responses reported in this paper most represent the attitudes, opinions, and preferences of retired white females, age 65 to 79, either married and widowed, living alone or with a spouse, and receiving an annual household income of less than $25,000.

Table 2 shows the current living arrangements of the respondents. Only 5.1% of those responding currently live in a retirement facility and none lives in a long-term custodial or nursing care facility. Most (79.0%) of those living in mixed-age housing live in a single-family house that they own. The large majority (87.7%) of those living in a retirement facility rents an independent unit in a multifamily dwelling. A

Table 1: Demographic and socioeconomic profile of mail survey respondents

Characteristic	Percent of Total (n = 3,327)
Age	
60–64	13.1%
65–69	20.7
70–79	51.6
80 and over	14.6
Sex	
Male	13.1
Female	83.6
Race	
White	97.7
Nonwhite	2.3
Education	
High school or less	56.8
Some college	27.2
College degree	8.1
Graduate school	7.9
Marital Status	
Married	41.4
Widowed	44.7
Divorced/separated/never married	13.9
Household Size	
1	49.6
2	42.6
3 or more	7.8
Employment	
Employed	11.0
Retired	68.3
Homemaker/disabled	20.7
Income	
Less than $15,000	50.1
$15,000–$24,999	23.2
$25,000–$34,999	11.4
$35,000 or more	15.3

larger proportion of those living in retirement facilities was living alone (77.1%) and had moved there relatively recently (45.3% within the last 5 years).

Table 2: Living Arrangements of Mail Survey Respondents

Living Arrangement	Percent of Mixed-Age Housing Residents (n = 2,456)	Percent of Retirement Housing Residents (n = 132)
Dwelling Type		
Single–family	79.0%	28.3%
Multiple–family	10.2	71.7
Other	10.8	—
Retirement Facility		
Independent living	—	87.7
Group/congregate	—	3.1
Assisted living	—	2.3
Continuing care	—	5.4
Ownership		
Own	85.9	30.9
Rent	11.8	67.1
Other	2.3	2.0
Length of Tenure (years)		
5 years or less	11.6	45.3
6–10	13.1	27.4
11–20	25.6	23.0
21–30	17.4	4.3
31–40	19.0	—
41 or more	13.3	—
Household Composition[1]		
Live alone	51.0	77.1
Live with spouse	41.4	16.3
Live with children	6.8	—
Live with others	6.3	7.2

[1] More than one may apply

C. Analysis of Mail Survey

The questionnaire recipients were asked to rate the importance of 35 attributes in deciding what type of retirement or long-term care facility to use on a 5-point scale from "Not at All Important" (1) to "Extremely Important" (5) and then to rate the various facilities on the extent to which the facilities possess each attribute on a 4-point scale from "Not at All" (1) to "Very Much" (4). These attributes are listed in Table 3.

To analyze the mail questionnaire respondents' ratings of the importance of long-term care and retirement housing attributes, the sample was divided into two groups: mixed-age housing residents and retirement housing residents. The average importance rating for each attribute was calculated for each group. These means were used to rank the attributes in order of importance. The means were also used to compare the difference in importance the two groups place on the attributes by use of a t-test of the equality of the means.

The respondents were also asked to indicate the degree to which they agreed, from "Strongly Disagree" (1) to "Strongly Agree" (5), with 33 statements concerning attitudes about living situations, housing facilities, and independence when choosing between in-home care and a nursing home. The statements are listed in Table 4.

The 33 statements were factor analyzed to identify their underlying dimensionality. Because all the items were developed for this research, exploratory factor analysis was employed using principal axis extraction and varimax rotation. Nine factors were extracted. The factor loadings were all greater than .5, as were all but one of the coefficient alpha measures of internal consistency. The scales with the corresponding items are presented in Table 4. The nine resulting scales can be grouped into three major categories: attitudes toward living with children, attitudes toward long-term care facilities, and attitudes toward alternative care and remaining independent. The mean summated scores of retirement housing residents and mixed-age housing residents were calculated for each factor to examine the differences in attitudes between each group using a t-test of the equality of the means.

The questionnaire asked whether the respondents were familiar with various long-term care and retirement housing options. Of those alternatives with which they were familiar, the respondents were also asked whether they had considered each not at all, somewhat, or quite a bit. Further, the average degree to which respondents in each group believed each type of housing contains the attributes from Table 4 was calculated.

The retirement facilities listed were independent living, group/congregate homes, assisted living, and continuing care communities. Independent living was defined as seniors-only, apartment-like facilities with no personal services. Group/congregate homes were defined as 5 to 20 people living independently with meals, planned activities, and limited medical care available. Assisted living was defined as 50 or more residents living in a facility providing companionship, meals, housekeeping, limited medical care, and assistance in performing daily living activities. Continuing care communities were defined as housing into which residents are admitted for independent living with progressive housing and services from group homes to nursing homes available as needed. Long-term care facilities included custodial care (unskilled nursing care provided 24-hours-a-day in a private home), intermediate care nursing home (limited supervision for those needing help in daily living activities, but not needing 24-hour care), and extended care nursing homes (24-hour nursing care provided with direct medical supervision).

Table 3: Mean importance of attributes in retirement and long-term care facilities

	Living Arrangement			
	Mixed-Age Housing	Retirement Housing	t	p
Safety Features	4.65[1]	4.65	1.006	.316
Acceptance of Medicare/Medicaid	4.39	4.36	0.648	.421
Ability to Stay Indefinitely	4.07	4.24	2.078	.150
Communication between Management and Residents	4.36	4.19	0.485	.486
Monthly Rental Fee	3.94	4.15	5.889	.015*
Access to Medical Services	4.39	4.14	0.039	.844
Quality of Food	4.39	4.04	3.189	.074
Private Kitchens in Apartment	3.57	4.02	0.131	.717
Size of Rooms	4.03	3.87	0.013	.907
Programs Encourage Independence	4.07	3.82	2.000	.157
Recreation	3.93	3.72	0.034	.853
Proximity to Shopping	3.55	3.69	1.940	.164
Proximity to Hospital	3.97	3.64	0.964	.326
Use Own Furniture	3.30	3.61	0.876	.349
Caring Environment	4.00	3.58	3.089	.079
Multiple Levels of Care	4.11	3.44	11.103	.001*
Planned Activities	3.69	3.41	3.584	.059
Maintenance Fees	3.47	3.39	0.330	.566
Proximity to Recreation	3.46	3.39	0.000	.996
A La Carte Services	3.68	3.37	4.895	.027*
Location within City	3.19	3.33	0.037	.847
Size of Facility	3.33	3.31	0.161	.688
Entrance Fees	3.57	3.28	4.826	.028*
Expulsion Privileges	3.26	3.23	0.289	.590
Therapy Available	3.68	3.10	8.052	.005*
Proximity to Family	3.71	3.05	15.043	.001*
Required Meals	3.78	3.05	23.531	.001*
Equity Accrual	3.50	2.98	1.629	.202
Communal Dining Area	3.26	2.96	4.172	.041*
Private Pay Residents Preferred	3.08	2.93	1.450	.229
Mix Independent and Assisted Residents	2.95	2.92	0.031	.860
Religious Affiliation	3.17	2.76	3.976	.046*
Ownership Transference	3.61	2.74	17.024	.001*
Required Services	2.64	2.48	1.729	.189
Purchase Option	3.01	2.28	12.531	.001*

[1]Means based on 5-point scale from "Not at All Important" (1) to "Extremely Important" (5).
*significant at .05 level.

Table 4: attitudes toward long-term care facilities and living situations: factor analysis results

Attitude Factor Name and Items	Factor Loading	Alpha Coefficient
Living with Children Would Create Conflict		.807
In-home care wouldn't be fair to my children	.565	
Living with children would threaten our relationship	.732	
Different generations do not mix well	.678	
In-home care would cause conflict within my children's family	.741	
I believe that it isn't right to live with children	.703	
I don't want to live with my children	.607	
Living with Children Would Make Me a Burden		.503
I don't want to be a burden to anyone	.700	
I believe my children have a right to independence	.582	
Living with Children Because they Want Me		—
My children want me to live with them	.734	
Nursing Home is Last Resort		.775
Nursing homes have bad reputations	.699	
A nursing home is the last resort	.603	
Once you enter a nursing home you may never leave	.652	
I would rather die than enter a nursing home	.564	
People in nursing homes usually retain dignity	−.691	
Nursing homes have improved in recent years	−.722	
Nursing Homes Too Structured and Lack Privacy		.697
I want the privacy of my own home	.569	
I don't feel ready for a nursing home yet	.512	
There are too many restrictions at a nursing home	.565	
Moving to a nursing home will make me feel old	.618	
In-home care lets me retain my dignity	.575	
Nursing Homes Provide Security, Services, and Companionship		.649
I desire the services provided by a nursing home	.657	
I want to live with people my own age	.618	
I want the security of knowing I'll be cared for	.707	
I expect to spend my old age in a nursing home	.460	
Live-In Help is Too Expensive or Not Available		.702
I will not be able to afford a nursing home	.520	
Having someone live with me would be too expensive	.760	
Not many people want to live-in with someone else	.722	
Finding someone who cares to live-in is almost impossible	.743	
Nothing Prolongs Independence		.599
There is little I can do to remain independent	.625	
Special products designed for seniors to prolong independence are too expensive	.790	
Special products designed to prolong independence are only for the very old	.787	
Assistance Needed in Daily Living Activities		.061
I currently require assistance with ADLs	.651	
I have no problem in getting around	−.720	

4. FINDINGS

A. Long-Term Care

The focus group participants perceived long-term health care in a traditionally narrow focus as "institutionalization in an acute-care facility or nursing home." Even those living in retirement communities that offer some personal care services did not think of their housing as a form of long-term care. They thought nursing homes to be the "worst thing that can happen" to someone. The responses to the mail survey produced three factors related to nursing homes and long-term care. One factor represented a positive view of nursing homes as a source of security, services, and companionship. This factor appears to serve as incentive for older people to move into a nursing home. The other two factors (housing of last resort, and structured and lacking privacy) represented negative traits of nursing homes which would discourage considering this type of long-term care. Analysis of mean summated scores on the nine attitude factors indicated that, in general, both residents of mixed-age housing and retirement facilities identified nursing homes with structure and lack of privacy. However, those already residing in a retirement facility felt significantly more positive about nursing homes providing needed services in an agreeable atmosphere, as is shown in Table 5.

Many focus group participants feared that financial constraints will make a nursing home the only choice later in life. Most of the retirement housing residents in the focus groups had made financial plans to avoid being forced to move into a nursing home in their old age. They either were already living in a private pay continuing care facility, planned to enter such a facility in the future, or were prepared to pay for personal care in their homes.

B. In-Home Care

All the focus group members felt more positively about using in-home care rather than institutionalization, but they had reservations, including:

- A preference and desire to remain independent

- A fear of becoming a burden on someone

- A fear of becoming a financial liability

- A fear of interfering with the private lives of others

- A concern for the quality of care received

Although many of those participating in the focus groups had provided personal care for one or more of their parents, none would consider having their children do the same for them. They felt such an arrangement is neither practical nor desirable. Their children's need for two incomes and the loss of traditional family values made this option desirable only if the elderly cannot afford an alternative. The national sample agreed, as is shown in Table 5. Two negative factors were identified that related to living with one's children: creating conflict and becoming a burden. These two factors inhibit living with one's children. This reluctance to move in with family members supports AARP's (1990) findings. Those who have moved to a retirement facility are significantly more negative about living with their children. They do not want to be a burden and threaten their relationship with their children. These findings are similar to the determination by Tell et al. (1987) that desire not to become a burden to family members is a major factor in choosing to move into a CCRC.

Many elderly feel unable to control their destiny. One factor revealed in the factor analysis related to independence represented the older respondents' resignation that they are unlikely to be able to prolong their independence. A second factor related to needing assistance with daily living activities. The survey respondents believed that live-in help was either too expensive or was not available. Those who live in retirement facilities were significantly less optimistic (as shown in Table 5) about the availability of live-in help, perhaps having experienced failed attempts to find such assistance.

Table 5: Summated group mean attitudes toward long-term care facilities and living situations

	Living Arrangement			
	Mixed-Age Hosuing	Retirement Housing	t	p
Long-Term Care				
Nursing Home is Last Resort	3.26[1]	3.18	1.026	.311
Nursing Homes too Structured/Lack Privacy	4.12	3.87	15.470	.001*
Nursing Home Provides Security/Services/Companionship	3.33	3.50	4.843	.028*
Alternative Care/Independence				
Alternative Care/Independence				
Live-in Help Too Expensive/Not Available	3.82	4.01	5.997	.014*
Nothing Prolongs Independence	2.57	2.41	3.908	.048*
Assistance Needed in Daily Living Activities	1.82	1.85	0.124	.725
Living with Children				
Living with Children Would Create Conflict	3.62	3.89	9.376	.002*
Living with Children Would Make me a Burden	4.44	4.58	4.257	.039*
Living with Children Because They Want Me	2.88	2.90	0.029	.864

[1]Group means based on 5-point scale from "Strongly Disagree" (1) to "Strongly Agree" (5).
*Significantly different at the .05 level.

C. Retirement Housing

Most of those participating in the focus groups, including residents of retirement communities, had limited knowledge of the range of retirement housing options, as other researchers have found (Festervand and Lumpkin, 1990; Harvard and Louis Harris, 1996). Despite industry growth and media coverage, most were not familiar with either congregate care or continuing care retirement facilities. However, after having those types of retirement housing explained, most participants were favorably impressed with the concepts.

Only one-fifth of the survey respondents living in mixed-age housing had considered moving to a retirement or long-term care facility, most often an independent living community (as shown in Table 6). However, even those considering moving are not aware of all their options. Of those who have considered retirement or long-term care facilities, more than 25% were unfamiliar with at least one of the housing alternatives available. Custodial care was the least familiar and least often considered form of housing.

Even those focus group participants who have moved into a retirement community see little distinction between alternative types of retirement housing. Those who do perceive a difference among housing offerings tend to place retirement housing into two categories: high-cost country club facilities and nursing homes.

Most of the focus group participants hold a relatively negative image of retirement housing. Residents of retirement housing were only nominally more positive about their residences. Complaints included "depressing environment" and "lack of com-

Table 6: Types of retirement and long-term care facilities considered by those currently living in mixed-age housing who have considered facilities

Type of Facility	Not Familiar	Familiar, but not Considered	Familiar & Consider Somewhat	Familiar and Consider Quite a Bit
Retirement Housing				
Independent living	25.1	19.9	32.5	22.5
Group/Congregate	28.8	39.4	19.8	12.0
Assisted Living	28.6	35.7	23.1	12.6
Continuing care	27.3	32.4	24.5	15.8
Long-Term Care Facilities				
Custodial care	31.3	46.5	11.5	10.7
Intermediate care nursing home	24.7	45.3	19.4	10.6
Extended care nursing home	27.0	45.5	13.8	13.8

Degree Considered (Percent of Total) (n = 467)

passion." The negative image arises from fear of hardships suffered by residents of failed projects, actual or perceived mismanagement, and the feeling that the industry has failed to create an affordable, acceptable retirement housing product. Most had moved to the retirement facility because they had no other options and were afraid to remain where they were and experience further physical or mental deterioration with no one to care for them. Nevertheless, if the financial resources were available, most focus group participants would prefer living in a retirement facility that provided services to any other housing alternative except remaining in their own home.

D. Supportive Products and Services

The participants in the focus groups generally were not familiar with the range of services provided by the more comprehensive facilities. Most expected the communities to offer planned recreation and meals; however, only residents of Lifecare communities were aware of the full scope of personal care services these facilities provide.

The services that focus group members valued the most were personal care services such as assistance in bathing, dressing, eating, cleaning, and mobility. The participants would prefer to provide their own transportation, meals, and recreation for as long as they are able to do so. The availability of a complete assortment of services was instrumental in the retirement housing selection by several focus group participants. They wanted the security of knowing that if and when such services were needed they would be readily available. These findings are similar to surveys of CCRC residents (Kichen and Roche, 1990; Tell et al., 1987) and those on a waiting list for supportive housing (Merrill and Hunt, 1990). Between one third and one half of the mail survey respondents would prefer retirement and long-term care facilities available at the same location, whereas just over one fourth would prefer separate retirement and long-term care facilities.

In the mail survey, both retirement facility and mixed-age housing residents generally agreed on which features are most important in choosing a retirement or long-term care facility (Table 3). The most important attributes to all respondents as a group were:

- Safety features
- Acceptance of Medicare and Medicaid
- Access to medical services
- The ability to stay in the facility indefinitely
- Communication between management and residents
- Quality of food

The safety features, medical services, and option for indefinite stay are similar to those preferred features found by Kichen and Roche (1990), Parr et al. (1988), and Regnier and Gelwicks (1981). This study, however, also found emphasis on qualitative features such as food quality and communication between staff and residents.

Those who have not yet moved into a retirement facility tend to place greater importance on more features than those who have experienced retirement housing living. Those still living in mixed-age housing placed significantly greater importance on *a la carte* services (only paying for services used), required meals (usually one or two per day), communal dining area, therapy available, multiple levels of care in one location, religious affiliation, entrance fees, ownership transference, and purchase option. Those already living in a retirement facility placed significantly greater importance on a monthly rental fee. Thus, everyone is agreed that medical services, safety features, and multiple levels of care that would allow aging in place are important. Those who have not chosen to move to a retirement facility appear to place greater importance on the ownership aspects of the housing asset than current rental retirement housing residents.

The most important factors focus group participants considered in evaluating facilities were location, cost, services, and atmosphere. Mail survey respondents living in mixed-age housing placed greater importance on proximity to family than those living in retirement housing. In terms of location, the focus group participants were looking for a facility close to their original residence, friends, and relatives, a location that offered the preferred climate and quality of life, or a location that offered the best value.

Cost was of greatest immediate importance to everyone. Most focus group participants thought all retirement facilities are too expensive. They wanted facilities to offer a wide range of services for which they would pay on an as-needed basis.

None of the focus group participants were receptive to care plans that include fees for all available services in the monthly charge regardless of whether the services are used. They would prefer to pay for services on an as-needed basis. Those already residing in retirement communities were more likely to consider rental fees of $600 to $1,500 as normal and acceptable. More nonresidents considered them excessive. The focus group participants did not like the idea of a large buy-in or endowment fee. Several felt that rental retirement housing was a bad investment. Once paid, all fees are lost with no equity accruing, no tax write-off possible, and no ownership transfer privileges available.

The mail survey respondents generally believed that all types of retirement housing and long-term care facilities offer the features they consider most important. No attribute was rated as important, but at the same time, as not being provided to the degree expected. Long-term care facilities were rated higher on the safety features, acceptance of Medicare/Medicaid, and access to therapy and a hospital. The retirement facilities were rated higher on size, availability of private kitchens, and proximity to recreation and shopping. Those who had not experienced retirement home living believed more strongly that retirement and long-term care facilities would provide the desired features (as shown in Tables 7 and 8). Again, the retirement housing residents' experience has shown them that not all facilities offer a full range of services.

Table 7: Rating of retirement and long-term care facilities on attributes by those currently living in mixed-age housing

Attribute	Independent Living	Group/ Congregate	Assisted Living	Continuing Care	Custodial Care	Intermediate Care Nursing	Extended Care Nursing
Safety Features	3.60[1]	3.59	3.60	3.63	3.57	3.65	3.69
Acceptance Medicare/Medicaid	3.25	3.27	3.36	3.41	3.46	3.57	3.60
Ability to Stay Indefinitely	3.36	3.21	3.22	3.29	3.19	3.27	3.37
Communication between Management and Residents	3.15	3.22	3.23	3.28	3.16	3.21	3.22
Monthly Rental Fee	3.27	3.30	3.23	3.25	3.17	3.25	3.25
Access to Medical Services	3.28	3.32	3.41	3.48	3.42	3.57	3.65
Quality of Food	3.20	3.33	3.38	3.38	3.35	3.41	3.44
Private Kitchen in Apt	3.37	2.71	2.63	2.43	2.09	1.87	1.80
Size of Rooms	3.15	2.92	2.84	2.77	2.60	2.58	2.59
Programs Encourage Independence	3.14	3.20	3.21	3.15	2.87	2.88	2.80
Recreation	2.88	3.04	3.00	2.99	2.68	2.75	2.69
Proximity to Shopping	3.17	3.03	2.89	2.67	2.31	2.17	2.08
Proximity to Hospital	2.96	2.92	3.00	3.11	3.09	3.22	3.31
Use Own Furniture	3.15	2.75	2.68	2.46	2.20	2.02	1.92
Caring Environment	3.04	2.93	3.12	3.22	3.15	3.20	3.34
Multiple Levels of Care	2.69	2.84	3.04	3.24	3.17	3.36	3.44
Planned Activities	2.55	2.85	2.86	2.93	2.68	2.83	2.78
Maintenance Fees	2.73	2.78	2.77	2.85	2.70	2.77	2.83
Proximity to Recreation	3.06	2.98	2.82	2.64	2.29	2.19	2.10
A La Carte Services	2.42	2.34	2.37	2.36	2.26	2.26	2.29
Location within City	2.75	2.61	2.62	2.62	2.56	2.61	2.61
Size of Facility	2.81	2.66	2.66	2.67	2.56	2.62	2.66
Entrance Fees	3.74	2.81	2.85	3.00	2.87	2.98	3.05
Expulsion Privileges	2.54	2.59	2.55	2.54	2.50	2.53	2.50
Therapy Available	2.51	2.64	2.90	3.09	3.02	3.31	3.42
Proximity to Family	2.99	2.84	2.89	2.89	2.94	2.94	2.96
Required Meals	3.39	2.86	3.10	3.26	3.34	3.48	3.57
Equity Accrual	2.62	2.35	2.24	2.19	2.01	1.97	1.99
Communal Dining Area	2.30	2.96	2.95	3.06	2.77	2.96	2.87
Private Pay Residents Prefer	2.57	2.51	2.47	2.49	2.41	2.43	2.45
Mix Independent & Assisted Residents	2.34	2.54	2.58	2.62	2.41	2.52	2.44
Religious Affiliation	2.55	2.48	2.49	2.52	2.43	2.45	2.49
Ownership Transference	2.64	2.24	2.11	2.03	1.86	1.81	1.83
Required Services	2.58	2.79	2.96	3.02	3.04	3.19	3.24
Purchase Option	2.45	2.07	1.94	1.89	1.69	1.65	1.65

[1]Means based on 4 point scale from facility has the attribute "Not at All" (1) to "Very Much" (4).

Table 8: Rating of retirement and long-term care facilities on attributes by those currently living in retirement housing

Attribute	Independent Living	Group/ Congregate	Assisted Living	Continuing Care	Custodial Care	Intermediate Care Nursing	Extended Care Nursing
Safety Features	3.71[1]	3.57	3.61	3.63	3.56	3.64	3.61
Acceptance Medicare/Medicaid	2.97	3.28	3.35	3.39	3.35	3.53	3.58
Ability to Stay Indefinitely	3.51	3.21	3.22	3.17	3.16	3.01	3.06
Communication between Management and Residents	3.27	3.15	3.17	3.21	3.03	3.14	3.07
Monthly Rental Fee	3.48	3.33	3.29	3.35	3.42	3.42	3.28
Access to Medical Services	3.24	3.24	3.36	3.45	3.43	3.50	3.64
Quality of Food	2.86	3.26	3.34	3.36	3.27	3.36	3.39
Private Kitchen in Apt	3.71	2.81	2.62	2.36	1.89	1.69	1.58
Size of Rooms	3.30	2.90	2.91	2.89	2.75	2.76	2.67
Programs Encourage Independ.	3.11	3.21	3.12	3.04	2.90	2.97	2.88
Recreation	2.93	3.03	2.91	3.04	2.73	2.69	2.60
Proximity to Shopping	3.50	3.17	2.88	2.67	2.28	2.02	1.99
Proximity to Hospital	2.95	2.86	3.00	3.09	3.13	3.24	3.31
Use Own Furniture	3.61	2.84	2.80	2.49	2.29	2.04	1.89
Caring Environment	3.09	2.76	3.08	3.20	2.99	3.21	3.28
Multiple Levels of Care	2.38	2.49	2.91	3.06	2.97	3.25	3.25
Planned Activities	2.68	2.87	2.87	2.96	2.73	2.83	2.78
Maintenance Fees	2.44	2.36	2.35	2.42	2.35	2.48	2.51
Proximity to Recreation	3.13	2.88	2.73	2.57	2.23	2.09	1.98
A La Carte Services	2.16	2.12	2.31	2.28	2.14	2.27	2.30
Location within City	3.09	2.63	2.67	2.66	2.50	2.59	2.56
Size of Facility	2.87	2.67	2.68	2.52	2.50	2.55	2.57
Entrance Fees	2.28	2.38	2.33	2.75	2.57	2.53	2.61
Expulsion Privileges	2.48	2.48	2.53	2.48	2.37	2.48	2.35
Therapy Available	2.35	2.32	2.74	3.03	2.87	3.18	3.26
Proximity to Family	2.79	2.64	2.75	2.69	2.77	2.89	2.96
Required Meals	1.95	2.65	2.90	3.15	3.34	3.44	3.52
Equity Accrual	2.07	1.74	1.74	1.64	1.56	1.54	1.48
Communal Dining Area	2.26	3.13	3.09	3.20	3.01	3.03	2.85
Private Pay Residents Prefer	2.21	2.07	2.15	2.26	2.28	2.25	2.31
Mix Independent and Assisted Residents	2.39	2.50	2.53	2.57	2.33	2.45	2.39
Religious Affiliation	2.25	2.01	2.00	2.04	1.97	2.05	2.04
Ownership Transference	2.01	1.59	1.51	1.42	1.36	1.28	1.28
Required Services	2.17	2.59	2.87	2.92	3.03	3.11	3.21
Purchase Option	1.88	1.58	1.51	1.46	1.31	1.28	1.26

[1] Means based on 4 point scale from facility has the attribute "Not at All" (1) to "Very Much" (4).

Atmosphere was described in terms of management's attitudes and physical facilities. Most participants wanted to find a facility with management that understands the needs of older adults, treats them with respect, and allows the residents to retain their dignity. In terms of physical facilities, they wanted a warm, light, and comfortable residence with an air of vitality. They preferred an apartment large enough to accommodate personal belongings, cooking facilities, and entertaining.

5. CONCLUSIONS

As the number of older residents grows, consumer demand for retirement housing and supportive services should increase. However, for government and private industry providers to successfully supply products seniors and their families want, they need to understand mature consumers' preferences and attitudes concerning housing and supportive service options.

The long-term care industry has responded to the needs of the heterogeneous segments of the increasing older population by offering consumers a wide variety of retirement housing and long-term care options. This response, in turn, has created a proliferation of labels that are not clearly defined or standardized, creating confusion for consumers. This confusion makes choosing the housing and long-term care offering most suitable to a consumer's needs difficult. Most of the consumers studied remain relatively uninformed about their housing and long-term care options. They do not understand what is offered by congregate care, continuing care retirement communities, and custodial care. Most continue to categorize retirement housing as either expensive country club facilities that they cannot afford or nursing homes—the housing of last resort, the place people go to die.

This research suggests the need for initiatives on the part of the retirement housing and long-term care industries, government agencies, and seniors groups to: (a) standardize the terms used to describe retirement housing options, and (b) effectively communicate the differences and benefits of each retirement housing and long-term care option. The development and positioning of clearly-differentiated long-term care products will help older consumers make informed choices that better satisfy their needs.

Government agencies, consumer groups, seniors organizations, and seniors housing providers have the opportunity to effectively educate consumers about alternatives to the dreaded nursing home. The developers and managers of housing facilities need to develop a coordinated marketing campaign to explain their type of housing facility and services they provide. They can also explain cost and financing arrangements so that more consumers will understand that they have the financial resources necessary to give them a choice of where they will live if and when they need supportive care. Such messages should be tailored to not only the potential senior residents, but also family members who influence the senior's housing decision.

When choosing a retirement home, consumers are looking for form, function, and atmosphere. They want a large enough unit to house their belongings and prepare their own meals. Consumers choosing a retirement facility want a range of support services available for their use—especially personal care services such as assistance in bathing, dressing, eating, cleaning, and mobility. They want the security of knowing if and when such services are needed, they would be readily available. However, few seniors interviewed in this study were aware of the range of services supportive housing may provide.

Physical security and medical services are also important. Because of their physical limitations, many residents are concerned about access to medical care and how they will pay for it. Many like the continuing care retirement community concept, which allows for several levels of care to be provided within one community. Thus, even if a resident's health deteriorates, he or she does not have to move very far. They can foresee living within the same community indefinitely. Residents show preferences for both long-term care facilities located separately from retirement housing and continuing care facilities that provide multiple levels of care in one location.

Financing is very important. More tenants are interested in moving to a housing facility with supportive services that allows the residents to pay for services as needed. Some are quite interested in purchase options—continuing as home owners rather than renters during retirement.

Not all mature consumers needing assistance with daily living activities will choose retirement housing. Many would prefer to maintain their current homes and pay for in-home services. Currently, many consumers believe that in-home care is either unavailable or unaffordable. Affordable in-home care options need to be expanded and their availability advertised.

Most of those surveyed do not want their children to provide personal care for them as they age. But some retirees want to live close to their previous residence, friends, and relatives. Others want to move to a home located in a milder climate that would provide an active outdoors life. Still others can be sold on a location that emphasizes low-cost retirement living.

ACKNOWLEDGMENTS

This research was funded by a grant to the second author from the AARP Andrus Foundation

REFERENCES

American Association for Retired Persons, *Understanding Seniors Housing for the 1990's*, Washington, DC: AARP, 1992.

American Association for Retired Persons, *Understanding Seniors Housing for the 1990s*, Washington, DC, AARP, 1990.

Branch, L. G., and A. M. Jette, A Prospective Study of Long-term Care Institutionalization Among the Aged, *American Journal of Public Health*, 1982, 72, 1373-79.

Cohen, M. A., E. J. Tell, C. E. Bishop, S. S. Wallack, and L. G. Branch, Patterns of Nursing Home Use in a Prepaid Managed Care System, *Gerontologist*, 1989, 29, 74-80.

Cohen, M. A., E. J. Tell, and S. S. Wallack, The Lifetime Risks and Costs of Nursing Home Use among the Elderly, *Medical Care*, 1986, 24, 1161-1172.
Coopers & Lybrand, *An Overview of the Assisted Living Industry*, Washington, DC: ALFAA, 1993.
Cohen, R. A., J. F. Van Nostrand, and S. E. Furner, *Chartbook on Health Data on Older Americans: United States, 1992*, Washington, DC: National Center for Health Statistics, 1993.
Crystal, S., C. Flemming, P. Beck, and G. Smolka, *The Management of Home Care Services*, New York: Springer, 1987.
Dey, A. N., *Characteristics of Elderly Home Health Care Users: Data from the 1994 National Home and Hospice Care Survey*, Advance data from Vital and Health Statistics, No. 279, Hyattsville, MD: National Center for Health Statistics, 1996.
Doty, P., Family Care of the Elderly: The Role of Public Policy, *Milbank Quarterly*, 1986, 64, 31-46.
Festervand, T. A., and J. R. Lumpkin, Positioning Retirement Housing Developments Via Perceptual Mapping, *Real Estate Finance*, 1990, 7:2, 78-82.
Gamzon, M., Seniors Housing in Focus, *National Real Estate Investor*, March 1996, 38:3, 63-64.
Harvard School of Public Health, and Louis Harris & Associates, *Long Term Care Awareness Survey*, Cambridge, MA: Harvard, 1996.
Hess, B. B., and E. W. Markson, *Aging and Old Age*, New York: Macmillan, 1980.
Hunt, M., The Design of Supportive Environments for Older People, *Journal of Housing for the Elderly*, 1991, 9:1/2, 127-40.
Hunt, M. and G. Gunter-Hunt, Naturally Occurring Retirement Communities, *Journal of Housing for the Elderly*, 1986, 3:3/4, 3-21.
Kane, R. A., and K. B. Wilson, *Assisted Living in the United States*, Washington, DC: AARP, 1993.
Kichen, J. M., and J. L. Roche, "Life-care Resident Preferences," in R. D. Chellis and P. J. Grayson, editors, *Life Care: A Long-Term Solution?*, 49-60, Lexington, MA: Lexington, 1990.
Kushman, J. E., and B. K. Freeman, Service Consciousness and Service Knowledge Among Older Americans, *International Journal of Aging and Human Development*, 1986, 23, 217-37.
McAuley, W. J., and R. Blieszner, Selection of Long Term Care Arrangements by Older Community Residents, *Gerontologist*, 1985, 25, 188-93.
Merrill, J., and M. E. Hunt, Aging in Place, *Journal of Applied Gerontology*, 1990, 9:1, 60-76.
Mindel, C. H., and R. Wright, Jr., Characteristics of the Elderly in Three Types of Living Arrangements, *Activities, Adaptation & Aging*, 1985, 6:4, 39-51.
National Center for Health Statistics, *Health, United States, 1994*, Hyattsville, MD: Public Health Service, 1995.
Newcomer, R., and S. Preston, Relationships Between Acute Care and Nursing Unite Use in Two Continuing Care Retirement Communities, *Research on Aging*, 1994, 16:3, 280-300.
Newcomer, R., S. Preston, and S. S. Roderick, Assisted Living and Nursing Unit Use Among Continuing Care Retirement Community Residents, *Research on Aging*, 1995, 17:2, 149-67.
Parr, J., S. Green, and C. Behncke, What People Want, Why They Move, and What Happens After They Move, *Journal of Housing for the Elderly*, 1988, 5:1, 7-32.
Porter, D. R., Developing Housing for Seniors, *Urban Land*, February 1995, 54, 17-22.
Regnier, V., and L. E. Gelwicks, Preferred Supportive Services for Middle to Higher Income Retirement Housing, *Gerontologist*, 1981, 21, 54-58.
Sherwood, S., H. S. Ruchlin, and C. C. Sherwood, "CCRCs: An Option for Aging in Place," in D. Tilson, editor, *Aging in Place*, 125-64, Glenview, IL: Scott, Foresman, 1990.
Soldo, B. J., In-Home Services for the Dependent Elderly: Determinants of Current Use and Implications for Future Demand, *Research on Aging*, 1985, 7, 281-304.
Strahan, G. W., *An Overview of Home Health and Hospice Care Patients: 1994 National Home and Hospice Care Survey*, Advance data from Vital and Health Statistics, No. 274, Hyattsville, MD: National Center for Health Statistics, 1996.
Tell, E. J., M. A . Cohen, M. J. Larson, and H. L. Batten, Assessing the Elderly's Preferences for Lifecare Retirement Options, *Gerontologist*, 1987, 27, 503-09.
U.S. Bureau of the Census, *Geographic Mobility: March 1992 to March 1993, Current Population Reports, P20-481*, Washington, DC: U.S. GPO, 1994.
U.S. Bureau of the Census, *Marital Status and Living Arrangements: March 1993, Current Populations Reports, P20-468*, Washington, DC: U.S. GPO, 1994.

U.S. Bureau of the Census, *Profiles of America's Elderly, Living Arrangements of the Elderly*, Washington, DC: U.S. GPO, 1993.

8

ADAPTING DEMAND METHODOLOGIES FOR ASSISTED LIVING MARKET ANALYSIS

Susan B. Brecht
Brecht Associates, Inc.

ABSTRACT

Although lax standards for feasibility studies were not exclusively to blame for the early failures of many traditional seniors housing communities, poor feasibility studies were frequently associated with poorly performing facilities. The perception of high risk and the reality of poor performance diminished the availability of capital. This article examines each component of the market feasibility study for assisted living, illustrating, where applicable, how it differs from traditional seniors housing. It identifies basic analytical issues that need further research—research designed to create a basis on which methodological techniques and standards can be established.

1. INTRODUCTION

The majority of published literature on market feasibility studies for traditional forms of seniors housing (continuing care retirement communities (CCRC), lifecare communities, congregate housing) primarily targets analytical techniques utilized to assess relatively independent elderly.[1] Those techniques incorporated benchmarks relating to the site evaluation, geographic definition of the market area expected to be served by the project, the appropriate minimum age, the relationship between income and project fees, the inclusion of comparable and competitive communities, projected absorption and fill period, and most significantly, acceptable levels of market penetration and market share. The latter indicators reflected, respectively, the proportion of age- and income-qualified households—net of existing and planned competition—required to fill the subject facility, and the percentage of all age/income-qualified households required to fill the subject and all other existing and planned communities. However, while the supply and demand equation that incorporates most of these components still forms the underlying basis for assisted living market feasibility studies, many of the elements of studies for this form of seniors housing require a different emphasis or methodology.

A. Definition of Assisted Living

Every state provides—through a wide variety of licensing categories of group settings—for services to be delivered to frail seniors who do not require nursing care. Those settings have many names, including but not limited to personal care, board and care, domiciliary care, adult care, and residential care. However, since the mid to late 1980s a movement has emerged to establish a framework from both a physical design and operational perspective that responds to the changing demands of senior consumers and those who care for them.

"Assisted Living" has been defined by the Assisted Living Federation of America (ALFA)[2] as a concept offering

> personalized assistance, supportive services and health care in a professionally-managed group living environment. Residents receive individualized assistance that is available 24 hours a day, and is designed to meet their scheduled and unscheduled needs. The setting is homelike and residential. For those who cannot live alone, this combination of housing, healthcare, services, and assistance with activities of daily living (ADLs) expands their ability to live dignified, meaningful lives.[3]

Arguably, many of the attributes of assisted living—according to ALFA's definition—are applicable to the various licensing categories that govern this level of care. However, it is the emphasis now placed on several elements that distinguishes con-

---

[1] Laughlin, James L. and S. Kelley Mosely, eds., Retirement Housing: A Step-by-Step Approach, New York: John Wiley & Sons, 1989. See also Brecht, Susan B., Retirement Housing Markets: Project Planning and Feasibility Analysis, New York: John Wiley & Sons, 1991 and Gimmy, Arthur E., MAI and Michael G. Boehm, Elderly Housing: A Guide to Appraisal, Market Analysis, Development, and Financing, Chicago: American Institute of Real Estate Appraisers, 1988.

[2] In 1996, ALFA changed its name. Previously it was known as the Assisted Living Facilities Association of America (ALFAA), under which name it issued several publications referred to throughout this paper.

[3] The Assisted Living Facilities Association of America and Coopers & Lybrand, An Overview of The Assisted Living Industry, October 1993.

temporary assisted living from its historical counterparts. Those elements include the "homelike and residential" setting in contrast to alternatives that were either nursing-home-like and institutional or conversions of existing residential properties not originally intended for a group setting. In addition, the emphasis on "dignified, meaningful lives" supported by assistance that meets "scheduled and unscheduled needs" further emphasizes the individualized concerns of the consumer rather than the convenience of the operator.

As the assisted living concept evolves, it appears to be filling a significant gap. For seniors who wish to remain in their homes as long as they are able, assisted living provides a noninstitutional option. For those frail seniors who do not require the medical care provided in the nursing home, assisted living represents an appropriate alternative.[4] This has been amply demonstrated—although not formally documented—by the transfer of seniors from nursing homes to assisted living communities described by staff at most assisted living communities.

B. Need for Establishment of Accepted Market Feasibility Standards

From the 1960s through the mid-1980s seniors housing development focused primarily on continuing care retirement communities and congregate housing. During that period, the approach to market feasibility analysis for these products went through a period of substantial change, leading eventually to a minimal set of standards that were accepted on an industry-wide basis by developers, sponsors, and most critically, the financial community.[5] In the early days of the seniors housing industry, assumptions were based more on hunches than on actual experience. When experience varied significantly from the assumptions on which feasibility studies were based, the results were unanticipated levels of "poor" performance that in some instances led to financial insolvency and bankruptcy.[6]

Assisted living is now in its formative stage, and at a point at which data on performance is just becoming available. Feasibility studies and the methodological standards for assisted living are therefore evolving as knowledge increases. Early studies for assisted living relied on many of the same types of assumptions that formed the basis for development of CCRCs or congregate housing. For example, utilization of a three- to five-percent penetration rate as an acceptable standard for project feasibility was simply applied to assisted living. In early feasibility studies, competition for assisted living was defined more narrowly than it is likely to be today, in much the same way that early studies of CCRCs only considered other CCRCs to be competitive, rather than encompassing a broader variety of seniors housing.

Understanding the differences between independent living and assisted living demand analyses will facilitate the articulation of a set of standard widely-accepted

---

[4] Spector, William, D., James D. Reschovsky, and Joel W. Cohen, Appropriate Placement of Nursing Home Residents in Lower Levels of Care, Cambridge, MA: The Milbank Quarterly, Vol. 74, No. 1, 1996.

[5] Gimmy, supra note 1; Brecht supra note 1.

[6] Office of Inspector General, Multi-Region Audit of the Insured Retirement Service Centers Program, (90-TS-111/112-0008), April 6, 1990.

benchmarks or practices in conducting market feasibility studies for assisted living. Establishing standards will allow those who commission such studies to become educated about what they should expect from the feasibility study. Equally importantly, this will create a framework for underwriting the financing of such facilities. Because of the potential for overdevelopment, it is critical that those who are actively involved in the industry—as well as those just entering it—have a generally agreed-upon basis for evaluation and decision-making.

2. SITE EVALUATION

A. Which Comes First: Site Selection or Target Market Identification?

In an ideal world, an organization would approach the development of an assisted living community by identifying the target market and its preferences, needs, and desires, and then selecting a site that meets the criteria established through that process. The feasibility consultant would be brought on board, under these circumstances, to do a study that would lead to the identification and selection of a site. Only rarely does an organization approach development in this way. The vast majority of studies are conducted once the site has been selected. As such, site evaluation becomes a component of market feasibility.

During the years in which seniors housing oriented towards the independent elderly emerged as a development trend, the philosophy relating to site selection reflected an increased understanding of the discretionary nature of the decision to move. As the industry matured, developers recognized that seniors who were relatively independent wanted to be able to easily maintain the activities that had sustained them before making the decision to move. As such, site selection became more attuned to supporting this notion. Most critically, those involved in the industry were finally disabused of the simplistic notion that "if you build it, they will come."

B. Criteria for Site Selection

The site of an assisted living community must meet several key criteria:

- It must be located in a neighborhood that is perceived as safe and attractive to the entire family making the decision;

- It must be easily accessible to adult children who will want convenience in visiting elderly relatives who reside there;

- It must reflect the socioeconomic target market being sought; and

- It must be accessible to shopping, places of worship, and medical services.

Despite the fact that selection of an assisted living community represents less of a lifestyle choice than the selection of an independent seniors housing community, the basic elements of good site selection—as illustrated by the latter two criteria—still must be observed. Site evaluation can be the first point at which feasibility is judged. For example, a site which is substantially inconsistent with the socioeconomic target market being sought may be judged inappropriate for the project being planned or may indicate a need to modify the market to be targeted.

The location of the site must be responsive to two audiences or market segments—senior prospects and their adult children—and in this way differs from site selection for independent living. It is most often the adult child who both initiate the search for this housing alternative and make the final decision. In interviews conducted by this author with marketing personnel at hundreds of assisted living communities, the interviewees indicated that the vast majority of initial contacts had been made by family members rather than by the prospective residents themselves. Therefore, in terms of weighting criteria, accessibility—particularly to adult children—may be considered to be a critical factor in site selection. A review of the zip codes of adult children for several assisted living communities currently in operation revealed that over 60% of the adult children resided within the local communities proximate to the assisted living community itself. Further, the ALFA 1996 Study[7] has indicated that 60% of family members of assisted living residents lived within 20 miles of the facility in which their elderly relative resided.

3. DEFINING THE MARKET AREA

Perhaps to even a greater extent than traditional seniors housing, assisted living is becoming a neighborhood business or service. ALFAA's 1993 survey results indicated that 74% of assisted living residents moved from within 15 miles or less of the facility.[7] This statistic reflects several factors that are shaping this industry:

- Unlike some examples of seniors housing, assisted living communities don't represent destination locations, drawing residents because of features such as alliances with colleges/universities, local amenities such as waterfront locations, or other leisure-oriented attractions.

- To the extent that assisted living is positioned, in part, as an alternative to a nursing home, market area draw may begin to emulate that of nursing homes by drawing from a very localized market area. This will be the case increasingly if the substantial number of assisted living communities being planned are actually built. With greater choice, seniors will be able to remain closer to home.

---

[7] The Assisted Living Federation and Coopers & Lybrand, An Overview of the Assisted Living Industry, 1996.

Specific site selection leads to specific geographic identity or orientation. The overstatement of the geographic market area is the single most critical error that can be made in a study, since it will ultimately lead to overstating the depth of the market for the project being evaluated. Unlike other forms of seniors housing for which substantial leasing or sales activities are required before financing is secured, assisted living is rarely preleased to any substantial degree. Market area determination must be made on the basis of detailed information gathered from local informants who are in a position to provide reliable information. These might include regional and local planners, representatives of organizations serving seniors (Area Agency on Aging, Council on Aging), and local Realtors, for example. The experience of other local assisted living communities that are already in operation can also provide vital information needed to develop specific parameters defining the market area.

Information obtained in defining the market area may indicate that both primary and secondary areas can be defined. The primary market area would include those locations expected to provide the largest proportion of the residents. The secondary market area may include locations proximate to the primary market area that are likely to produce some residents (perhaps 10% to 20%), but that are not as closely oriented to the project location as those incorporated into the primary market area. In cases where the orientation of such areas is in no way connected to a project location, there may not be a definable secondary market area.

4. ANALYSIS OF DEMOGRAPHIC TRENDS

A. Overall Population Trends

The larger context for the analysis of a target market for assisted living is set by evaluating general population trends for the defined geographic market area. Typically, population trend data is examined for the current decade and may also incorporate trends from the previous decade. Population growth is considered to be indicative of a reasonably healthy economic environment and of an area's ability to retain and attract residents. Overall population losses may be an initial indicator of an area's decline and may, unless corrected, impact long-term viability of new developments, including assisted living.

B. Analysis of Target Market Characteristics

While the resident is the only end user in assisted living, there are actually two target markets: residents and their adult children. Thus, market studies for assisted living must focus attention on both.

1. The Prospective Resident

An analysis of projected changes during the trend period in total elderly population and households (typically beginning with age 70 or 75 and above) and household composition (i.e., a comparison of one-person households and those with two or more persons) begins the process of estimating the size of the target market. Residents of assisted living communities are, according to the 1996 ALFAA study, typically single women of approximately age 85. Less than three percent of all residents in responding facilities were married and living with their spouses.

Household income for targeted elderly households must be evaluated. For this purpose, Census data is readily available, cross referencing household income by age of householder. Although a detailed profile of assets is not really available for narrowly-defined geographic market areas, information on housing tenure and housing values is. The home is typically a senior's primary asset[8], and one which, until sold, is not income producing as other assets are likely to be. An approximation of elderly housing values can be obtained from the Census and updated through the Multiple Listing Service available through most Realtors and is an important additional indicator of the economic potential of the target market. The Census also provides information on the proportion of elderly households that are homeowners and renters.

In order to truly segment and describe the elderly target market it is necessary to cross tabulate householders data by age, income, housing tenure, and household type or size. Sources for such data as householder by age and income on a specific localized basis are available through the Census Bureau and commercial vendors like Claritas. However, while organizations like Claritas can aggregate such data for a geographic area defined in a wide variety of ways, obtaining Census data directly must be done on a place-by-place basis. In addition, vendors like Claritas offer a specific profile of elderly trends not only for the base year of the Census but for the current year and five years hence.

2. Analysis of Adult Children Market

Although no widely-accepted formulas have yet been developed directly relating the size and economic status of the adult child market with demand for assisted living units, most studies still carefully examine this segment of the market. There are some organizations, such as Sunrise, which consider the adult child market (typically considered to be those age 45 to 64) as an equally-strong indicator of market potential as the elderly market itself. A trend analysis that considers this pool of households will frequently reflect the economic conditions of a given market. For example, markets which are experiencing significant economic growth may show extremely robust growth in this age segment because organizations are relocating personnel in this age group to the area. Other economically-depressed markets may be demonstrating losses in this age segment as households leave the area to find employment elsewhere.

---

[8] U.S. Bureau of the Census, Household Wealth and Asset Ownership: 1991, Current Population Reports, P70-34, Washington, DC: U.S. Government Printing Office, 1994.

C. Analysis of Housing Market

Because of the potential importance of the home in the economic equation of assisted living affordability, a review of the overall condition of the residential real estate market is an important component of the analysis. An examination of housing values and their pattern of growth or decline, as well as the ability to sell homes within a reasonable time period, becomes critical. Many developers of seniors housing from the late 1980s and early 1990s will recall the negative impact of that period's real estate depression on filling and refilling units. The problem of a housing market in decline is just as real for assisted living communities—which do not require an entrance fee—as it was for continuing care retirement communities that did require such a fee. Psychologically, seniors resist moving until their home is sold, whether or not they require the additional financial resources made available from the sale of a home.

5. QUALITATIVE INTERVIEWS

Most market feasibility studies for assisted living communities do not include survey research with the prospects because of the difficulty of obtaining valid results. Until a move to an assisted living community becomes imminent, seniors and their younger family members frequently are in a state of denial or do not recognize the dimensions of the need. As such, responses to surveys and focus group discussions—unless held with those on the verge of making the decision to move—don't often reflect the reality of what will be needed versus "what might be nice someday if and when we actually need this type of thing." This does not mean, however, that some form of qualitative research should not be incorporated into a feasibility study. With the building pressure that may lead to a move, there will be increased interactions with representatives of the types of organizations that provide services, advice, and counsel to aging seniors and their families.

The 1996 ALFA study revealed that besides family members—who represented the largest single referral source (24%)—health care professionals collectively comprised 35% of referrals, lead by hospitals (15%), physicians (11%), nursing homes (6%), and home health agencies (2%).[9] As such, interviews with representatives of each of these potential referral sources—as well as clergy, financial advisors, and attorneys—can be useful in assessing several key issues. The first is the extent to which it appears that those who are in a position to refer understand the concept of assisted living and are able to differentiate it from a nursing home. Second is gaining an understanding of what the needs and desires of these prospective residents might be. In addition, such interviews can illuminate potential barriers to the move including affordability, acceptability of specific locations, and attitudes towards purchasing services. This type of feedback can be critical to assessing feasibility. For example, a study may reveal that while the market appears to have the demographic depth to

---

[9] ALFA, supra note 7.

support a project, the biases and attitudes held by seniors about spending money on themselves may make it difficult for them to choose to move to an assisted living community or may preclude it altogether. Certainly most seniors would prefer to remain at home if possible, but there can be demonstrable attitudinal differences from market to market about the acceptability of choosing to move. In one market where we conducted a study for an assisted living facility, many seniors had moved on a full-time basis to small vacation homes that they had enjoyed during their working years. This blue-collar market was characterized, by many key informants, as having created a second generation of working class family members who, hard pressed to acquire even the modest vacation homes of their parents' era, counted on inheriting the vacation homes in which parents now resided full time. Pressure was placed by children on their parents to "hang on" to the home and not sell it. This type of dynamic certainly influenced the nature of the market for assisted living in this particular community.

6. ANALYSIS OF COMPETITIVE FACTORS

An element of increasing complexity in assisted living market analysis is the evaluation of the competitive environment. Unlike market studies for independent living units in congregate facilities and CCRCs, the assisted living facility faces a more complex array of direct and indirect competition. All facets of competition must be considered.

A. Direct Competition

The most obvious form of competition will be other assisted living facilities, although not all will compete directly. Before the analysis of direct competition begins, it is important to establish criteria for those facilities that are to be considered. Most organizations planning a project have a fairly well-developed idea about the socio-economic target market that they intend or hope to serve. If this is the case, criteria for establishing what is competition should consider other facilities serving a similar group. Establishing criteria regarding the minimum size of facilities to be considered competition is also a factor. In many markets, assisted living facilities may range from Mom-and-Pop operations that serve a small population in a converted single-family home to larger communities built specifically for use as assisted living. If at all possible, once criteria have been set and existing competition identified, a visit should be arranged with each direct competitor, particularly if a detailed market study is being conducted (telephone surveys are sufficient for preliminary analyses). A visit to an existing property obviously allows a more thorough analysis and an opportunity to observe the details of the physical plant, and to a certain extent, the condition of the residents and the attitude of the staff towards those residents. The following types of information should be gathered:

- Sponsorship and location

- Economic and geographic target market

- Number/type/size of units

- Payment plans/prices

- Services/amenities included in fee, in addition to fee

- Availability of other levels of care

- Occupancy level, waiting list, and turnover rates

- Resident profile including place or origin, age, income, source of referrals

- Absorption during fill period (for newer facilities)

- Marketing information

- Expansion plans, if any.

Data gathered from representatives of operational competitive facilities should include the number of operational beds and licensed beds in order to avoid the potential for overestimating the supply within a given market, since not all licensed beds are always considered operational, due often to preferences for private versus semi-private accommodations.

Of equal importance is information on planned projects. Planned projects can be identified through a variety of sources including representatives of existing facilities, municipal zoning/planning offices, and state licensing and regulatory representatives. Information on planned projects should include as much detailed information as possible, including a description of the planned facility and its fee structure, as well as its status in terms of regulatory approvals, financing, and timing.

B. Indirect Competition

1. Assisted Living Programs and Services for Independent Living Residents in Retirement Communities

With increasing regularity, independent living components of retirement communities are either facilitating residents' arrangements for home care services designed to support the need for personal care assistance or are establishing their own in-house capacity to deal with these needs. Survey research conducted by this author during the last two years in over 100 retirement communities has indicated that a range of 10% to 50% of independent-living residents may be receiving such additional support in order to delay or obviate the need to move to a higher level of care. The lines, therefore, between levels of care are blurring. From the perspective of estimating market depth, arguably, those independent-living residents receiving such care, are no longer truly part of the market for a move to an assisted living community, and may be more likely to remain in their apartments or cottages until nursing care is required.

2. Home Health Services

As alluded to above, home health care services can forestall the move to assisted living, and may be perceived, in that light, as a form of competition. The substantial increase in, availability of, and reimbursement for home health care services during the last decade has undoubtedly altered the patterns of movement from home to alternative living environments, helping seniors to stay at home longer. Discussions with marketing directors at all levels of care reveal that the majority is witnessing increasing age and frailty of residents at the point of moving into the community.

Ultimately, home care is not the right solution for many. Services are costly, particularly when they are required on a chronic basis, and not reimbursable when not prescribed by physicians. The social isolation of being homebound eventually becomes a problem for some seniors, and the assisted living community offers a healthy alternative. Finally, home care services work best when a family support system exists to maintain the senior. Burnout due to the frequent dual pressures of both child and elder care conspire to turn adult children into the primary target market for assisted living communities despite the fact that they are not the end users.

7. QUALIFYING THE MARKET USING FRAILTY INDICATORS

A. Why Age and Income Qualifications Are Not Enough

1. Differentiation Between Independent Living and Assisted Living Residents

The traditional methodologies considered acceptable for estimating market depth for independent living units in retirement communities are based primarily on utilizing age and income screens. To a certain extent, further modifiers—including housing tenure and household type—are used by some analysts. The process of sizing the market examines residents at the point of move-in rather than later in their tenure, when additional care may be needed. Although residents of retirement communities may be aging in place and obtaining additional support services, the criteria for admission to an independent living unit at most communities require residents to function without substantial assistance.

By contrast, assisted living communities typically are serving elderly residents who require a much greater level of support than do independent living residents. Assisted living operators indicate that at the point of move-in, the vast majority of residents require assistance with activities of daily living (ADLs) such as bathing, dressing, eating, toileting, and transferring. There are differences of opinion regarding how many areas of ADL assistance are typical of new residents, with some arguing that as many as three are the norm. Other assisted living communities have required residents be relatively independent and require occasional assistance with as few as one ADL.

As such, estimations of the size of the assisted living target market, when considering the end users, should take frailty level into consideration. Utilization of some measure of assistance with ADLs or instrumental activities of daily living (IADLs) such as meal preparation, shopping, and managing money, has become more widely accepted and expected in feasibility studies for assisted living.

2. Potential for Overstating Size of Market

The risk in not utilizing frailty measures in estimating the size of the assisted living market is that overstatement of market depth can lead to overbuilding. This assuredly was the case for independent living demand studies in the 1970s and early 1980s when studies frequently misjudged such factors as target market age and geographic draw. Greater understanding of the market led to more exacting standards regarding such assumptions. So too, with assisted living, experience is modifying analytical standards, and baseline assumptions for assisted living in many studies acknowledge resident frailty through the application of measures of frailty identified through national studies.

B. Measures of Frailty

1. Activities of Daily Living (ADLs)

a. What Are They? Dependence on others in performing certain physical activities is considered to be an indicator of functional limitations, and is viewed as an indicator of the need for health services. Although the national studies that have been conducted identify over 40 indices that use varying lists of activities to assess ADLs[10], most include the following:

- Bathing

- Dressing

- Getting out of bed (transferring)

- Feeding oneself

---

[10] Weiner, Joshua M, Raymond J. Hanley, Robert Claire, and Joan Van Nostrand, Measuring the Activities of Daily Living: Comparison Across National Surveys, Journal of Gerontology, Vol 45, No. 6, 1990.

- Toileting (continence)

Other measures frequently included in the basic ADLs are walking and getting outside. A total of eleven national surveys have estimated the size of the elderly population with ADL difficulties, reflecting that a range of 5.0% to 8.1% of the elderly (65+) noninstitutionalized population is receiving help with at least one ADL limitation. There are substantial differences among the national surveys, as noted in the study by Wiener, et al.. In spite of these differences, trends across the studies tend to be similar although levels may differ. For example, there is a relationship between age and need for assistance. And women are more likely to need assistance than men.

What is unclear is which of these studies may be the most appropriate for use in estimating the size of the market for assisted living. As the Weiner analysis illustrates

> policy analysts and researchers need to think carefully about what questions they are trying to answer. In addition, to avoid confusion in reporting their results, they need to specify in greater detail than they have previously how they defined ADL disabilities and which data elements they used.[11]

At this point in the development of methodologies for estimating market depth for assisted living, there is no real concurrence on the most appropriate measures or indicators of ADLs. The only area in which consensus is likely is that studies of noninstitutionalized populations are likely to be more appropriate than those which measured ADL dependencies among institutionalized populations, since the latter usually reflects nursing home patients.

b. ADL Profile of Assisted Living Residents. In their 1996 survey of assisted living facilities, ALFA and Coopers & Lybrand indicated that participating facilities reported that residents demonstrated an average of 3.0 ADL deficiencies, with the highest percentage of residents requiring assistance with bathing and medication reminders (the latter is actually considered an instrumental activity of daily living).[12]

It should be noted that these statistics reflect the characteristics of the existing resident population, not characteristics of those at the point of move-in. As such, lower levels of ADL assistance may be typical of the population who are considering or actually making the move.

2. Instrumental Activities of Daily Living (IADLs)

a. What Are They? Another frequently used measure of limitation is the need for assistance with IADLs, typically viewed as more complex tasks including such things as:

- handling personal finances

---

[11] Ibid.
[12] ALFA, *supra* note 7.

- preparing meals
- shopping
- doing housework
- traveling/getting around in the community
- using the telephone
- taking medications

Survey research indicates that approximately 17.5% of people age 65+ had IADL limitations and those limitations most frequently experienced are the ability to get around in the community and going shopping. Few with IADL limitations managed without assistance.[13]

b. Are IADLs an Appropriate Indicator of a Potential Assisted Living Resident? Arguably, the need for IADL assistance is an excellent indicator of a potential assisted living resident. Most residents of such communities are likely to need help with at least one or more IADLs. And the services offered in most assisted living communities are designed to provide support for at least some IADLs such as shopping, getting around the community, preparing meals, doing light housework, and taking medications.

While IADL assistance requirements may not be correlated yet to demand for assisted living communities, they do present an opportunity to better understand and profile prospective residents. This can be important in designing the appropriate service package, and in general, appreciating the nature of the disabilities that residents may ultimately have, if not at the point of move-in, eventually during a period of residency.

3. 1990 Census Mobility and Self-Care Measures

a. What Are They? In 1990, the U.S. Bureau of the Census gathered data from respondents age 65 and older on mobility and self-care limitations. Estimates of persons with such limits were made based on responses to questions in the Census regarding whether respondents had a health condition lasting six months or more which resulted in limitations in mobility or self care. By asking these questions the Census Bureau attempted to measure the number of older people with ADL limitations.

---

[13] J. Leon and T. Lair, Functional Status of the Noninstitutionalized Elderly: Estimates of ADL and IADL Difficulties. DHHS Pub. No. (PHS) 90-3462 (June 1990). National Medical Expenditure Survey Research Findings 4, Agency for Health Care Policy and Research, Rockville, MD: Public Health Service.

b. Can They Be Correlated to Need or Demand for Assisted Living? While the proportions of seniors responding affirmatively to the Census Bureau's questions regarding mobility and self-care vary by geographic area, the national statistics indicated that 13.2% reported mobility limits only, 4.9% reported self care limits only, and 12.4% reported limits with both.[14] It should be pointed out, however, that the Census inquired as to whether the respondent had difficulty, not whether they had received help with these limitations. As such, it may not be appropriate to compare the Census data with that gathered through the various national surveys on ADLs described earlier in this paper since many of the latter results reflected those receiving help with ADLs.

8. CURRENT METHODOLOGIES USED TO ESTIMATE MARKET DEPTH

Demand analysis for any type of housing or services is built upon a series of assumptions designed to estimate the total size of the target market. Methodologies used in establishing the size of the market for assisted living—studies that utilize only age and income screens—do not differentiate the assisted living target market from the independent living target market. However, in order to more accurately establish the potential depth of the market, demand analyses may use additional criteria designed to reflect the particular characteristics of the assisted living resident. Most methodologies in use today use some combination of the following variables. While the variable may be incorporated in the analysis, the way in which each is used is not necessarily consistent across methodologies.

A. Demand Methodology Variables

1. Minimum Age

Most studies being done today assume that residents will be at least 75 at the point of moving to an assisted living community. This recognizes that although many residents are in their early to mid 80s, a number are also between the ages of 75 and 80. A more conservative approach to setting the minimum age for an analysis would be to use 80, although few studies appear to be making this assumption.

2. Minimum Income

Since pricing has a direct impact on utilization, a minimum income level must be established, in order to size the market able to afford the proposed assisted living community. If the sponsor/developer has not established the economic target market

---

[14] U.S. Department of Commerce, Economics and Statistics Administration, Bureau of the Census, 1990 Census of Population and Housing.

for the proposed assisted living community, an analysis might be conducted estimating the size of various economic segments. In such cases, income ranges might be established in order to identify the size of each market segment. However, for studies being conducted when the economic target market has been identified, the following factors may be considered in establishing minimum income:

a. Differentiation in income by household type: A substantial difference exists between income levels of married couple households and households consisting of a male or female living alone. According to a report published in 1991 by the U.S. Bureau of the Census[15] the following comparison can be made:

	Age 75+ Households	
Income Range	Married Couples	Living Alone
Less than $20,000	48.5%	85.7%
$20,000 to $34,999	28.4%	10.9%
$35,000 or more	23.0%	3.4%

While these proportions obviously vary from market to market, the substantial differences reflect the potential for overstating the size of market from an income qualification perspective, if income is not differentiated by household type. Although standard data reports produced by national data vendors such as Claritas do not differentiate income levels by household type, this information is available on data tapes from the 1990 Census. In addition, highly segmented demographic data on seniors is available through a Cincinnati-based organization called Project Market Decisions in its SMART Report series.

b. Unit price: If price parameters have been established for different types of units, it is typical to use a weighted average monthly fee. If not, the price for the majority of the units may be used.

c. Rent/income ratio: Once the average fee has been established, it is common to make an assumption regarding the proportion of a resident's income that can be expected to be spent on that monthly fee. Given the service package for assisted living communities that typically includes all meals and snacks—as well as assistance with activities of daily living—many studies assume that approximately 75% to 85% of a resident's monthly income will be spent on the community's monthly fee. Minimum income can then be calculated by multiplying the monthly fee by twelve and dividing that sum by 75% to 85%. Discussions with some multifacility providers who are beginning to gather data on issues such as rent/income ratio indicate that many residents

---

[15] DeNavas, C. and E. Weiniak, U.S. Bureau of the Census, Money Income of Households, Families and Persons in the United States: 1990, Current Population Reports, Series P-60, No. 174, Washington, DC: U.S. Government Printing Office, July 1991.

may be spending more than 85% on the monthly fee and, in fact, are spending a portion of their liquid assets to support residency. But to date, no national data has been developed to either support or refine this assumption.

d. Differentiating between owner/renters: Increasingly, studies are differentiating between the seniors who are homeowners and renters in establishing minimum income standards. As has been documented nationally, approximately 75% of seniors are homeowners and the majority of them own their homes mortgage-free. Examination of localized data in numerous markets reveals that home ownership tends to increase with income. As such, owners who sell their homes when moving to an assisted living community are very likely to have considerable additional income available to them, once the proceeds from the sale of the home are invested. Analysts differentiating between the minimum income required by owners and renters are taking this additional income into consideration in establishing minimum income for owners. Clearly a set of assumptions must be made about the amount of cash available for investment after the sale of the home and the interest level at which that cash will be invested.

3. Market Area Draw

Most studies delineate the proportion of residents expected to be drawn from the defined primary and secondary market areas for the proposed assisted living community. The determination of exactly what percentage to use is another area where the judgment of the analyst is required. The basis for such a decision can be informed by the experience of local competitors to the extent that they exist and that such information is shared with the analyst. In markets where the first assisted living community is the subject of the study, analysts must rely more heavily on information from interviews and on such factors as the degree of migration of adult children to an area. Where the latter is prevalent, a larger proportion of units may be filled from nonlocal seniors who move at the behest of their children. Regardless, it is prudent to be relatively conservative in making such an assumption. This is particularly true given the fact that data vendors such as Claritas have already reflected projected in- and out-migration in their current estimates and future projections of population. As most analysts will agree, if the local market is not sufficient to support the majority of the assisted living community's units/beds, the project takes on a much greater level of risk. An assumption of local market area draw ranging from 60% to 90% is not uncommon for not only the first, but most—if not all—facilities.

4. Competition

Although some seniors may transfer from one assisted living community to another, it is relatively atypical and most studies assume that once a resident has moved to an assisted living community she will remain there. As such, units/beds in facilities deemed by the analyst to be competitive must be addressed in attempting to establish the size of the available market for a new facility. Traditionally, in studies conducted for independent living, both existing and planned units are considered in sizing the available market. Different methodologies may vary the proportion of competitive units used to calculate net market depth, but typically the majority of competitive units are considered.

This exercise is less simple with assisted living, particularly if the analysis is based on households rather than population. The Census defines households as including

> all the persons who occupy a housing unit. A housing unit is a house, an apartment, a mobile home, a group of rooms or a single room that is occupied as separate living quarters. Separate living quarters are those in which the occupants live and eat separately from any other persons in the building.[16]

In addition, the Census identifies another segment of the population as residing in group quarters which, among other things, includes "nursing, convalescent and rest homes, such as soldiers', sailors', veterans', and fraternal or religious homes for the aged, *with or without nursing care.*"[17] As such, to the extent that assisted living facilities may have been captured by the 1990 Census as group quarters, their residents were not included in the Census count of elderly households. Therefore, excluding them from available households is inappropriate, since they were not among this universe when the Census was taken. Although arguably it is more conservative to simply assume that all assisted living communities counted their residents as members of households rather than among the population in group quarters, this may be a vastly overconservative assumption in many markets. It is possible, of course, to determine whether an assisted living facility that was in operation in 1990 may have been counted as group quarters by examining the Census information on a tract or block level.

5. Frailty Qualifications

Reflecting to the earlier discussion of measuring frailty levels, many studies now employ assumptions regarding a prospective resident's need for assistance with ADLs, IADLs, or both. At this point, however, there is no consistency across the various methodologies being used regarding which measures of either are best suited to assisted living demand analysis. There are arguments both for and against the use of frailty qualification that go beyond the fundamental question of which measures are most appropriate. Using a measure of frailty to size the market reflects an approach which attempts to accurately reflect the size and characteristics of the target market. Anecdotal evidence in most markets indicates that assisted living residents in most facilities have remained at home for as long as possible before moving and are increasingly frail upon entry. On the other hand, some providers argue that they are serving a proportion of residents—albeit relatively small—that has moved in order to be in a more supportive environment, but that does not require assistance with ADLs or IADLs. In certain states like New York, licensing categories such as Adult

---

[16] U.S. Department of Commerce, Economic and Statistics Administration, Bureau of the Census, 1990 Census of Population and Housing.
[17] Ibid.

Homes—established to serve seniors who are not, strictly speaking, "independent"—mandate that residents require only a minimal amount of supervision or assistance.

6. Household Size

One pattern that is clear regarding assisted living residents is that they are, for the most part, single individuals, rather than married couples. Although independent living communities may draw from 20% to 40% couples, depending on a variety of factors, assisted living communities to date rarely have more than 5%, if that, among their residents. As such, the potential exists for oversizing the market by including all married couples. This is particularly true for assisted living communities targeting middle- to upper-income residents because higher income segments will include a greater proportion of couples than lower income segments. Again, while information varies between markets, national statistics indicate the following breakdown by household type in 1990.

Living Arrangements of the Elderly(75+)[18]	
Alone	41.6%
With Spouse	40.1%
With Other Relatives	15.6%
With Nonrelatives Only	2.7%

Again, these statistics vary with income, but in general, they reflect the fact that a substantial proportion of the 75+ market may, in fact, not be part of the market for assisted living as long as this option remains unpopular among married couples.

B. Using Market Penetration Rates in Quantitative Demand Methodologies for Assisted Living

The quantitative methodologies used to size the market and evaluate market depth for independent living units have come to rely on a widely-accepted standard referred to as "market penetration." Market penetration typically refers to the proportion of qualified households required to fill a planned project once the market has been qualified by age and income, and competitive units, both existing and planned, have been subtracted from the qualified household pool. Penetration levels of 3% to 5% of the net qualified market have become considered as the acceptable norm by most organizations analyzing, developing, or financing independent living units.

Unfortunately, no such norms have evolved yet for the assisted living market. As can be appreciated by the discussion on the variability regarding which assumptions

---

[18] Arlene F. Saluter, U.S. Bureau of the Census, Marital Status and Living Arrangements: March 1990, Current Population Reports, Series P-20, No. 450, Washington, DC: U.S. Government Printing Office, May 1991.

are used to size the market, the use of penetration rates begins to lose meaning. Many analysts agree that, to the extent a penetration rate is used at all, it is likely to be significantly higher than that used for independent living analysis. Penetration rates ranging as high as 20% to 35% have been observed in various studies for assisted living communities. Factors supporting the acceptability of a higher penetration rate include the greater degree of screening that may be used to size the market and the need-driven nature of the assisted living move decision (i.e., more will choose this option because they need it rather than want it). Despite this, widely agreed-upon standards for penetration, or some other final capture rate measure are still elusive.

9. ABSORPTION

Absorption or fill-rate projections are critical in forecasting the financial performance of an assisted living facility. Overly aggressive fill-up forecasts can result in inadequate capitalization of start-up costs and, potentially, loan defaults. As such, absorption should be carefully considered and conservatively projected. There are a number of factors that should be taken into account by the market feasibility study, to the extent possible, given the point at which the study is conducted.

- Experience of competitive facilities: Information on fill rates from newer competitive facilities, if they exist, can be used to project the subject property's absorption pace. This information, however, needs to be evaluated within the context of the competitor's location, the experience of its staff, and the comparability of its pricing, services, and design.

- Experience of project marketing team: If a study is being conducted when the entire project team has been assembled, the experience and track record of the marketing staff or consultants is a factor to be considered in projecting absorption. In addition, for organizations that have already developed and filled other similar assisted living communities, the statistics on their other properties can be considered.

- Preopening marketing: Most assisted living facilities do not prelease as substantial a proportion of units as is the case with independent living, where a minimum of 50% preleasing is typical, if not required. However, if preleasing is anticipated, this will have a positive impact on the rate at which the project fills, particularly in the early months.

- National Surveys: ALFA's 1996 survey indicated an average of 18.4 months to reach stabilized occupancy.[19] In addition, a study was conducted in 1996 ex-

---

[19] ALFA, supra note 7.

amining absorption from 1990 to 1996, indicating a simple overall net absorption rate of 5.3 units per month.[20]

When projecting absorption, the impact of turnover must be factored in so that fill rates, net of turnover, are used. Given the relatively frail nature of residents in assisted living facilities, turnover typically begins during the initial fill period. The 1996 ALFA Study indicated that participating facilities experienced a 38% annual turnover rate.[21]

10. CONCLUSIONS

Market feasibility studies for assisted living communities, while similar in some respects to those conducted for independent living, vary in numerous significant ways. The lessons learned from the failures of many seniors housing communities in the 1980s should point to the need for the establishment of sound baseline data and demand methodologies that take this data into consideration. Given the pace of development of assisted living communities during this decade and the increasing number of multifacility providers, the types of data needed to establish baselines should be available. Collaboration between providers and analysts will be necessary to establish standards. Although the performance of individual providers is and should be considered proprietary, an organization such as ALFA, with its extensive membership base, could be the catalyst for a study designed to collect data that could be aggregated and evaluated for the purpose of helping all involved in this burgeoning industry to better understand it, and by doing so, enhance the potential for its future success.

---

[20] Seniors Housing Absorption Study: 1990 to 1996.
[21] ALFA, supra note 7.

9

SENIORS HOUSING INVESTMENT:
HOW PENSION FUNDS CAN OBTAIN SUPERIOR RETURNS, ACHIEVE PORTFOLIO DIVERSIFICATION, AND PROVIDE FUNDS FOR A NEEDED HOUSING PRODUCT

L. Robin DuBrin
President and Chief Executive Officer
Columbia DuBrin Realty Advisors, L.L.C.

ABSTRACT

Seniors housing investment offers pension funds solid real estate returns and portfolio diversification. This emerging segment fills a void in the continuum between private residences and nursing homes, and is supported over the long term by a strong demographic trend. To date, pension funds have been reluctant to invest in seniors housing. For increased activity, funds will need to learn the merits of the business, how to classify assets, how to quantify risk, and how to evaluate investment quality. The seniors housing industry needs to produce standardized information that facilitates institutional investment. Given these efforts, successful investing in seniors housing is possible.

1. INTRODUCTION

Fundamentally, institutional investors desire good returns on their investments. This has been the primary driver for their investments in real estate; it has historically generated these superior returns and it is this track record that has lead to increasing volumes of investment dollars being placed in real estate. Additionally, the theory that real estate investments are counter cyclical in nature to other types of investment programs has added to investment in real estate.[1] Unfortunately, the result of this flood of capital to real estate is that it is increasingly difficult to find top quality investment opportunities in the traditional real estate sectors; what remains to fund are more marginal projects. Moreover, as quality investments have become harder to find, institutional investors have been left with little ability to diversify their real estate investment portfolios. As publisher Geoffrey Dohrmann (1994) so aptly stated:

> [t]he sheer volume of money that pension funds will be depositing over the next 10 years does have some interesting implications for those seeking investment capital. Clearly, there isn't enough institutional grade property left in the market to absorb it all. (Pension funds already own most of what they have defined as being "institutional" in quality.) This means they are going to have to begin altering their investment parameters.

The answer to this investment dilemma is seniors housing. To the institutional investor, not only does this sector offer the potential of good returns on investments, but it could provide excellent portfolio diversification. It is a sector of the real estate industry that is beginning to emerge, bolstered by a strong underlying demographic trend and a clear benefit to the frail elderly. For the seniors housing industry, investment by pension funds would provide the much-needed capital that will allow it to keep pace with the increasing demand for its services.

Some institutions have recognized and benefited from the investment opportunities in seniors housing. However, much of the investment community—particularly the pension funds—has been slow to learn about the tremendous potential of this industry over the next thirty years. The potential residents of independent, congregate care, assisted living, and special needs facilities and their families understand the benefit of seniors housing and its different levels of services. Unfortunately, what is easily embraced by the seniors housing community and its consumers, has not been grasped by the investment community well enough to loosen all the investment capital needed to fill the demands.

We have found, that when fully explained, the concept of a range of seniors care alternatives does make sense to the investment community. They begin to understand that there is a need for an intermediate housing product that fills the void between a high-maintenance private residence and the expensive, medically-intensive nursing home. Moreover, as they study demographic trends over the next thirty years, they see an increasing market almost unparalleled in potential.

---

[1] Given the real estate investment environment of the 1980s, many have questioned the counter cyclical theory.

2. DEMOGRAPHIC TRENDS

We, as a population, are much older than we have ever been in our history and we are only getting older. The general population has substantially shifted over the past 90 years. The number of seniors over 65 is ten times greater than it was in 1905. From 1950 to 1970 alone, the elderly population grew by 66% (U.S. Department of Commerce, 1993). In 1905, the adult population that was 65 and older comprised only 3.5% of the overall population—approximately 4 million. By 1970, there were 18.8 million people; in this category in 1980, 25.5 million; and in 1990, there were 31.1 million people aged 65 and older. The growth between 1970 and 1980 was 26%, and between 1980 to 1990 the population grew 18.1%. By the year 2050, the same population is predicted to be 78.9 million, greater than a 100% increase.

Figure 1 shows the aging population growth trends from 1910 to 2050. The numbers on the right side reflect the numbers of seniors 65 and older in millions.

Furthermore, the oldest of the elderly are living longer. This means additional growth in the frail elderly population. The "85 and older" population was approximately 122,000 in 1900. By 1940, that segment of the population had grown to 365,000. In 1990, there were 3,021,000 persons aged 85 and older—approximately a 825% increase in 45 years. By the year 2030, the U. S. Census Bureau predicts we will have more than 8,381,000—a 275% increase—and, by 2050, we will have 17,652,000 seniors 85 and older—almost a 210% increase.

Because of these dramatic changes in the demographics of our population, support for seniors housing investment can be heard from the general public. The informed general public believes it is a needed commodity and many people that we speak with when discussing the seniors housing business tell us they think it is a socially-redeeming endeavor to provide this type of housing. Providing seniors with good affordable housing is a goal of many who are in this business from lenders to operators.

3. INSTITUTIONAL ACTIVITY

The amount of institutional activity in this investment area has begun to show significant evidence of acceptance as an investment, although the pension funds still have not *jumped* in with both feet. The following is exemplary of many of the investors in seniors housing:

Figure 1. Population Over 65 Years of Age (In Millions)

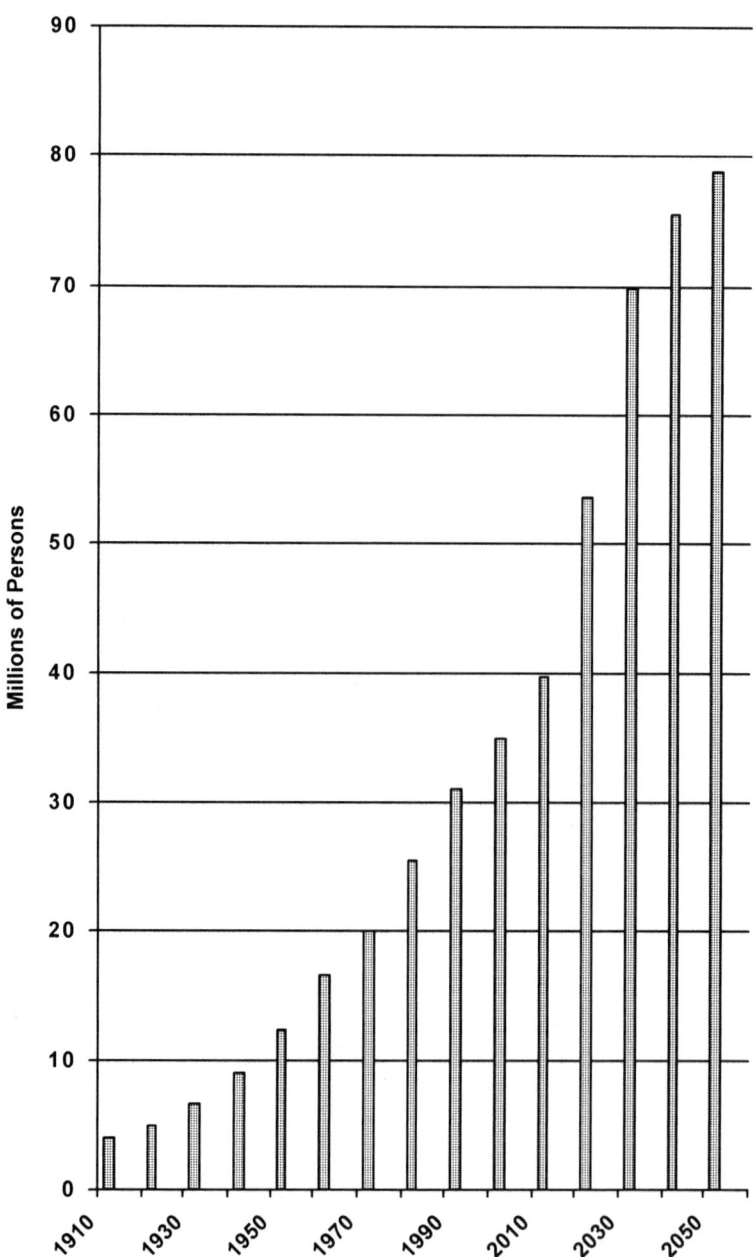

Source: US Department of Commerce, 1993:2-2

- An Alabama pension fund has set up a new seniors housing development program to begin funding in 1997 and other pension funds are looking at investing in seniors housing as a specific investment.[2]

- Many investment advisors have begun to look at this product as an alternative to conventional real estate. Generally, though, they have not devoted the resources to develop a quality investment program and management team.

- Banks, which had virtually abandoned this market after the late 1980s, are now back and bullish.[3]

- SouthTrust has investments in over 42 states. They are expanding their programs through their recent venture in PRN Mortgage Capital, LLC.[4]

- NatWest, Smith Barney, Alex. Brown, J.C. Bradford, and others have taken more than thirteen seniors housing (Assisted Living) companies public in 1993-1996. Legg Mason has a dedicated health care REIT analyst.

- Nomura Securities has provided in excess of $200 million in seniors housing debt for a major seniors housing operator, Holiday Retirement Corporation.[5]

- Healthcare REITs have financed in excess of $1 billion in credit facilities and mortgages for seniors housing operators in 1995. Meditrust alone has predicted to finance that amount in 1996.[6]

- Insurance companies including Equitable, Prudential, Pacific Mutual, Sun Life, and others provided more than $300 million in funding in 1995.

- Fannie Mae began a seniors housing mortgage program with their DUS Lenders in 1995.

- Columbia DuBrin Realty Advisors, founded in 1994, as the first investment advisor to focus on the seniors housing industry, has provided services for acquisitions, dispositions, investment analysis, and joint ventures, as well as debt and equity financing in seniors and health care products for assets in excess of $300 million.

---

[2] Interview with David Bronner, CEO, Retirement Systems of Alabama, December 1996. Several corporate funds did invest in independent living facilities through First Chicago in the early 1980s and CalPERS commissioned a report on seniors housing, which was not completed, to help them determine whether seniors housing should be in their portfolio. No allocation has been made (Interview with Sheryl Pressler, CEO, CalPERS, October 1996).
[3] Lenders Session, October 1996, National Investors Conference.
[4] Interview with John Cathey, Health Care Lending, SouthTrust Bank, November 1996.
[5] Interview with Ray Anthony, Nomura Securities and Thilo Best, VP, Holiday Retirement.
[6] Interview with Steve Press, VP of Acquisitions, Meditrust, October 1996.

In summary, lenders of all types have accepted investment in the seniors living and long-term-care industries as a viable option with a substantial majority of firms viewing the industry as equal to or superior to investing in conventional real estate.

4. PENSION FUND INVESTMENT EVALUATION PROCESS AND SENIORS HOUSING

Since there is much evidence for a growing demand, coupled with positive discussion throughout the investment community about seniors housing, why are so few pension funds taking the plunge? The answer to pension fund reluctance is found in the most fundamental assumptions and questions pension funds employ when evaluating investments:

1. Does seniors housing fulfill the fund's investment criteria and asset allocation needs?

2. How is the investment product type evaluated and the risk quantified?

3. Is the investment sized appropriately so that it won't require a lot of management?

A. Does seniors housing fulfill the fund's investment criteria?

Pension funds generally work with consultants, or "gatekeepers," who provide asset allocations, and advisors, who acquire, advise, and asset manage the investments. Both help the pension fund determine how to allocate their assets in their investment portfolio. Consultants may be engaged to set up a particular asset diversification program or asset allocation for a particular fund. They are more readily used by public pension funds. Advisors, after responding to requests for proposals from funds and consultants, actually invest the allocated funds.

Pension funds sometimes have an objective to spread their allocations among different asset classes to spread the risk of loss and enhance investment returns. The asset classes may include stocks, bonds, commodities, real estate, mortgages, alternative investments, venture capital, opportunistic investment programs, derivatives, and other investment products. Each investment product has various risk components and profiles. Some pension funds are very conservative in their investment objectives and, as a goal, look to invest a portion of their assets within their geographic or economic community, while others employ wide diversification to help meet their requirements to invest billions of dollars in order to maximize returns and to spread risks. Sometimes politics plays a part in investment decisions. Note, however, that the trustees of pension funds are generally considered fiduciaries, and as such they may be subject to personal liability for their decisions. They, therefore, want to make sure that all investments meet the investment guidelines set out by the funds' asset allocations, enabling legislation, and any other criteria that may be approved by the investment board/trustees, such as reasonable protection of the pension funds' assets by assuring the quality and the prudence of the investment.

Seniors housing may fit into one or more of the pension funds' investment categories,[7] including a direct real estate investment through a purchase of real estate, fixed income or mortgages (securitized or direct), alternative investment, an opportunistic program, a direct equity placement within an operating company that owns and operates seniors housing, or an investment in a fund that has one of the aforementioned programs with a seniors housing component. The advisors work with consultants and pension funds to help educate them on the merits of seniors housing and to help them define which category the investment might best fit to fulfill a particular pension fund's investment portfolio requirements or asset allocations.

When a pension fund needs to invest, under its investment allocation directives, in a particular asset class for which seniors housing qualifies, the consultant and advisor may recommend a specific investment when it meets the minimum or better standards required by the fund for that investment class (i.e., risk, return based upon quantifiable risk adjustment, length of investment period and size of investment, etc.). The investment may be placed in the form of a commingled account, where more than one investor pools its investments into a fund which might invest in one or more properties, mortgages or other seniors housing investments; or the investment might be placed in a separate account, an account owned by one pension fund investor. The commingled accounts may be structured as limited liability companies, limited or general partnerships, corporations, private REITs, or other appropriate legal structures. The commingled accounts may be the direction that some small pension funds might employ to approach this kind of investment, while a larger fund might prefer a separate account where they have more control. The type of account, commingled or separate, depends upon the particular fund's investment criteria and what is popular at investment time. For example, commingled accounts are not as popular as they have been in the past, because of the issues of control and liquidity.

B. How is the investment product type evaluated and the risk quantified?

The key question facing investors evaluating seniors housing is whether their investment is more real estate asset, or more a business. Resolving this question is important because pension fund investors have specific categories in which they place their investments. Since seniors housing has both an operational and a real estate component, it does not easily fit into the existing boxes. To illustrate, look at pension fund real estate portfolios, and you will generally find they are comprised of core real estate. Seniors housing as an asset class is not, at this time, in the core portfolio of

---

[7] Seniors Housing may or may not be unde the heading of real estate investment in pension funds.

any pension fund.[8] So with very few examples, how have they attempted to quantify risk?

In their struggle to make sense of seniors housing investments, some institutional investors have treated independent and congregate care facilities as just another form of apartment investment and management, while assisted living and special needs facilities have been lumped with nursing home projects. Unfortunately, neither is accurate. Seniors housing differs from other classes of real estate in how it is managed, marketed, researched, and developed. Moreover, it requires a whole new scope of experiences and expertise from advisors, operators, and investors.

The principal reason why pension funds have struggled with the correct placement of seniors housing in their portfolios is that that very placement drives the evaluation and risk assessment of the investment. If understood incorrectly, the funds risk subpar investments. To avoid this outcome, what is needed is a better way of evaluating investments and dealing with the issue of risk in seniors housing.

Pension fund managers, accustomed to dealing with more traditional real estate, will want answers to these questions: How are the risks of seniors housing investments quantifiable if there are no reliable reports and studies? How can the risk/return trade-offs be assessed? If seniors housing is more of a business than core real estate, then what returns should a pension fund look to receive? How should one look at the market for this product? Is there more risk and if so can the fund be compensated for that additional risk? I will outline how these questions have begun to be addressed.

Generally, the pension fund investor looks for a quantifiable risk. To assist in this quantification, they want to see research and industry standards such as fill-up rates, lease and rental rates, profit margins, level of occupancy or vacancy, and the type and size of operations. The issue to be addressed for the pension investment officers, trustees, and their real estate consultants is how this risk differs from other real estate investments. They want to know what issues are specific to this asset class, how they should evaluate the risks, and how they are to be compensated for any additional risk. They also want to know whether they will require additional staff to manage the investment and relevant costs.

Those pension fund investors who are quite comfortable with real estate investment and have categorized seniors housing as simply another type of real estate product will probably apply core real estate guidelines and will rely on research and standards that are not specific to seniors housing. This real estate approach is chosen because it is familiar and data are available. Until the last couple of years, there has been a dearth of research on the performance of seniors housing. With the recent studies by the American Seniors Housing Association (1994, 1995 and 1996), National Investment Conference (Mueller and Laposa, 1996, and NIC, 1994), and Coopers and Lybrand (1993, 1994, 1995, and 1996), more information specific to seniors housing is being generated. However, while these reports are good sources of information related to a segment of seniors housing operators, they have not been fully

---

[8] Core real estate is defined as commercial real estate: office, retail, warehouse, and more recently, multifamily housing. Information regarding composition of core real estate portfolios comes from CDRA research completed in November 1996.

representative of the market because many of the very qualified operators did not respond to the request for information, citing that it takes too much time to complete the surveys or voicing concern that the information they provide may give away operating secrets.[9] Studies, based on a full cross-section of the industry, would show that seniors housing can be competitively managed to provide good investment returns.[10]

In 1996, the NIC and Price Waterhouse, LLP, allocated research funds and time for a report on *The Investment Case For Seniors Living And Long Term Care Properties In An Institutional Real Estate Portfolio,* which, on first review of the preliminary report, will continue the positive trend of information and research needed to satisfy the institutional investor. Additionally, the Special Issue Monograph of the Journal of Real Estate Research, sponsored by NIC and the American Real Estate Society, is devoted to the seniors housing and long-term-care topics and was published in 1997. What this additional research shows is that there have been overwhelming successes by seniors housing operators, such as Holiday Retirement, Leisure Care, Capital Seniors Living, and others, all who have created profitable enterprises that have provided good investment returns.

As more research and industry information are published, investors will become increasingly aware that investment in seniors housing is more than a core real estate investment; it has a large corresponding operational component. With this operational aspect come issues related to identifying the market and providing the right kinds of operating programs for a particular seniors housing product. The traditional and well-documented ways of examining market demand, competition, and the attendant management of competitive risk do not seem to be easily applied to seniors housing. For example, if you are looking at investing in an assisted living facility, do you just research the existing assisted living facilities or do you research the congregate care, special needs, and skilled nursing facilities? The research most likely, if done properly, will include all of the facilities and this takes more work. It requires on-site visitation to determine the actual seniors housing product, as many people call their facilities by names such as assisted living—popular with Wall Street—that may really be more like congregate care in the services provided. A congregate care property may more directly compete with assisted living because of home health care options and an independent facility may really be assisted living. Finally, one or more of the properties may have a mix of tenants and a menu of services, which makes the research more complicated.

Researching the market potential requires a different approach to looking at consuming populations. Demographics have to be segmented for the analysis of this particular asset type. For instance, some seniors housing markets are quite successful as import markets when the adult children of the seniors move their parent(s) in from out of town to be near them. However, the local demographics, as looked at in traditional real estate analyses, would show an overbuilding in the market. There are also

---

[9] This industry has a history of jealously guarding its proprietary information.

[10] Note that the Executive Director of ASHA, David Schless, has indicated that their 1995 report's statistical pool is much more representative of the market; if this holds true for the future, there will be more accurate statistical information to provide annual industry trends.

the characteristics of particular markets and racial groups and communities that may or may not tend to like seniors housing more than others.

What further complicates market research and operational analyses is that many operators have their own formulas for successfully researching the market and hold this information as proprietary. Additionally, some do not want to divulge how they successfully charge for their services and the processes by which they manage risk. This closefisted environment makes it difficult to assemble the typical institutional reports and studies of the market, pricing, success of the investment, and track record of the seniors housing industry, as well as specific types of properties and known operators with track records that pension fund investors want to see.

Another operational issue facing pension fund investors is that many seniors housing operating companies have not had the longevity nor have they been of the size—either in number of units or net worth—that would be typical of the institutional investors' criteria. As a result, most operators have not been faced with complying with institutional standards of reporting. Look-back records for their operations and properties may be incomplete or incorrectly formatted. Fortunately, as more of the seniors housing companies go public, the less the accounting and reporting issues will be a problem.

Finally, in addition to the real estate and operational risks associated with the targets of investment, pension funds need to tackle the risk created by a lack of advisors experienced directly in the seniors housing investment arena. Pension advisors or asset managers have typically had no experience in seniors housing and, therefore, have no track record with this investment product or with pension funds investing in the product. The advisors quite simply have not had the expertise in seniors housing needed to diversify into this product type and there is a serious learning curve to understand and properly invest in this product.

Since pension funds generally do not invest directly, but go through their advisors, who are fiduciaries to the funds, the difficulty in assembling the expertise and access to pension funds is significant. In fact, it may be the biggest problem of all because the consultants have not had experience in the product either. If they do not understand the product or feel comfortable with it, they will not recommend seniors housing to the client. This is generally because of the consultant's fiduciary relationship to the pension funds and correspondent liability if they make poor investment recommendations, especially if the decisions are based upon an investment of which the consultant lacks knowledge. Therefore, because pension funds generally do not go out and investigate new ways to invest their money[11] and the investment advisors and consultants have little or no experience, it is an uphill educational process.

The lack of choice in knowledgeable advisors in the seniors housing product type produces another risk to some pension funds because it does not give them an alternative advisor. The funds want to know who will asset manage a property or portfolio of assets (properties, mortgages, etc.) for them if, for whatever reason, a particular advisor does not work. They want to have viable options for asset management of the investment by other advisors.

---

[11] CalPERS has been a noted exception.

There is the additional problem that if no one specializes in the product type, who will take the time or have the knowledge to educate the pension funds about seniors housing as an investment category? Or, gather the information necessary to satisfy the funds' need to have the reports and studies they desire? As an overall statement, though, the interest of pension funds in seniors housing exists; investment is simply a matter of time.

C. Is the investment sized appropriately?

Seniors housing is a specialized type of real estate that takes a level of knowledge and expertise that an investment manager who is involved successfully in other investment products (e.g., core real estate) does not have the time or the need to conquer. It takes time and money to diversify and train managers and marketers to develop a new product, and to have the expertise necessary to properly advise and manage the product.

Additionally, because the seniors housing product is a niche product and is typically smaller than most core real estate, it will take more resources to acquire and manage than the core real estate programs. With this understanding, the issues then become: How does an advisor price this additional cost and how do they justify it to the pension fund when the funds are not familiar with the management costs of this type of investment product? Will the funds allow a higher fee than they do for their core real estate? If a $70 million investment has ten properties rather than one, will it cost more to manage? The advisor must educate investors on these additional issues.

Because this type of investment product is smaller in monetary terms than those in which a pension fund typically invests, institutional interest may waver. Pension funds, which typically invest in large shopping centers and office buildings, are accustomed to single real estate investments that are larger than $20 million. Depending on the type of product—be it assisted, congregate, or independent, and whether it is a "stand-alone" facility—the average product size is between 60 and 140 units, which may equate to a value of $4-$15 million. This raises the issue that, on an individual investment, which may be considered small, what kinds of resources do the pension funds need to allocate for oversight of the investment? The smaller the investment, the more resources that may have to be allocated to the oversight of the investment resulting in a need to counterbalance the cost with higher returns. Pension funds, their consultants, and advisors will need to determine whether or not the return is adjusted for the additional cost in time and human resources and is therefore worthwhile.

5. SUMMARY AND CONCLUSIONS

The seniors market is ripe for investment. The market has begun to mature. Successful investment in this industry is possible. Holiday Retirement Corporation, the largest congregate care provider in the nation, has achieved great success, with assets worth in excess of a billion dollars under management and owned in various partnerships. They have an organization and professionalism an institutional investor can appreciate and can invest in without concerns about justifying the quality of the operator or worry about successful management of the investment product. There are several other success stories as well (*Chain Reactions*, 1996).

To provide better communication with pension funds, however, successful seniors housing operators and investment advisors need to provide information in two categories: real estate and operating company performance. General real estate and operating information about seniors housing as a whole should be accumulated across the industry on a nondisclosure basis and then disseminated.

Operators need to be aware that there is a standard of reporting which pension funds require—audited statements. Many pension funds are requiring reporting in compliance with Association of Investment Management and Research (AIMR) guidelines. The funds require the investment advisor to supply this kind of information on all properties they hold on behalf of a pension fund. Supplying these reports in the formats desired by the investing entity will be crucial.

Operators may also need to take precautions against the obstacle of too much success. When pension funds begin investing in seniors housing, the capital markets for seniors housing may become flooded. Over the years there has been an ebb and flow of pension fund money into various industries that has changed the character of those industries. While many in the seniors housing industry may see this not as a risk, but as an opportunity for exponential growth in their market share, it will be essential to the continuing health of the industry to maintain a strong focus on quality control and limits based on human resources, expertise, and well-defined market conditions.

Should the capital flooding occur, not only will investors require knowledgeable advisors who can match them with the best operators to create quality investments, but operators will face the same questions all real estate owners and developers face: Is the market being over-built? Is there too much competition and how can I survive the onslaught of investment money creating more and more seniors housing projects? If these potential problems are handled well, then operators also stand to win in this investment environment.

Advisors who wish to enter the seniors housing arena should be aware that the learning curve on their part—not to mention on the part of the funds they approach—is a long and steep one. Pension funds demand that their advisors have direct experience in the particular market niche being presented for investment. Acquiring this expertise requires a sizable investment of time, effort, and financial commitment.

Educating investors, operators, and others on this investment opportunity is a long process. As with other relatively new ideas, the pioneers in this work will have an uphill struggle. But seniors housing is a concept that makes a great deal of sense. It fills a market need and provides an excellent investment opportunity. Clearing the obstacles is possible with the right direction, a strong commitment, and a long-term outlook.

Seniors housing operators need advocates such as ASHA, NIC, Assisted Living Federation of America and National Association of Seniors Living. They need to help dedicate the time and resources to create the research needed for seniors housing investment with the pension funds. The operators need to become more focused on the business aspect of operating their facilities so that they run a professional organization and business for which investors can quantify and ameliorate their risk. Those in the investment community need to work closely with the trade associations and the industry to help develop the reports and research necessary to analyze the seniors housing market. Together, seniors housing operators and institutional investors can create a solid financial future in housing our nation's senior population.

ACKNOWLEDGMENT

The author wishes to thank Glenn Mueller, now of Legg Mason, Robert Kramer of NIC and David Schless of ASHA for encouraging her to write about the pension funds' requirements for investing, and the possibilities for investing in seniors housing with pension funds.

REFERENCES

American Seniors Housing Association, *Selected Seniors Housing Transactions: 1985-1993*, Washington, DC: American Seniors Housing Association, 1994.

Chain Reactions: The CLTC 75-Plus, *Contemporary Long Term Care* 19, no. 12, December 1996, 35-47.

Coopers and Lybrand, *The State of Seniors Housing: 1995,* Washington, DC: American Seniors Housing Association, 1995.

Coopers and Lybrand, *The State of Seniors Housing: 1994,* Washington, DC: American Seniors Housing Association, 1994.

Dohrmann, Jeffrey, The Only Band in Town, *Real Estate Capital Markets Report,* Summer 1994, 43.

Mueller, Glenn R. and Steven P. Laposa, *The Investment Case for Seniors Living and Long Term Care Properties in an Institutional Real Estate Portfolio: A Critical Analysis*, Annapolis, MD: National Investment Conference, 1996.

1994 NIC Lender and Investor Survey Results: Financing Preferences and investment Trends for the Senior Living and Long Term Care Industries, Annapolis, MD: National Investment Conference, 1994.

US Department of Commerce. *Sixty Five Plus in America.* Current Population Reports: Special Studies Publication PS23-178RV prepared by Cynthia M. Taeuber, Economics and Statistics Administration, Bureau of the Census, Washington, DC, 1993.

10

PENSIONS AND SENIORS HOUSING

Stephen Roulac
The Roulac Group

Providing capital to seniors housing involves many important public policy considerations. A quarter century ago, then SEC Commissioner William Casey warned of "barriers which will deprive housing and other types of real estate development of access to the full market and prevent capital from moving to the soundest and most attractive developments." The unfamiliarity with seniors housing investment by pension funds has been a barrier to capital being available to this sector of the economy. The "Investment Case" report represents a major step toward removing that barrier, so that capital can more readily flow to sound and attractive investment opportunities.[1]

Previously, the demand for seniors housing and its associated capital requirements have been more the subject of myth and misimpression than grounded in the reality of rigorous examination and insight. This research study meaningfully advances the dialogue by contributing information, analyses, and insights never before available.

This study does not presume to provide all of the answers. Rather, it serves as a starting point for further consideration, with an agenda of concerns that can enable participants to make more informed decisions. The data generated and communicated in this research study are most useful to those who are currently participating or considering participating in the production and financing of seniors housing. Especially

---

[1] The Roulac Group served as editorial advisor for the "Investment Case" research undertaken by Price Waterhouse on behalf of the National Investment Conference for the Senior Living and Long Term Care Industries. They critiqued the research output and commented on drafts of the research report.

helpful are the frameworks and ways of thinking about how seniors housing is linked to traditional investing concepts and to real estate investments, specifically. The report also provides an extensive bibliography of data and research currently available on seniors housing.

The subject of this research is both important and timely. The combined forces of changing demographics, declining traditional family configurations (such as parents living with adult children), and emerging new family structures (such as working spouses not able to care for aging parents) mean that seniors live longer, more independently, and in different housing environments than their predecessors. Since housing continues to be the dominant expense for all citizens, the implication in the growth of the number of seniors is consequently a strong need for capital to fund seniors housing for many decades.

Who will provide capital to fund needed seniors housing? One source that has been identified as a logical capital provider is pension funds. Just as the seniors housing sector is experiencing great change, pension funds are likewise going through a reevaluation process concerning real estate. Indeed, at this writing, pension fiduciaries are being challenged to craft the appropriate role for real estate in their portfolios. Questions concerning the proper allocation of total investment dollars to real estate; portfolio composition within the real estate allotment; recommended investment strategy, and many more issues are certainly daunting and often confusing. Perhaps more so than most other real estate investment capital providers, pension funds need guidance on strategic and policy considerations, so understanding the overall context of the senior living and long term care market is essential.

The market demand for seniors housing previously has not been understood. This study answers questions about demand by analyzing demographics, specifically: Who makes up the market? And what are their attributes? The research identifies a general structure of the market and a classification of the different property types within it. Particularly valuable are the market segmentation models that provide an informative means of thinking about seniors housing. In addition, this research provides specific demand information using national forecasts, then presents a sensitivity analysis based on current, conservative, and optimistic trends. It also includes an informed assessment of current supply based on a thorough review of available data.

One powerful consideration that might encourage pension funds to invest in the nation's infrastructure of retirement housing is a social one: because pension fiduciaries manage the capital of working individuals, in order to provide for future retirement of those workers, it makes sense for pension funds to invest in properties that serve corresponding retirement housing needs. However, as appealing as a particular investment might be from a social perspective, that purpose alone is insufficient to justify commitment of pension capital. Pension fund managers must also meet the fiduciary obligation of the prudent man standard, based upon the class of investment activity and the particular investment. This research provides solid information about the economic potential—with a balanced view of both the risks and returns—of investing in this specialized real estate sector.

From the institutional perspective, investing in seniors housing involves answering two questions: What does your capital buy? And where does your return come from?

These questions, although simple at face value, are fundamental to those considering what is involved in seniors housing. Basically, seniors housing is a combination of:

1. Real estate: an investment in tangible property; and

2. Services: including equipment and personal property, which in seniors housing assume a much larger role than in traditional real estate; and systems and procedures involved in delivering services and managing the seniors housing facility.

Thus, seniors housing blends elements that are most often thought of as separate and disparate:

1. The housing asset, which may be rented or owned;

2. Hotel-type services (known as "congregate services" in the seniors housing industry), particularly having to do with meal preparation, maid services, social activities, and recreation;

3. Assistance with daily living (ADL) activities: personal care services such as bathing, dressing, eating, walking, toilet use; and

4. Medical services: which can range from daily care like medication reminders to more advanced, specialized, and sophisticated healthcare.

From the pension fund perspective, there is recognition of a new agenda for real estate investing. Historically, pension funds were primarily concerned with core real estate, consisting of offices, industrial, retail, and apartments. Indeed, initially, many pensions were reticent even to participate in apartments, fearing that "direct contact" with tenants—as differentiated from the more impersonal and removed interaction with business entities in the other three core property types—was susceptible to conflict and controversy, and deemed inappropriate to pension trustees and staffs. Another reason institutions declined to invest was that the investment size in each unit was considered too small. More recently, apartments have not only gained a strong following, but more specialized property types such as hotels, mini-warehouses, timberlands, etc., outside the main core have been increasingly accepted and now account for larger portions of pension portfolios.

It is safe to say that some years ago, the idea of pension investing in senior living and long term care properties would have been improbable—or at least so alien as to not receive a fair hearing. Today, pensions have changed to become more receptive to a universe of investment possibilities, reflecting both the maturity of the institutional real estate investing sector and mirroring the specialized investing strategies that characterize corporate securities, such as the popularity of mutual funds. The study's findings suggest that the industry currently is—and within the next 5-, 10-, or 15-year investment horizon still will be—characterized by a transition away from smaller, less-rationalized operators and away from noninstitutional sources of capital flowing to individual operations. The inefficiencies of the current capital markets coupled with rising, demographic-driven demand might mean that above-average returns can be earned on employed capital. As a result, if seniors housing and long term care properties are added to an institutional portfolio, the overall portfolio returns might be increased without comparable increases in risk. The combination of pension funds and seniors housing is an idea whose time has come.

11

THE INVESTMENT CASE FOR SENIOR LIVING AND LONG TERM CARE PROPERTIES IN AN INSTITUTIONAL REAL ESTATE PORTFOLIO

Glenn R. Mueller
Real Estate Research Group Head
Legg Mason Wood Walker Inc.

Steven P. Laposa
National Director of RE Research
Price Waterhouse LLP

ABSTRACT

The Investment Case for Seniors Housing by Institutional Investors study describes the expanding seniors housing industry, explores the demand and supply of space in the industry, and examines the risk and return potential of investments that might be made by institutional investors in seniors housing real estate. The study breaks new ground in proposing industry standard definition categories and in estimating future potential demand. It also attempts to provide a comprehensive analysis of the data available on existing supply—a daunting task due to the lack of standard definitions and dearth of comprehensive supply data available in the seniors housing industry. The study then reviews the potential risks of investing in seniors housing and concludes with the reasons why institutional investors may find seniors housing an attractive investment alternative, including an estimate of the amount of capital that may be needed in this growing industry.

Three issues are highlighted in this study and warrant institutional investor review and analysis. Interested institutional investors who allocate time and resources to educate internal staff and learn of the opportunities in the seniors housing industry, could profit by understanding 3 main issues:

- The seniors housing industry will require large capital infusions over the next 30 years. The gross capital size of the seniors housing marketplace is estimated to grow from $86 billion in 1996 to $126 billion in 2005, to $490 billion in 2030. Traditional sources of capital may not be sufficient to meet this need.

- The seniors housing market is emerging and is expected to grow in a linear fashion through 2010, then grow exponentially from 2010 to 2030. This growth should offer institutional investors an opportunity to include an additional asset allocation to their portfolios which currently meets a minimum market size requirement, and is expected t o grow substantially in capital needs in the short term.

- The stability of future seniors housing demand, through aging of the population, should be independent of economic and business cycles, thus offering diversification benefits for the portfolio. Other institutional investment concerns, such as the systematic risks of seniors housing returns, generally appear favorable over the long term.

1. SENIORS HOUSING PROPERTY TYPE CATEGORIES DEFINED

Seniors housing provides a wide range of real estate services and care under many different names. The plethora of definitions have been placed into four categories for this study.

Category A is *real estate* with no additional services provided. Seniors who are healthy and active and need no support or care have a number of options for places to live. These include staying in their current home, or moving to an active adult community or seniors-only apartment complex. They may own or rent the real estate they inhabit.

Category B is *real estate* with *services* such as meals, transportation, and housekeeping. These services are unskilled services that can be contracted for independently or purchased with the housing. Thus, people who own their homes may purchase these services in their own homes one at a time or contract with a home care provider or other provider for these services. When provided in a seniors facility, housing units in this category are most commonly referred to as independent living units.

Category C is *real estate* with *services* and *ADL care*. ADL (activities of daily living) care includes such things as meal preparation, laundry, bathing, dressing, toilet use, eating, medication reminders and IADLs (instrumental activities of daily living) such as handling finances, phone use, shopping, and medication administration. People in this category may also need some minor medical care (such as administering drugs) or have a physical or cognitive disability. When provided in a senior facility, housing units in this category are most commonly referred to as assisted living units.

Category D is *real estate* with *services*, *ADL care*, and *medical care*. Medical care includes such things as specific disease care, non-ambulatory care (bed ridden), and intensive medical care. These facilities have been traditionally referred to as skilled nursing facilities or nursing homes.

A number of seniors-focused real estate facilities have evolved over the past decade including active adult communities, seniors apartments, congregate care facilities (CCF), assisted living facilities (ALF), skilled nursing facilities (SNF) and continuing care retirement communities (CCRC). A description of the care giving business as well as the real estate's physical description is undertaken to help explain the reasons for certain building design requirements. Many of the real estate facilities built today include more than one category of care unit type. Currently, the income derived from seniors housing is not broken down by the industry into a real estate component and a services or care-giving component, making the returns that a real estate investment might receive difficult to identify. Additionally, the percentage of costs paid by residents for housing and services changes dramatically for each seniors housing type—from mainly housing to mainly services and care. This transition from mainly housing to mainly care and the property type definitions are summarized in Figure 1.

2. DEMAND FOR SENIORS HOUSING

The size of demand for seniors housing is not well defined or well understood, as there are too many different definitions and studies with conflicting statistics to produce reliable numbers for the U.S. as a whole. This study attempts to reconcile where the elderly population currently resides as a base case for developing its future estimates of demand. Table 1 summarizes the reconciliation attempt that reveals owner occupied, nursing home, board and care, independent living and age restricted non-care demand estimates from the 1990 census.

Figure 1. Senior Living Categories

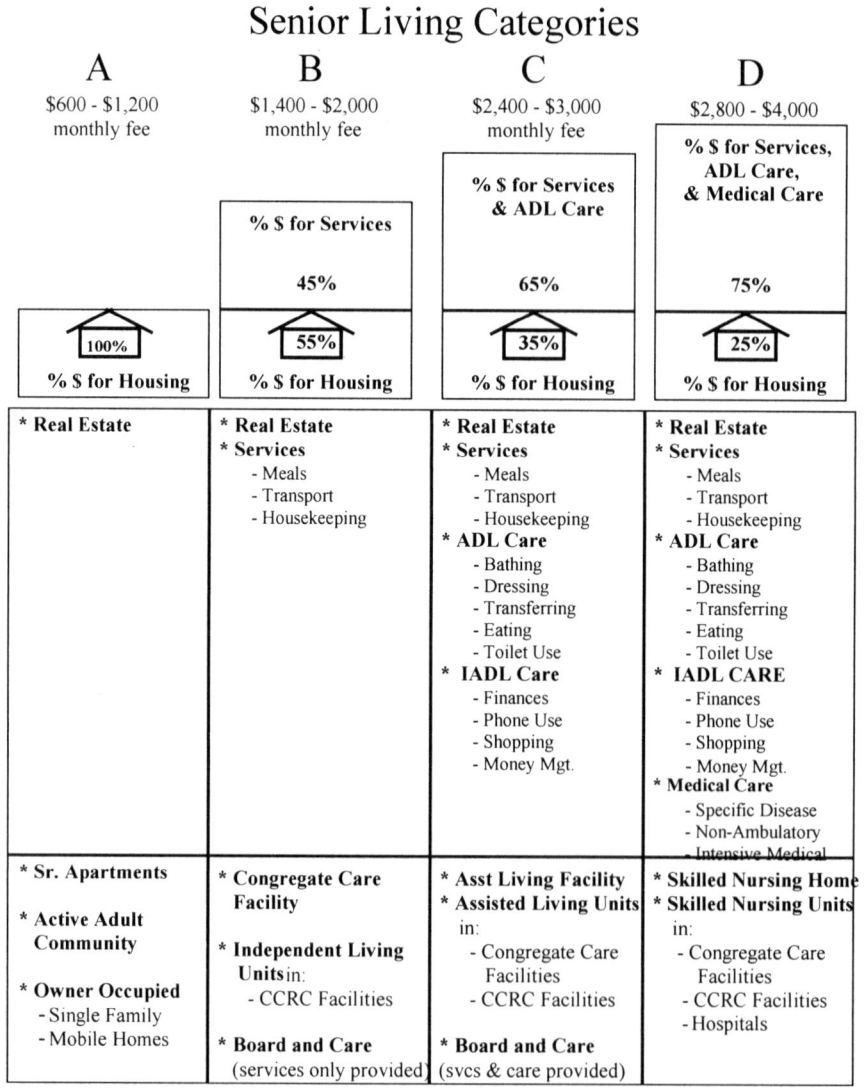

Demographic data shows that the growth of the elderly 65+ population in the U.S. has increased dramatically in the 20th century and will continue to grow from 31 million people in 1990 (12% of population) to 77.7 million people by 2030 (20% of population). This large growth must be studied more carefully, though, as the elderly population broken into 10 year age cohorts tells a different story. The oldest population age cohort—85 years and over—has the highest growth rate of the seniors group but is also the smallest in absolute numbers.

Table 1. Estimated Elderly Population in 1990 by Seniors Housing Property Type

Population (000)	Source & Notes
31,079	1990 Census Bureau (revised 1990 figure)
- 23,309	Owner-occupied population (Population x 75%-1990 home ownership rate 65+)
= 7,770	Rental population
	Total population less owner occupied
1,318	Nursing home population (65 and older), of which 34.3% were private pay (452,000)
560	Board and care and assisted living (65 and older), of which 67% were private pay (374,000)
751	Independent living unit population
2,629	Subtotal independent living or care-oriented senior rental housing
232	Age restricted, no care elderly population
4,909	Remaining seniors in non-age restricted, no care rental units (No reported care rentals, less subtotal seniors housing)

Source: US Census Bureau, Dept. of Health and Human Services, Research Triangle Institute, NIC, Price Waterhouse LLP (See full report for details)

3. MODEL

The overall demand for seniors housing is a relatively straightforward modeling task since future demand estimates are based on existing population data. The demand model needs to account for the timing of when seniors will require and accept seniors housing living arrangements, including the senior rental housing segment. However, determining which type of seniors housing will be needed (gross demand), and subsequently used (effective demand), is a complex task with a number of additional assumptions. In this demand model used to estimate elderly population by the four seniors housing property types, four steps are developed to estimate probability classifications based on the demand indicators of age, health, housing choice, and income. All assumptions about mortality rates, immigration, and other demographic factors are embedded in the Census Bureau's numbers for both current statistics and forecasts.

This seniors housing demand model uses the probabilities of demand available on health, housing choice, and income data for seniors found in current literature and statistics, throughout the future estimate period. Therefore, it is a constant demand model because the ratios and proportions are constant for each future period. For example, home ownership rates by elderly age groups are the same in 2030 as home ownership rates in 1996. The net result of the demand model is an estimate of the population with incomes greater than $25,000 that will need the four specific seniors housing property type categories (Figure 2).

Figure 2. Income Distribution Classification & Seniors Housing Category

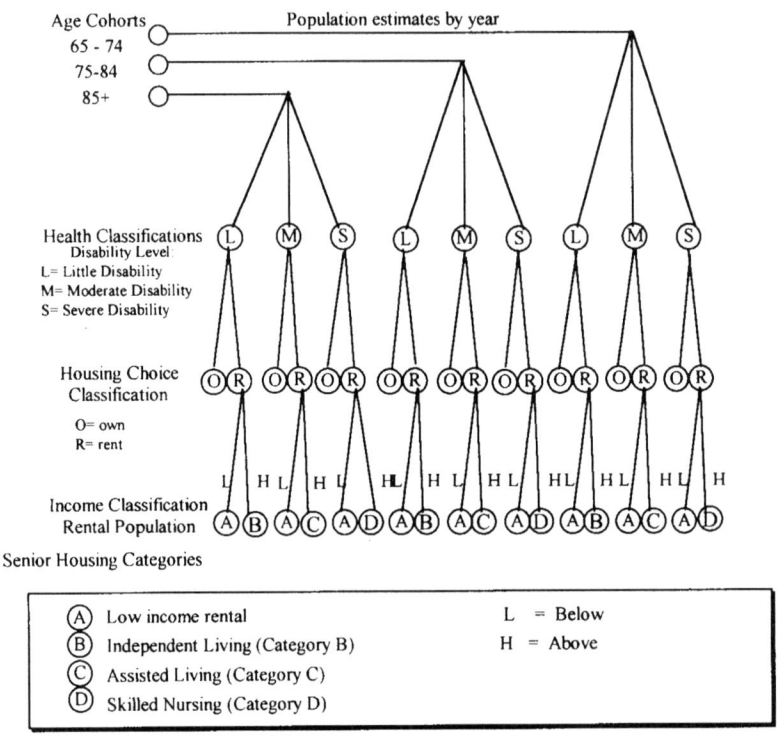

After analyzing age cohorts, health conditions (including disabilities), home ownership, and income levels, this study develops a base demand model that assumes current seniors housing use rates will continue into the future, giving a base demand estimate of potential growth for the industry. This base demand model finds the current effective demand for all three seniors housing categories to be 1.78 million people and growth that will double to over 3.7 million people by 2030 (Figure 3). The next four years, through 2000, will bring demand of about 100,000 people. Additionally, an optimistic and conservative demand model is also developed assuming different growth rates for the main assumption variables in the demand model which are health, housing choice, and income of the elderly.

THE INVESTMENT CASE FOR SENIOR LIVING

Figure 3. Base Case Estimate of Effective Demand for Seniors Housing Categories Elderly Population over $25k Income

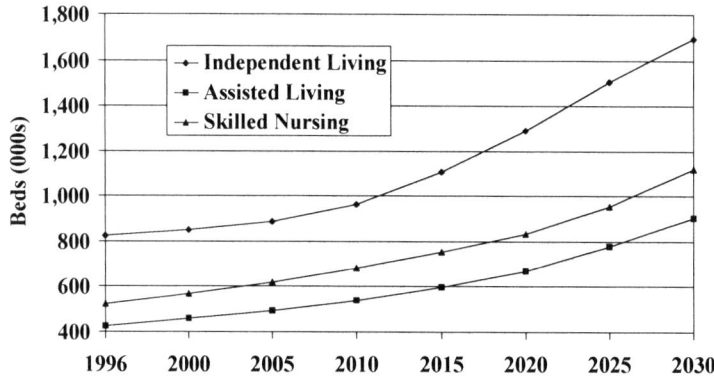

Thousands of Beds

Base	1996	2000	2005	2010	2015	2020	2025	2030
Independent Living	826	849	887	963	1,108	1,292	1,507	1,694
Assisted Living	427	457	492	537	597	671	778	903
Skilled Nursing	524	567	619	681	752	834	957	1,120
Subtotal	1,778	1,873	1,997	2,181	2,457	2,797	3,242	3,717

Source: Price Waterhouse LLP

Note: Skilled nursing includes private pay residents—approximately 34% of total skilled nursing demand.

4. SUPPLY

The supply estimates in the seniors housing industry vary widely due to the young age of the industry, lack of consistent definitions, and lack of national data collection efforts. Most data has been collected on a state or regional level, and definitions vary due to local regulations. Although efforts to collect seniors housing supply estimates have improved in recent years, current estimates fall short of describing the seniors housing industry.

1990 Census data and other supply estimate surveys performed in the early 1990s present a reasonable picture of the distribution of elderly population by seniors housing facility type. Board and care and assisted living facilities accounted for the majority of seniors housing facilities in 1990, followed by skilled nursing facilities, congregate, and CCRCs (Table 2).

Table 2. Estimated Distribution of Renter-Occupied Population, 1990 By Seniors Housing Facility

Seniors Housing Facility Type	Estimated # of Facilities	Elderly Resident Population
Skilled Nursing Facilities	17,000	1.318 million
Board and Care/Assisted Living	24,589	0.560 million
Congregate and CCRC	5,381	0.751 million
Total	**46,970**	**2.629 million**

Source: Price Waterhouse LLP, National Investment Conference on Senior Living and Long Term Care Industries

5. VALUATION

The value of seniors housing facilities varies widely due to the different locations, services provided, and sizes of facilities. Although valuation procedures are similar to those used in other real estate property types, the relatively small size of the properties and the risks associated with running the service and care portions of the facilities place capitalization and return rates at higher levels than other real estate property types. This means that expected returns from these property types have been and are currently higher than other real estate investment alternatives (Table 3).

Table 3. 1996 Seniors Housing Investment Return Survey

Facility	Overall Capitalization Rate Range (%)	Overall Capitalization Rate Average (%)	Internal Rate of Return Range (%)	Internal Rate of Return Average (%)	Equity Dividend Rate Range (%)	Equity Dividend Rate Average (%)
Age Restricted Apartments	7–12	9.9	11–13	13.5	8–13	10.7
Unlicensed Congregate Living	9.5–12	10.6	12–18	14.0	10–20	14.5
Licensed Assisted Living	10–14	11.2	12–20	15.0	10–25	16.5
Licensed Skilled Nursing-LT	11–16	12.9	13–19	15.0	10–25	18.2
Continuing Care Retirement Community	10–15	11.7	12–20	14.5	12–25	16.5

Source: Senior Living Valuation Services, Inc., *Seniors Housing Investment* Spring 1996, Volume 3, adjusted responses (less the highest 5% and lowest 5% of respondents. Survey results may still indicate presence of distressed seniors housing pricing.

In 1995 the acquisition price of seniors housing properties ranged from $33,800 average per bed for skilled nursing to $74,200 average per bed for assisted living (Table 4). At the same time, average development costs were estimated at $74,800 average per bed for assisted living, leading to the conclusion that prices are currently high enough to justify new construction in these facilities.

Table 4. Seniors Housing Price per Unit ($) in 1991 and 1995

Property Type	Average 1991 Price ($)	Average 1995 Price ($)	1995 Low Price ($)	1995 High Price ($)
Independent & Congregate	37,800 per unit	50,700 per unit	14,000 per unit	116,000 per unit
Assisted Living	27,500 per bed	74,200 per bed	39,000 per bed	100,000 per bed
Skilled Nursing	29,000 per bed	33,800 per bed	15,000 per bed	73,000 per bed

Source: Capital Valuation Group, unpublished report, 1996

6. RISKS AND RETURNS

While the major risk for any individual facility is its location (demand is highly variable by location) and acceptance in its local community, there are also many psychological hurdles that must be overcome. Nursing homes have been perceived in the past as less than desirable by many seniors. The residential nature of the independent living must be presented to seniors, and assisted living facilities must be promoted to seniors, as well as their adult children who are the major decision makers in many cases. According to a recent Harvard Medical School study, the awareness of seniors housing alternatives is rather low at only 50%. Also, if home healthcare becomes more accepted and attractive, the possibility of seniors staying in their own homes will increase. Improvements in health and home-ownership rates, and a decline in income levels could also hurt the demand for seniors housing.

The return to a real estate investor is also highly dependent upon the successful operation of the property and service and care-delivery system. Changes in current funding levels by the government of Social Security and Medicare reimbursement is also a risk that would change the ability of many seniors to afford these institutional-quality housing options. Another risk is the affordability of these units in the future.

The historic returns of real estate investments in seniors housing are difficult to construct due to the lack of private market data. However, some public market data is available. On the debt side, defaults on government-sponsored bonds in different seniors housing property types have been declining over the past 5 years. On the equity side, three public health care REIT indices (NatWest Healthcare, Alex. Brown & Sons Healthcare, and the National Association of Real Estate Investment Trusts

(NAREIT) Healthcare), have produced returns between the S&P 500 and the Russell 2000 small cap stock index (but with higher return volatility). The two seniors housing company return series (the Irving Levin Long Term Care, and the Facility Based Long Term Care) show very strong returns with higher standard deviations, which may be due to the small size of the stocks and high growth of these companies (Figure 4).

Figure 4. Risk vs Return 1991-1995 Healthcare and Other Investments

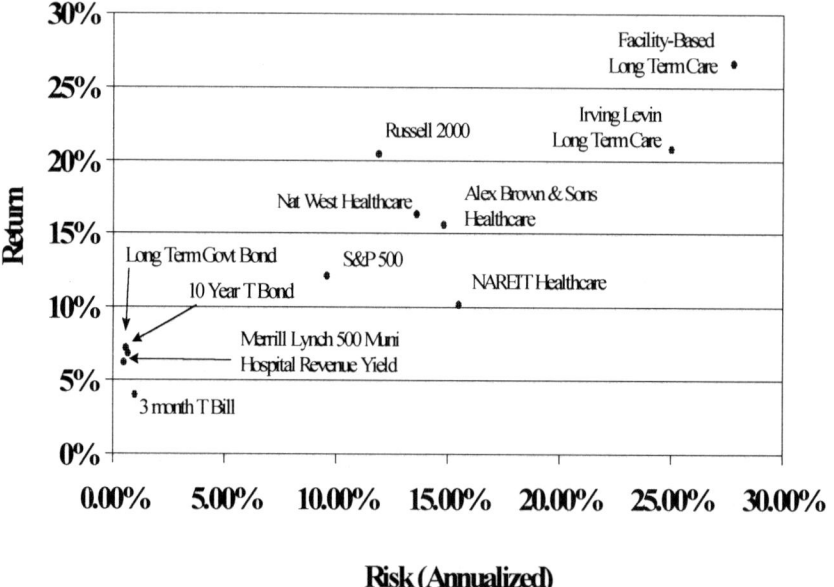

Source: Federal Reserve, Ibbotson & Associates, Alex. Brown & Sons, NatWest, NAREIT, Irving Levin, Merrill Lynch, Price Waterhouse LLP

7. CONCLUSION

The question before the institutional investor community is whether there is an opportunity for investment in seniors housing. Using the population growth estimates of the U.S. Census for seniors, this study develops a demand estimate for institutional investment in the major seniors housing property categories. Taking the demand estimate (developed in Figure 3) times the current transaction prices for seniors housing gives a current institutional market size of $86 billion. Thus, the institutional-quality seniors housing market is already larger than the public REIT equity market. Using the base case model for demand growth and a 3% inflation in building costs per year, the seniors housing industry is estimated to grow by $16 billion to 2000 and should grow to over $490 billion in the next 35 years (Figure 5). This growth represents a large capital investment opportunity for institutional investors in both the near term and the long term.

Figure 5. Gross Institutional Capital Size of the Seniors Housing Market Place 1996 to 2030

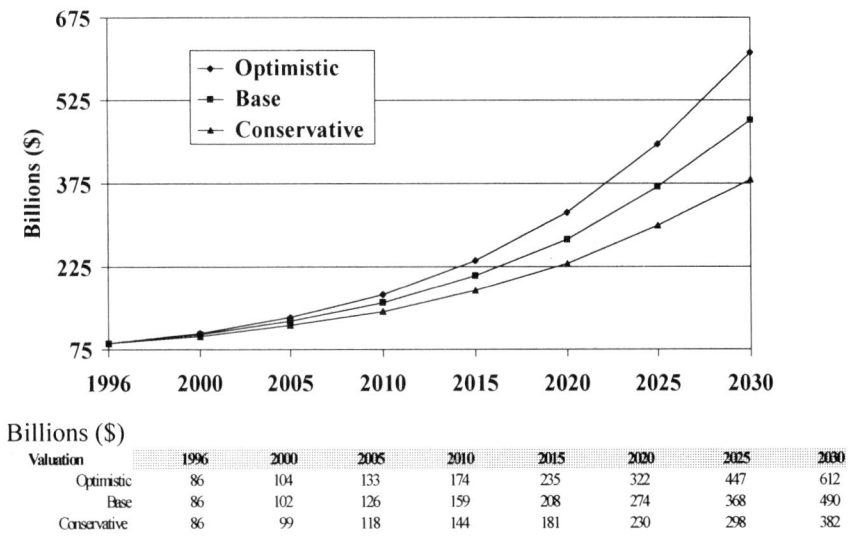

Valuation	1996	2000	2005	2010	2015	2020	2025	2030
Optimistic	86	104	133	174	235	322	447	612
Base	86	102	126	159	208	274	368	490
Conservative	86	99	118	144	181	230	298	382

While the future sources of return and risk of oversupply are not yet well understood, the little public and private data available points toward high returns with moderate to high levels of risk. This information leads to the conclusion that there is certainly room for institutional investor investment and influence in the seniors housing arena. This 120 page study has attempted to provide a base of information that will produce more questions, research, and interest from the institutional investor community, with a goal of improving the capital market opportunities for seniors housing in the future. The study is available from NIC in Annapolis, MD.

12

QUANTIFYING THE SUPPLY OF SENIORS HOUSING

Michael A. Anikeeff
Allan L. Berman Real Estate Institute
John Hopkins University

James E. Novitzki
Department of Information Technology
Johns Hopkins University

ABSTRACT

The 1991 National Health Provider Inventory[1] is a survey of nursing homes, board and care homes, hospices, and home health care agencies. Previous studies have investigated the supply of nursing homes and board and care homes on a national and regional basis (see Delfosse, 1991 and Sirrocco, 1994). This study uses new data from the survey to investigate the data on a state-by-state basis. Since nursing homes and board and care facilities are regulated by the states, the different relationships found between region and supply of seniors housing in earlier studies are explained in this finer-grained analysis.

---

[1] 1991 is the most recent census rather than sample survey

1. INTRODUCTION

In order to provide a benchmark for estimating the supply of seniors housing and long term care facilities, we examined the National Health Provider Inventory (NHPI). This survey was conducted by the Bureau of the Census under the direction of the National Center for Health Statistics (NCHS); 46,942 nursing homes and board and care facilities responded (see Appendix). The NHPI was one of a series of similar surveys conducted since 1967. The survey was previously known as the Inventory of Long Term Care Places (ILTCP), which was conducted in 1986. Earlier, it was called the National Master Facility Inventory (NMFI), which was conducted eight times, the first in 1967 and the last in 1982. The earlier studies also covered nursing homes and board and care homes.

The 1991 study includes information on home health care, which was not included in earlier surveys. Data from the survey is published in periodic reports from the National Center for Health Statistics. The national and regional data in this report have been presented in an earlier study (Sirocco, 1994); however, since states set policy for nursing homes and other seniors housing facilities, an analysis by state is useful for developers and investors trying to determine the existing supply of seniors housing. This is important for projecting future need and future competition.

This paper will review the definitions used in the survey and then examine the following:

- the number of nursing homes and board and care homes by state

- the number of beds and residents by state, by type of facility

- the size of the nursing homes and board and care homes by the number of beds, by state

- the breakdown of beds in each state by for profit, nonprofit, or government ownership

- occupancy rates in board and care and nursing homes by state

- the number of residents 65 and older in nursing homes and board and care homes by state

- the number of beds per thousand residents over 65

- number per 1,000 residents over 65 that use nursing homes, board and care homes, and home health service by geographic region

2. DEFINITIONS

This section provides a definition of terms as they are used in the NHPI survey.

1. Nursing home. A nursing home is a facility with three or more beds that is either licensed as a nursing home, certified as a nursing facility under Medicare or Medicaid, identified as a nursing care unit in a retirement center, or otherwise determined to provide nursing or medical care.

2. Freestanding nursing home. This is a nursing home that is neither structurally connected to, nor organizationally considered part of the hospital.

3. Hospital-based nursing home. A nursing home that is part of a hospital organizationally or structurally.

4. Board and care home. This is a generic term used to describe a residential setting that provides either routine general protective oversight or assistance with activities necessary for independent living to mentally- or physically-limited persons.

5. Bed. A nursing home or board and care home bed is one that was set up and staffed at the time of the survey. Beds for day-care-only patients were not included. For hospitals and retirement centers, only the beds in their nursing home units were included.

6. Resident. A resident is a person who has been formally admitted to, but not discharged from, a nursing home or board and care home, and who stayed in the home the night prior to the survey.

7. Ownership. Ownership refers to the type of organization that controls and operates the home. Proprietary homes are operated under private commercial ownership. Nonprofit homes are operated under voluntary or nonprofit auspices which may or may not be church related. Government ownership refers to homes operated by federal, state, or a local government.

8. Occupancy rate. Occupancy rate is the percentage of beds that was occupied by residents at the time of the survey. It is computed by dividing total residents by total beds.

Those interested in the specific technical aspects of the survey method and data collection techniques are referred to Sirrocco, 1994.

3. NUMBER OF NURSING HOMES AND BOARD AND CARE HOMES

The data on the number of nursing homes and board and care facilities are summarized in Table 1. The 1991 NHPI study identified 15,511 nursing homes, of which 14,744 were freestanding and 767 were hospital-based. There were 31,431 board and care facilities, of which 18,262 were not for the mentally retarded. Subsequent to discussion of Table 1, the data will reflect the market for seniors housing by deleting certain nursing and board and care homes from the analysis. The nursing homes addressed will be the freestanding facilities, because the hospital-based facilities were owned primarily by government and nonprofit entities.[2] Further, the board and care facilities addressed will exclude the homes for the mentally retarded. Only 10.8 percent of the residents in homes for the mentally retarded are over 65 years old.

Table 1. Nursing homes and board and care homes, United States, 1991

Type of Facility	Facilities	Beds	Residents
All Facilities	46,942	2,098,336	1,891,257
Nursing Homes	15,511	1,615,586	1,478,217
Freestanding	14,744	1,559,394	1,426,320
Hospital-Based	767	58,292	51,897
		482,650	413,040
		362,014	302,820
Retarded			
For the Mentally Retarded	13,169	120,836	110,220

Source: Sirrocco, 1994

The states with the most freestanding nursing homes are California (1,133), Texas (1,030) and Ohio (869). Note that Illinois (758) and Pennsylvania (690) outrank New York (536) and Florida (552). States with the largest number of board and care homes not for the mentally retarded include California (3,722), Florida (1,104), Pennsylvania (1,033), and interestingly, Michigan (1,749).

---

[2] 63 of the 767 hosiptal-based facilities were privately owned, and only 4,819 of the 51,897 residents were in hosiptal-based homes were private.

Table 2. Number of beds, residents in nursing homes, and board and care, by state, 1991

State	NRSHM	NHBDS	NHRES	B&CHM	B&CBDS	B&CRES
U.S.	14,744	1,558,300	1,426,719	18,262	362,014	302,820
Northeast	2,654	328,435	313,022	3,180	85,999	74,441
Maine	130	9,192	8,864	215	3,060	2,768
New Hampshire	79	7,493	7,074	135	1,680	1,329
Vermont	50	3,478	3,332	138	2,215	1,830
Massachusetts	554	50,133	47,604	311	6,321	5,767
Rhode Island	104	9,915	9,440	52	1,029	920
Connecticut	240	27,983	26,836	119	2,543	2,298
New York	536	94,884	92,484	864	30,911	27,544
New Jersey	307	39,970	37,302	313	9,756	8,174
Pennsylvania	654	85,387	80,086	1,033	28,484	23,811
Midwest	5,137	518,917	468,730	4,004	64,154	54,317
Ohio	869	82,516	76,944	402	5,197	4,234
Indiana	528	55,701	46,022	50	1,707	1,396
Illinois	758	95,465	85,052	96	3,400	3,064
Michigan	469	48,886	44,593	1,749	21,300	18,190
Wisconsin	405	48,710	44,886	521	7,443	6,464
Minnesota	399	42,001	39,927	342	5,826	5,017
Iowa	423	34,521	31,897	128	5,053	4,340
Missouri	525	51,652	44,888	392	9,408	7,556
North Dakota	70	6,056	5,810	43	1,014	910
South Dakota	122	8,448	8,060	61	397	331
Nebraska	209	17,846	16,177	85	2,389	2,005
Kansas	360	27,115	24,474	135	1,020	810
South	4,708	501,798	458,047	4,791	105,603	87,628
Delaware	45	4,101				
DC	18	3,010				
Virginia	217	26,324				
West Virginia	107	9,792				
North Carolina	283	28,259				
South Carolina	132	13,122	12,601	252	5,449	4,810
Georgia	324	35,011	33,500	505	5,528	4,532
Florida	545	63,752	59,169	1,104	34,674	27,529
Kentucky	271	25,685	24,452	310	3,968	3,442
Tennessee	275	32,493	30,989	263	4,505	3,799
Alabama	197	21,323	20,467	201	3,189	2,645
Mississippi	147	14,431	14,091	78	1,407	1,131
Arkansas	221	21,076	19,775	77	2,612	1,815
Louisana	298	35,550	31,781	51	812	697
Oklahoma	386	32,421	27,386	55	1,800	1,435
Texas	1,030	108,285	90,168	218	4,786	3,899
West	2,245	208,520	186,920	6,287	106,258	86,434
Montana	70	5,713	5,181	66	1,233	1,101
Idaho	57	4,887	4,342	88	1,696	1,429
Wyoming	25	2,243	1,982	20	592	438
Colorado	176	17,609	14,979	205	4,183	3,698
New Mexico	62	5,933	5,462	134	1,767	1,501
Arizona	112	13,265	11,723	217	4,736	3,692
Utah	82	6,292	5,209	46	1,380	1,250
Nevada	27	3,171	2,908	74	897	812
Washington	269	26,506	24,198	473	9,303	8,489
Oregon	183	14,382	13,036	927	7,718	6,886
California	1,133	105,781	95,300	3,722	70,059	54,722
Alaska	11	780	704	15	175	149
Hawaii	38	1,958	1,896	300	2,519	2,267

Source: NHPI

4. NUMBER OF BEDS AND RESIDENTS

In Table 2 we examine the number of beds and the number of residents per nursing home and board and care home. Note that this table contains all residents regardless of age. A table for those over 65 will be presented later. The number of beds and number of residents are closely related. Nursing homes had 1,559,394 beds and 1,426,719 residents, whereas board and care homes had 362,014 beds and 302,820 residents. States with the largest number of nursing home beds include Texas (108,285), California (105,781), Illinois (95,465), New York (94,884), and Pennsylvania (85,387). The states with the most board and care beds were California (70,059), Florida (34,674), New York (30,911), Pennsylvania (28,484), and Michigan (21,300).

5. FACILITY SIZE BY NUMBER OF BEDS

Table 3 illustrates nursing home and board and care home size by number of beds. The data reveals that approximately 90 percent (13,069) of the nursing homes have between 25 and 199 beds. The average size of a nursing home is 100 beds. In Figure 1, the states with the highest average number of beds per nursing home are New York (177), District of Columbia (167), Pennsylvania (131), New Jersey (130), Maryland (128), and Virginia (121). The states with the largest numbers of nursing homes with over 200 beds are New York (184), Illinois (120), Pennsylvania (84), Wisconsin (59), and California (50). The states with the smallest average size nursing homes are Hawaii (52 beds), South Dakota (69), Alaska (71), Maine (71), and Vermont (70).

Board and care homes are smaller than nursing homes, and it is interesting to see how much smaller. We find that over 80 percent of them have fewer than 25 beds. The national average size of a board and care home is 20 beds. The state with the lowest average number of beds is South Dakota (7). Several states had an average size of eight beds: Kansas, Delaware, Oregon, and Hawaii. The states with the largest average size facilities included Iowa (39), New York (36), Virginia (36), Illinois (35), Indiana (35), and Arkansas (34).

6. OWNERSHIP OF FACILITIES

A. Nursing Homes

The number and percentage distribution of nursing homes by for-profit, nonprofit, and government ownership is reported in Table 4 and Figure 3. In the United States, there are 14,744 nursing homes, of which 10,522 are for profit (71.4 percent), 3,497 are nonprofit (23 percent), and 725 are government owned (4.9 percent). The states

Table 3. Nursing home and board and care home size by number of beds, 1991

	Average Beds			Actual NH Beds				Actual B&C Beds			
	NURHM	B&Cnmr	<25	25-99	100-199	200+	<25	25-99	100-199	200+
US	100.69	20.10	11.10	140.90	118.75	21.92	288.94	57.67	9.25	2.43
Northeast	108.44	22.00	14.56	110.11	129.44	40.78	251.33	85.33	11.89	4.78
Maine	71	14	4	102	22	2	176	36	2	1
New Hampshire	95	12	5	38	30	6	121	14	0	0
Vermont	70	16	9	26	14	1	113	25	0	0
Massachusetts	90	20	40	272	221	21	221	88	2	0
Rhode Island	95	20	7	52	38	7	46	5	0	1
Connecticut	117	21	6	95	121	18	85	33	0	1
New York	177	36	10	125	217	184	589	188	60	27
New Jersey	130	31	20	78	165	44	209	86	14	4
Pennsylvania	131	28	30	203	337	84	702	293	29	9
Midwest	95.92	21.25	15.92	225.00	154.00	33.17	287.67	39.83	4.92	1.33
Ohio	95	13	50	400	355	64	360	38	4	0
Indiana	105	34	10	268	206	44	30	14	6	0
Illinois	126	35	6	338	294	120	50	40	4	2
Michigan	104	12	57	157	216	39	1,649	78	16	6
Wisconsin	120	14	15	f181	150	59	476	40	5	0
Minnesota	105	17	9	213	149	28	285	47	5	5
Iowa	82	39	8	312	96	7	50	69	8	1
Missouri	98	24	24	250	226	25	280	105	6	1
North Dakota	87	24	1	47	21	1	27	15	1	0
South Dakota	69	7	3	102	17	0	59	2	0	0
Nebraska	85	28	4	154	44	7	58	22	4	1
Kansas	75	8	4	278	74	4	128	8	0	0
South	108.71	19.94	7.47	118.53	135.88	15.06	214.35	57.59	8.59	1.29
Delaware	91	8	6	15	23	1	67	4	1	0
Maryland	128	11	9	65	110	28	212	26	2	0
DC	167	15	1	7	4	6	96	5	3	1
Virginia	121	36	10	74	109	24	173	149	15	3
West Virginia	92	11	4	56	45	2	196	25	1	0
North Carolina	100	25	22	102	151	=8	480	198	20	0
South Carolina	99	22	8	67	51	6	193	53	6	0
Georgia	108	11	6	117	181	20	474	29	2	0
Florida	117	31	13	168	326	38	751	268	70	15
Kentucky	95	13	23	121	117	10	261	44	5	0
Tennessee	118	17	6	111	140	18	223	38	1	1
Alabama	108	16	4	85	99	9	178	20	3	0
Mississippi	98	8	4	70	68	5	64	13	1	0
Arkansas	98	34	2	114	98	7	40	34	2	1
Louisiana	119	16	4	93	181	20	41	10	0	0
Oklahoma	84	33	0	253	127	6	28	24	3	0
Texas	105	22	5	497	480	48	167	39	11	1
West	89.23	17.92	9.00	113.85	56.38	7.46	413.69	55.08	12.31	3.31
Montana	82	19	3	46	19	2	55	6	5	0
Idaho	86	19	2	34	19	2	70	16	2	0
Wyoming	90	30	1	16	7	1	15	2	3	0
Colorado	100	21	6	85	76	9	167	32	3	2
New Mexico	96	13	2	30	29	1	121	12	1	0
Arizona	118	22	3	31	71	7	165	44	6	2
Utah	77	30	3	54	25	0	31	11	4	0
Nevada	117	12	4	154	44	7	58	22	4	1
Washington	99	20	10	137	109	13	357	102	13	1
Oregon	79	8	15	107	59	2	877	43	6	1
California	93	19	49	764	270	50	3,158	416	113	35
Alaska	71	12	0	09	1	1	14	1	0	0
Hawaii	52	8	19	13	4	2	290	9	0	1

Source: NHPI

Figure 1. Average Beds in Nursing Homes

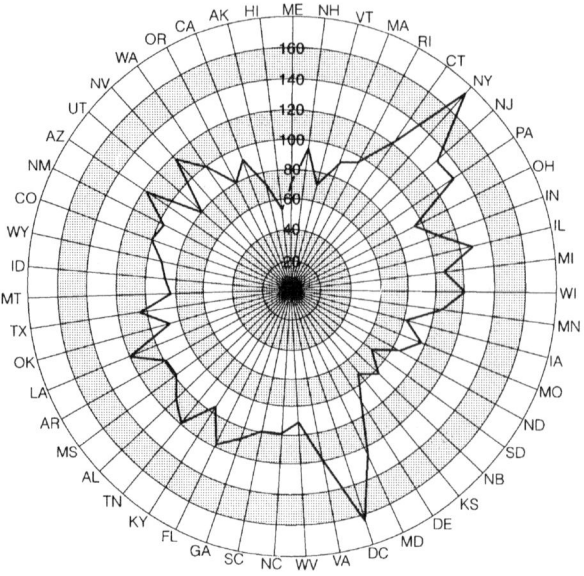

Source: NHPI, author

Figure 2. Average Beds in Board and Care Homes

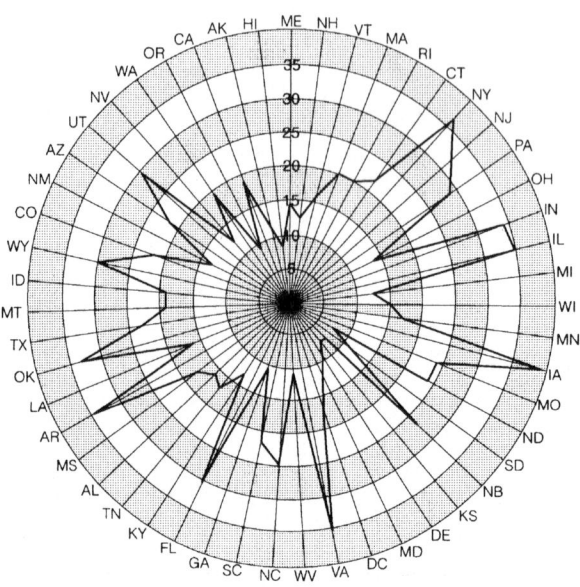

Source: NHPI, author

with the largest number of for-profit nursing homes are California (930), Texas (876), Ohio (676), Illinois (506), and Massachusetts (445). The states with the largest number of nonprofit nursing homes are Pennsylvania (265), Illinois (215), California (192), New York (189), and Minnesota (182).

Table 4. Number and percent distribution of nursing homes by type of ownership and state: United States, 1991

	Number of Nursing Homes				Percent of Nursing Homes[1]			
	Total	Profit	Non-profit	Gov't	Total	Profit	Non-profit	Gov't
United States	**14,744**	**10,522**	**3,497**	**725**	**100.0**	**71.4**	**23.7**	**4.9**
Alabama	197	159	30	8	100.0	80.7	15.2	4.1
Alaska	11	1	5	5	100.0	9.1	45.5	45.5
Arizona	112	71	38	3	100.0	63.4	33.9	2.7
Arkansas	221	187	20	14	100.0	84.6	9.0	6.3
California	1,133	930	192	11	100.0	82.1	16.9	1.0
Colorado	176	127	41	8	100.0	72.2	23.3	4.5
Connecticut	240	190	48	2	100.0	79.2	20.0	0.8
Delaware	45	28	16	1	100.0	62.2	35.6	2.2
DC	18	5	9	4	100.0	27.8	50.0	22.2
Florida	545	420	116	9	100.0	77.1	21.3	1.7
Georgia	324	255	49	20	100.0	78.7	15.1	6.2
Hawaii	38	23	10	5	100.0	60.5	26.3	13.2
Idaho	57	42	9	6	100.0	73.7	15.8	10.5
Illinois	758	506	215	37	100.0	66.8	28.4	4.9
Indiana	528	421	99	8	100.0	79.11	18.8	1.5
Iowa	423	248	165	10	100.0	58.6	39.0	2.4
Kansas	360	231	99	30	100.0	64.2	27.5	8.3
Kentucky	271	199	63	9	100.0	73.4	23.2	3.3
Louisiana	298	243	47	8	100.0	81.5	15.8	2.7
Maine	130	106	21	3	100.0	81.5	16.2	2.3
Maryland	212	140	62	10	100.0	66.0	29.2	4.7
Massachusetts	554	445q	97	12	100.0	80.3	17.5	2.2
Michigan	469	312	115	42	100.0	66.5	24.5	9.0
Minnesota	399	174	182	43	100.0	43.6	45.6	10.8
Mississippi	147	122	15	10	100.0	83.0	10.2	6.8
Missouri	525	385	112	28	100.0	73.3	21.3	5.3
Montana	70	37	16	17	100.0	52.9	22.9	24.3
Nebraska	209	109	60	40	100.0	52.2	28.7	19.1
Nevada	27	26	1	-	100.0	96.3	3.7	0.0
New Hampshire	79	45	21	13	100.0	57.0	26.6	16.5
New Jersey	307	209	81	17	100.0	68.1	26.4	5.5
New Mexico	62	37	23	2	100.0	59.7	37.1	3.2
New York	536	306	189	41	100.0	57.1	35.3	7.6
North Carolina	283	224	51	8	100.0	79.2	18.0	2.8
North Dakota	70	9	60	1	100.0	12.9	85.7	1.4
Ohio	869	676	162	31	100.0	77.8	18.6	3.6
Oklahoma	386	333	43	10	100.0	86.3	11.1	2.63
Oregon	183	140	37	6	100.0	76.5	20.2	3.3
Pennsylvania	654	341	265	48	100.0	52.1	40.5	7.3
Rhode Island	104	85	19	-	100.0	81.7	18.3	0.0
South Carolina	132	99	21	12	100.0	75.0	15.9	9.1
South Dakota	122	41	76	5	100.0	33.6	62.3	4.1
Tennessee	275	198	51	26	100.0	72.0	18.5	9.5
Texas	1,030	876	140	14	100.00	85.0	13.6	1.4
Utah	82	64	14	4	100.0	78.0	17.1	4.9
Vermont	50	37	11	2	100.0	74.0	22.0	4.0
Virginia	217	152	56	9	100.0	70.0	25.8	4.1
Washington	269	210	52	7	100.0	78.1	19.3	2.6
West Virginia	107	87	18	2	100.0	81.3	16.8	1.9
Wisconsin	405	199	147	59	100.0	49.1	36.3	14.6
Wyoming	25	12	8	5	100.0	48.0	32.0	20.0

[1]Excludes hospital-based facilities

Source: NHPI

States with the highest percentage of for-profit nursing homes (Figure 3) are Nevada (96.3 percent), Texas (85), Oklahoma (86.3), Arkansas (84.6), Mississippi (83) and California (82). The states with highest percentage of nonprofit nursing homes are North Dakota (85.7 percent), South Dakota (62.3), District of Columbia (50), and Minnesota (45.6).

Figure 3. Nursing Home Percent Ownership for Profit

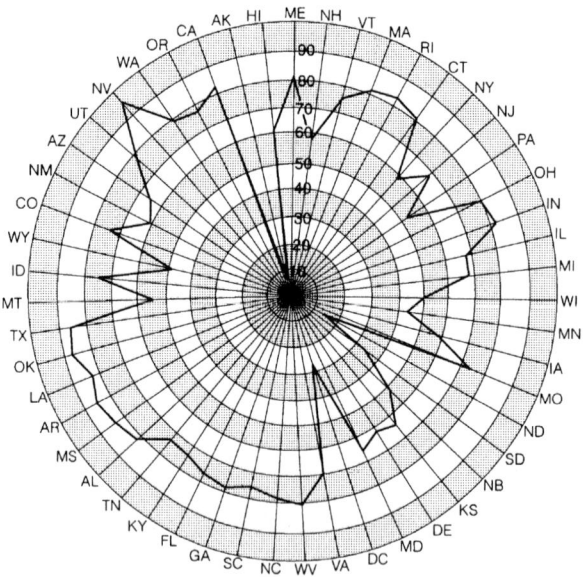

Source: NHPI, author

B. Nursing Beds

The 1,558,300 [3]nursing home beds (table 5) in the United States are primarily owned by for-profit firms (1,085,813, or 69.7 percent). Nonprofit entities owned 372,272, or 23.9 percent of the beds, and government agencies owned 100,215, or 6.4 percent. The largest number of for-profit beds are located in Texas (92,591), California (89,184), Illinois (64,707), Ohio (60,567), New York (50,422), Florida (49,422), Indiana (42,702), Pennsylvania (38,830), Massachusetts (38,742), and Missouri (36,382). These ten states contain over half of the for-profit nursing home beds in the country.

---

[3] Note this differs from 1,559,394 reported in Table 1

Table 5. Number and percent distribution of nursing home beds by type of ownership and state: United States, 1991

	Number of Nursing Home Beds				Percent of Nursing Home Beds			
	Total[1]	Profit	Non-profit	Gov't	Total[1]	Profit	Non-profit	Gov't
United States	1,558,300	1,085,813	372,272	100,215	100.0	69.7	23.9	6.4
Alabama	21,323	17,028	3,100	1,195	100.0	79.9	14.5	5.6
Alaska	780	35	509	236	100.0	4.5	65.3	30.3
Arizona	13,265	8,844	4,149	272	100.0	66.7	31.3	2.1
Arkansas	21,706	18,792	1,603	1,311	100.0	86.6	7.4	6.0
California	105,781	89,184	15,671	926	100.0	84.3	14.8	0.9
Colorado	17,609	13,482	3,386	741	100.0	76.6	19.2	4.2
Connecticut	27,983	22,524	5,129	330	100.0	80.5	18.3	1.2
Delaware	,101	2,612	1,367	122	100.0	63.7	24.6	31.7
DC	3,010	1,314	741	955	100.0	43.7	33.3	3.0
Florida	63,752	49,422	12,843	1,487	100.0	77.5	20.1	2.3
Georgia	35,011	27,130	6,065	1,816	100.0	77.5	17.3	5.2
Hawaii	1,958	1,229	702	27	100.0	62.8	35.9	1.4
Idaho	4,887	3,743	729	415	100.0	76.6	14.9	8.5
Illinois	95,465	64,707	24,911	5,847	100.0	67.8	26.1	6.1
Indiana	55,701	42,702	10,727	2,272	100.0	76.7	19.3	4.1
Iowa	34,521	18,736	14,381	1,404	100.0	54.3	41.7	4.1
Kansas	27,115	17,857	7,639	1,619	100.0	65.9	28.2	6.0
Kentucky	25,685	18,395	6,680	610	100.0	71.6	26.0	2.4
Louisiana	35,550	29,782	4,500	1,268	100.0	83.8	12.7	3.6
Maine	9,192	7,079	1,752	361	100.0	77.0	19.1	3.9
Maryland	27,163	18,039	7,641	1,483	100.0	66.4	28.1	5.5
Massachusetts	50,133	38,742	10,126	1,265	100.0	77.3	20.2	2.5
Michigan	48,886	31,392	12,900	4,594	100.0	64.2	26.4	9.4
Minnesota	42,001	17,825	19,946	4,230	100.0	42.4	47.5	10.1
Mississippi	14,431	12,056	1,096	1,279	100.0	83.5	7.6	8.9
Missouri	51,652	36,382	12,609	2,661	100.0	70.4	24.4	5.2
Montana	5,713	3,213	1,105	1,395	100.0	56.2	19.3	24.4
Nebraska	17,846	8,762	5,334	3,750	100.0	49.1	29.9	21.0
Nevada	3,171	3,099	72	-	100.0	97.7	2.3	0.0
New Hampshire	7,493	4,020	1,248	2,225	100.0	53.7	16.7	29.7
New Jersey	39,970	27,576	8,930	3,464	100.0	69.0	22.3	8.7
New Mexico	5,933	3,600	1,989	344	100.0	60.7	33.5	5.8
New York	94,884	50,422	35,155	9,307	100.0	53.1	37.1	9.8
North Carolina	28,259	22,677	5,199	383	100.0	80.2	18.4	1.4
North Dakota	6,056	746	5,256	54	100.0	12.3	86.8	0.9
Ohio	82,516	60,567	17,880	4,069	100.0	73.4	21.7	4.9
Oklahoma	32,421	28,221	3,145	1,055	100.0	87.0	9.7	3.3
Oregon	14,382	10,860	3,205	317	100.0	75.5	22.3	2.2
Pennsylvania	85,387	38,830	31,928	14,629	100.0	45.5	37.4	17.1
Rhode Island	9,915	8,014	1,901	-	100.0	80.8	19.2	0.0
South Carolina	13,122	'9,851	1,581	1,690	100.0	75.1	12.0	12.9
South Dakota	8,448	2,664	5,519	265	100.0	31.5	65.3	3.1
Tennessee	32,493	23,215	5,010	4,268	100.0	71.4	15.4	13.1
Texas	108,285	92,591	14,888	806	100.00	85.5	13.7	0.7
Utah	6,292	4,602	1,446	244	100.0	73.1	23.0	3.9
Vermont	3,478	2,639	594	245	100.0	75.9	17.1	7.0
Virginia	26,324	19,149	6,123	1,052	100.0	72.7	23.3	4.0
Washington	26,506	21,246	5,001	259	100.0	80.2	18.9	1.0
West Virginia	9,792	7,754	1,798	240	100.0	79.2	18.4	2.5
Wisconsin	48,710	21,315	16,283	11,112	100.0	43.8	33.4	22.8
Wyoming	2,243	1,147	780	316	100.0	51.1	34.8	14.1

[1] Excludes hospital-based facilities.
Source: NHPI

C. Ownership of Board and Care Homes

The 18,262 board and care homes in the United States (table 6) are predominantly owned by for-profit organizations (13,734). Nonprofit homes make up only 20.2 percent or 3,683 homes, while government agencies control 845 homes, or 4.6 percent. Private board and care home ownership is more concentrated than private nursing home ownership. Table 6 shows a significant number of the for-profit homes are concentrated in just five states: California (3,244), Michigan (1,389), Florida (909), Oregon (847), and Pennsylvania (818). These states account for over half (52 percent) of the for-profit board and care facilities in the country.

Figure 4. Board & Care Percent Ownership for Profit

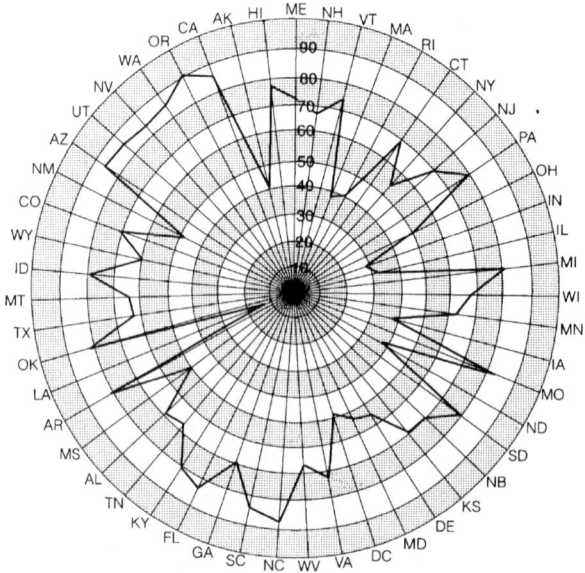

Source: NHPI, author

D. Board and Care Beds

If we examine the actual number of beds controlled by for-profit firms, we find in Table 7 that of the 362,014 beds in the United States, 261,642 (72.3 percent) were for profit, 87,188 were nonprofit, and 13,184 were government owned. Figure 4 shows that the for-profit beds are concentrated in six states: California (59,855), Florida (27,595), New York (20,180), Pennsylvania (19,414), North Carolina (15,771), and Michigan (14,782). Over 60 percent of the inventory of private board and care beds can be found in these six states. The difference between the state rankings in ownership of homes and ownership of beds is explained by the size of the facilities in these states. New York and North Carolina have fewer but larger facilities than Oregon, for example.

Table 6. Number and percent distribution of board and care homes by type of ownership and state: United States, 1991

	Number of Board and Care Homes[1,2] with Ownership				Percent of Board and Care Homes[1,2] with Ownership			
	Total	Profit	Non-profit	Gov't	Total	Profit	Non-profit	Gov't
United States	18,262	13,734	3,683	845	100.0	75.2	20.2	4.6
Alabama	201	138	53	10	100.0	68.7	26.4	5.0
Alaska	15	6	7	2	100.0	40.0	46.7	13.3
Arizona	217	186	28	3	100.0	85.7	12.9	1.4
Arkansas	77	60	15	2	100.0	77.9	19.5	2.6
California	3,722	3,244	394	84	100.0	87.2	10.6	2.3
Colorado	204	144	58	2	100.0	70.6	28.4	1.0
Connecticut	119	82	36	1	100.0	68.9	30.3	0.8
Delaware	72	40	25	7	100.0	55.6	34.7	9.7
DC	105	52	43	10	100.0	49.5	41.0	9.5
Florida	1,104	909	178	17	100.0	82.3	16.1	1.5
Georgia	505	351	86	68	100.0	69.5	17.0	13.5
Hawaii	300	233	39	28	100.0	77.7	13.0	9.3
Idaho	88	74	12	2	100.0	84.1	13.6	2.3
Illinois	96	30	60	6	100.0	31.3	62.5	6.3
Indiana	50	14	29	7	100.0	28.0	58.0	14.0
Iowa	128	47	58	23	100.0	36.7	45.3	18.0
Kansas	136	94	32	10	100.0	69.1	23.5	7.4
Kentucky	310	248	38	24	100.0	80.0	12.3	7.7
Louisiana	51	6	44	1	100.0	11.8	86.3	2.0
Maine	215	156	52	7	100.0	72.6	24.2	3.3
Maryland	240	129	84	27	100.0	53.8	35.0	11.3
Massachusetts	311	117	179	15	100.0	37.6	57.6	4.8
Michigan	1,749	1,389	279	81	100.0	79.4	16.0	4.6
Minnesota	342	212	105	25	100.0	62.0	30.7	7.3
Mississippi	78	38	24	16	100.0	48.7	30.8	20.5
Missouri	392	330	56	6	100.0	84.2	14.3	1.5
Montana	66	41	25	-	100.0	62.1	37.9	0.0
Nebraska	85	59	20	6	100.0	69.4	23.5	7.1
Nevada	74	62	9	3	100.0	83.8	12.2	4.1
New Hampshire	135	91	42	2	100.0	67.4	31.1	1.5
New Jersey	313	217	90	6	100.0	69.3	28.8	1.9
New Mexico	134	64	63	7	100.0	47.8	47.0	5.2
New York	864	458	344	62	100.0	53.0	39.8	7.2
North Carolina	698	606	54	38	100.0	86.8	7.7	5.4
North Dakota	43	16	26	1	100.0	37.2	60.5	2.3
Ohio	402	203	157	42	100.0	50.5	39.1	10.4
Oklahoma	55	44	10	1	100.0	80.0	18.2	1.8
Oregon	927	847	56	24	100.0	91.4	6.0	2.6
Pennsylvania	1,033	818	193	22	100.0	79.2	18.7	2.1
Rhode Island	52	21	22	9	100.0	40.4	42.3	17.3
South Carolina	252	210	35	7	100.0	83.3	13.9	2.8
South Dakota	61	48	6	7	100.0	78.7	9.8	11.5
Tennessee	263	171	83	9	100.0	65.0	31.6	3.4
Texas	218	132	58	28	100.0	60.6	26.6	12.8
Utah	46	39	6	1	100.0	84.8	13.0	2.2
Vermont	138	103	32	3	100.0	74.6	23.2	2.2
Virginia	340	244	73	23	100.0	71.8	21.5	6.8
Washington	473	405	57	11	100.0	85.6	12.1	2.3
West Virginia	222	146	43	33	100.0	65.8	19.4	14.9
Wisconsin	521	348	160	13	100.0	66.8	30.7	2.5
Wyoming	20	12	5	3	100.0	60.0	25.0	15.0

[1] Excludes 8,578 nonresponding board and care homes.
[2] Excludes 13,169 board and care homes for the mentally retarded.
Source: NHPI

Table 7. Number and percent distribution of board and care home beds by type of ownership and state: United States, 1991

	Number of board and care home beds[1,2]				Percent of Board and care home beds[1,2]			
	Total	Profit	Non-profit	Gov't	Total	Profit	Non-profit	Gov't
United States	362,014	261,642	87,188	13,184	100.0	72.3	24.1	3.6
Alabama	3,189	1,985	1,110	94	100.0	62.2	34.8	2.9
Alaska	175	77	74	24	100.0	44.0	42.3	13.7
Arizona	4,736	4,049	654	33	100.0	85.5	13.8	0.7
Arkansas	2,612	2,044	542	26	100.0	78.3	20.8	1.0
California	70,059	59,855	9,391	813	100.0	85.4	13.4	1.2
Colorado	4,183	2,356	1,780	47	100.0	56.3	42.6	1.1
Connecticut	2,543	1,656	885	2	100.0	65.1	34.8	0.1
Delaware	581	207	356	18	100.0	35.6	61.3	3.1
DC	1,550	434	1,051	65	100.0	28.0	67.8	4.2
Florida	34,674	27,595	6,887	192	100.0	79.6	19.9	0.6
Georgia	5,528	4,182	743	603	100.0	75.7	13.4	10.9
Hawaii	2,519	1,998	384	137	100.0	79.3	15.2	5.4
Idaho	1,696	1,306	336	54	100.0	77.0	19.8	3.2
Illinois	3,400	1,177	1,836	387	100.0	34.6	54.0	11.4
Indiana	1,707	824	490	393	100.0	48.3	28.7	23.0
Iowa	5,053	1,541	2,405	1,107	100.0	30.5	47.6	21.9
Kansas	1,020	584	400	36	100.0	57.3	39.2	3.5
Kentucky	3,968	3,015	848	105	100.0	76.0	21.4	2.6
Louisiana	812	127	665	20	100.0	15.6	81.9	2.5
Maine	3,060	2,062	971	27	100.0	67.4	31.7	0.9
Maryland	2,759	1,069	1,482	208	100.0	38.7	53.7	7.5
Massachusetts	6,321	3,105	2,916	300	100.0	49.1	46.1	4.7
Michigan	21,300	14,782	5,015	1,503	100.0	69.4	23.5	7.1
Minnesota	5,826	2,784	2,553	489	100.0	47.8	43.8	8.4
Mississippi	1,407	806	439	162	100.0	57.3	31.2	11.5
Missouri	9,408	7,697	1,587	124	100.0	81.8	16.9	1.3
Montana	1,233	428	805	—	100.0	34.7	65.3	0.0
Nebraska	2,389	1,859	477	53	100.0	77.8	20.0	2.2
Nevada	897	702	181	14	100.0	78.3	20.2	1.6
New Hampshire	1,680	1,118	520	42	100.0	66.5	31.0	2.5
New Jersey	9,756	6,867	2,838	51	100.0	70.4	29.1	0.5
New Mexico	1,767	718	960	89	100.0	40.6	54.3	5.0
New York	30,911	20,180	9,366	1,365	100.0	65.3	30.3	4.4
North Carolina	17,275	15,771	1,091	413	100.0	91.3	6.3	2.4
North Dakota	1,014	166	736	112	100.0	16.4	72.6	11.0
Ohio	5,197	2,397	1,610	1,190	100.0	46.1	31.0	22.9
Oklahoma	1,800	1,525	245	30	100.0	84.7	13.6	1.7
Oregon	7,718	6,640	1,144	144	100.0	83.7	14.8	1.5
Pennsylvania	28,484	19,414	8,239	830	100.0	68.2	28.9	2.9
Rhode Island	1,029	638	315	76	100.0	62.0	30.6	7.4
South Carolina	5,449	4,073	1,191	185	100.0	74.7	21.9	3.4
South Dakota	397	290	87	20	100.0	73.0	21.9	5.0
Tennessee	4,505	2,645	1,653	207	100.0	58.7	36.7	4.6
Texas	4,786	3,256	1,241	289	100.0	68.0	25.9	6.0
Utah	1,380	1,144	224	12	100.0	82.9	16.2	0.9
Vermont	2,215	1,577	615	23	100.0	71.2	27.8	1.0
Virginia	12,225	8,747	3,049	429	100.0	71.6	24.9	3.5
Washington	9,303	7,993	1,230	80	100.0	85.9	13.2	0.9
West Virginia	2,483	1,613	624	246	100.0	65.0	25.1	9.9
Wisconsin	7,443	4,488	2,851	104	100.0	60.3	38.3	1.4
Wyoming	592	256	96	240	100.0	43.2	16.2	40.5

[1] Excludes 8,578 nonresponding board and care homes.
[2] Excludes 13,169 board and care homes for the mentally retarded.

Source: NHPI

7. OCCUPANCY

Table 8 shows that in 1991, nursing homes had a nationwide occupancy rate of 91.5 percent and board and care homes an occupancy rate of 83.6 percent.

Mississippi had the highest nursing home occupancy rate (97.6%), followed by New York (97.4), Hawaii (96.8), North Carolina (96.1), and South Carolina (96.0). The states with the lowest nursing home occupancy rates were Indiana (82.6%), Utah (82.7), Texas (83.2), and Oklahoma (84.2).

The states with the highest occupancy rates in board and care homes were Washington (91.2%), Massachusetts (91.2), District of Columbia (90.8), Nevada and Utah (both 90.5), Connecticut (90.3), Maine (90.4), and Illinois (90.1). States with low occupancy rates for board and care homes are New Hampshire (79.1%), Kansas (79.4), Florida (79.3), Arkansas (69.4), Oklahoma (79.7), Wyoming (73.9), Arizona (77.9), and California (78.1).

8. SENIOR RESIDENTS AND SUPPLY OF SENIORS BEDS

In our current context, we are concerned with individuals over 65. Therefore, it is important to segregate the nonseniors from the seniors when analyzing nursing homes and board and care facilities. In this survey, 92 percent of nursing home residents nationwide were over 65 years of age, and 68 percent of board and care residents were over 65. This is a national average, but appears to hold at state levels (Delfosse, 1995).

In Table 9 we examine the number of nursing homes and board and care home beds per 1,000 individuals 65 years and over. We look at the type of home, provide data by state, and provide a combined nursing home and board and care bed rate. Compare the data in Table 10 on residents in nursing homes and board and care homes over 65 years of age. In the U.S. there are 49 nursing home beds per 1,000 persons over 65, and there are 41.5 residents in nursing homes per 1,000 persons over 65. The previous occupancy data demonstrated that the national occupancy rate is 91.5 percent. Thus, without the younger residents this figure would be 81 percent.

Nationally, there are 11.4 board and care home beds per 1,000 persons over age 65. And only 6.5 per 1,000 persons over 65 are residents of board and care homes. Occupancy is 83 percent—not 57 percent—because of the younger residents.

The states that have highest number of nursing home beds per 1,000 persons over 65 are in the North Central Midwest: Indiana (78.7), Wisconsin (73.7), Minnesota (75.5), Iowa (80.1), Missouri (71.2), South Dakota (82.0), Nebraska (79.0), and Kansas (78.4). Does a substantial supply of nursing home beds negatively impact the

Table 8. Percent occupancy rates of nursing homes and board and care homes by type of home and geographic region and division: United States, 1991

	Percent Occupancy Rates	
	Nursing Homes[1]	Board and Care Homes[2,3]
United States	**91.5**	**83.6**
Northeast	**95.3**	**86.5**
New England	95.3	83.5
Middle Atlantic	95.2	86.0
Midwest	**90.3**	**84.6**
East North Central	89.8	85.4
West North Central	91.2	83.5
South	**91.1**	**82.9**
South Atlantic	94.4	83.3
East South Central	95.8	84.2
West South Central	85.4	78.3
West	**89.6**	**81.3**
Mountain	87.6	84.4
Pacific	90.4	80.7
Northeast		
New England		
Maine	96.4	90.4
New Hampshire	94.4	79.1
Vermont	95.8	82.6
Massachusetts	94.9	91.2
Rhode Island	95.2	89.4
Connecticut	95.9	90.3
Mid-Atlantic		
New York	97.4	89.1
New Jersey	93.3	83.7
Pennsylvania	93.7	83.5
Midwest		
East North Central		
Ohio	93.2	81.4
Indiana	82.6	81.7
Illinois	89.0	90.1
Michigan	91.2	85.3
Wisconsin	92.1	86.8
West North Central		
Minnesota	95.0	86.1
Iowa	92.3	85.8
Missouri	86.9	80.3
North Dakota	95.9	89.7
South Dakota	95.4	83.3
Nebraska	90.6	83.9
Kansas	90.2	79.4

Table 8. Percent occupancy rates of nursing homes and board and care homes by type of home and geographic region and division: United States, 1991 *(continued)*

	Percent Occupancy Rates	
	Nursing Homes[1]	Board and Care Homes[2,3]
South		
South Atlantic		
Delaware	92.1	86.0
Maryland	94.2	86.0
District of Columbia	95.7	90.8
Virginia	94.6	84.2
West Virginia	95.1	80.3
North Carolina	96.1	88.6
South Carolina	96.0	88.2
Georgia	95.6	81.9
Florida	92.8	79.3
East South Central		
Kentucky	95.1	86.7
Tennessee	95.3	84.3
Alabama	95.9	82.9
Mississippi	97.6	80.3
West South Central		
Arkansas	91.1	69.4
Louisiana	89.3	85.8
Oklahoma	84.4	79.7
Texas	83.2	81.4
West		
Mountain		
Montana	90.6	89.2
Idaho	88.8	84.2
Wyoming	88.3	73.9
Colorado	85.0	88.4
New Mexico	92.0	84.9
Arizona	88.4	77.9
Utah	82.7	90.5
Nevada	91.7	90.5
Pacific		
Washington	91.2	91.2
Oregon	90.6	89.2
California	90.0	78.1
Alaska	90.2	85.1
Hawaii	96.8	89.9

[1] Excludes hospital-based facilities.
[2] Excludes 8,578 nonresponding board and care homes
[3] Excludes board and care homes for mentally retarded
Source: NHPI

Table 9. Beds per 1,000 persons over 65 years of age

State	Nursing Homes	Board & Care	Combined Rate
US	**51.5**	**10.8**	**62.3**
Northeast	**53.1**	**13.5**	**66.6**
Maine	55.7	18.5	74.2
New Hampshire	58.1	13.0	71.1
Vermont	51.1	32.6	83.7
Massachusetts	60.7	7.7	68.4
Rhode Island	65.7	6.8	72.5
Connecticut	61.9	5.6	67.5
New York	40.2	13.1	53.3
New Jersey	38.3	9.3	47.6
Pennsylvania	46.0	15.3	61.3
Midwest	**70.9**	**8.5**	**79.4**
Ohio	75.7	3.6	61.1
Indiana	78.7	2.4	81.1
Illinois	65.8	2.3	68.1
Michigan	43.3	18.8	62.1
Wisconsin	73.7	11.3	85.0
Minnesota	75.5	10.5	86.0
Iowa	80.1	11.7	91.8
Missouri	71.2	13.0	84.2
North Dakota	65.1	10.9	76.0
South Dakota	82.0	3.9	85.9
Nebraska	79.0	10.6	89.6
Kansas	78.4	2.9	81.3
South	**48.5**	**9.3**	**57.8**
Delaware	50.0	7.1	57.1
Maryland	51.3	5.2	56.5
District of Columbia	38.6	19.9	58.5
Virginia	38.5	17.9	56.5
West Virginia	36.0	9.1	45.1
North Carolina	34.2	20.9	55.1
South Carolina	32.3	13.4	45.7
Georgia	52.3	8.3	60.6
Florida	26.2	14.3	40.5
Kentucky	54.4	8.4	62.8
Tennessee	41.6	7.2	58.8
Alabama	40.2	6.0	46.2
Mississippi	44.8	4.4	49.2
Arkansas	61.3	7.4	68.7
Louisiana	75.0	1.7	76.7
Oklahoma	75.4	4.2	79.6
Texas	61.6	2.7	64.3
West	**36.7**	**13.0**	**49.7**
Montana	52.9	11.4	64.3
Idaho	39.1	13.5	52.7
Wyoming	45.8	12.7	57.9
Colorado	51.8	12.7	64.1
New Mexico	35.3	10.5	45.8
Arizona	26.7	9.5	36.2
Utah	40.6	8.9	49.5
Nevada	23.1	6.5	29.6
Washington	45.0	15.8	60.8
Oregon	35.9	19.2	55.1
California	33.2	22.0	55.2
Alaska	32.5	7.3	39.8
Hawaii	15.1	19.4	34.5

Source: NHPI

QUANTIFYING THE SUPPLY OF SENIORS HOUSING

Table 10. The estimated number of residents 65 years of age and over in nursing homes and board and care homes, and number per 1,000 population 65 years of age and over by type of home, geographic region, division and state: United States, 1991

	Nursing Homes		Board and Care Homes	
State	Residents	Number per 1,000 Population	Residents	Number per 1,000 Population
US	1,318,059	41.5	206,551	6.5
Northeast	294,565	41.8	51,015	7.2
Midwest	430,857	54.8	30,864	3.9
South	423,807	38.7	61,916	5.7
West	168,784	28.7	63,192	10.7
Northeast				
Maine	8,473	51.4	1,998	12.1
New Hampshire	6,794	52.7	984	7.6
Vermont	3,144	46.2	1,401	20.6
Massachusetts	44,641	54.0	3,148	3.8
Rhode Island	9,110	60.3	494	3.3
Connecticut	24,687	54.6	1,543	3.4
New York	87,432	37.0	18,249	7.7
New Jersey	34,873	33.4	4,932	4.7
Pennsylvania	75,411	40.6	18,266	9.8
Midwest				
Ohio	70,666	49.3	2,126	1.5
Indiana	41,925	59.2	653	0.9
Illinois	75,547	52.1	1,730	1.2
Michigan	40,799	36.1	11,783	10.4
Wisconsin	41,065	62.1	4,140	6.3
Minnesota	37,568	67.6	1,313	2.4
Iowa	30,365	70.5	1,840	4.3
Missouri	41,793	57.6	4,649	6.4
North Dakota	5,535	59.5	784	8.4
South Dakota	7,719	74.9	190	1.8
Nebraska	15,236	67.4	1,393	6.2
Kansas	22,639	65.4	253	0.8
South				
Delaware	3,541	43.2	288	3.5
Maryland	23,572	44.6	1,401	2.6
District of Columbia	2,687	34.4	539	6.9
Virginia	23,027	33.8	7,337	10.8
West Virginia	8,797	32.3	1,567	5.8
North Carolina	25,087	30.4	11,368	13.8
South Carolina	11,686	28.8	3,137	7.7
Georgia	30,426	45.5	3,109	4.6
Florida	56,157	23.1	21,852	9.0
Kentucky	22,555	47.8	2,105	4.5
Tennessee	28,832	45.8	2,769	4.4
Alabama	18,899	35.7	1,494	2.8
Mississippi	13,067	40.6	674	2.1
Arkansas	17,866	50.5	1,315	3.2
Louisiana	28,277	59.7	73	0.2
Oklahoma	25,431	59.1	593	1.4
Texas	83,900	47.7	2,457	1.4
West				
Montana	4,774	44.2	909	8.4
Idaho	3,908	31.3	1,051	8.4
Wyoming	1,853	37.8	330	6.7
Colorado	13,600	40.0	2,777	8.2
New Mexico	5,078	30.2	553	3.3
Arizona	10,772	21.7	2,685	5.4
Utah	4,517	29.1	1,060	6.8
Nevada	2,550	18.6	531	3.9
Washington	22,259	37.8	6,024	10.2
Oregon	12,118	30.2	5,798	14.5
California	85,052	26.7	39,966	12.5
Alaska	540	22.5	15	0.6
Hawaii	1,763	13.6	1,493	11.5

supply of board and care beds? Three of the above-referenced states have low ratios for board and care beds per 1,000 residents over 65: Indiana (2.4), South Dakota (3.9), and Kansas (2.9), while the board and care ratios for the other states in this group average 10 to 11 beds per 1,000 persons over 65.

The states with the lowest ratio of nursing home beds per 1,000 persons over 65 are in the South and West: Hawaii (15.1), Nevada (23.1), Florida (26.2), Arizona (26.7), Alaska (32.5), and California (33.2). In some cases, states with low ratios of nursing home beds to population had ratios of board and care home beds that exceeded the national average of 11 per 1,000; specifically, these are Oregon (19.2), California (22), Hawaii (19.4), and Florida (14.3). However, Alaska (7.3), Nevada (6.5), and Arizona (9.5) had low ratios for board and care home beds as well as for nursing home beds.

The states with the highest ratio of board and care home beds to 1,000 persons over age 65 are Vermont (32.6), California (22), North Carolina (20.9), District of Columbia (19.9), Hawaii (19.4), Oregon (19.2), and Michigan (18.8). States with low ratios of board and care home beds are Louisiana (1.7), Illinois (2.3), Indiana (2.4), Texas (2.7), Kansas (2.9), and Ohio (3.6).

The combined ratio of nursing home beds and board and care home beds per 1,000 persons over 65 in Table 9 gives the following ranking: Iowa (91.8), Nebraska (89.6), Minnesota (86.0), South Dakota (85.9), Wisconsin (85), and Missouri (84.2). The states with the lowest combined ranking are Nevada(29.6), Hawaii (34.5), Arizona (36.2), Alaska (39.8), and Florida (40.5).

Does having a large number of nursing home and board and care home beds per 1,000 persons over age 65 impact occupancy? In the high-ratio group, Iowa, Minnesota, South Dakota, and Wisconsin had better-than-average occupancy in nursing homes and board and care homes. However, Missouri had less-than-average and Nebraska had about-average occupancy.

On the other hand, does a low number beds per 1,000 in nursing homes and board and care homes affect occupancy? Nevada had high occupancy in board and care homes and above-average occupancy in nursing homes. Hawaii had high occupancy in nursing homes and above-average occupancy in board and care homes. Arizona had lower-than-average occupancy in nursing homes and board and care homes. Alaska had about-average occupancy, while Florida had higher-than-average occupancy in nursing homes but was among the lowest in board and care home occupancy.

The results suggest that the usage of nursing homes and board and care homes differs by location. In the next section we examine this more closely.

QUANTIFYING THE SUPPLY OF SENIORS HOUSING

9. SENIORS USE OF NURSING HOMES, BOARD AND CARE HOMES, AND HOME HEALTH CARE

The use of nursing homes, board and care homes, and home health care by region is summarized in Table 11. The data on home health care were added to the previously-presented state data from Table 10 to provide a more comprehensive picture. The table shows that in the U.S., for every 1,000 people 65 years of age and older, about 77 people were either in nursing homes (41.5), in board and care homes (6.5), or receiving home health care (29). However, there are significant regional differences. The Northeast (91 persons per 1,000) used all three services—with more home health care—than the other regions. One could speculate that this reflects the high use of home health care in New York. In addition, the Midwest was also above the national average with a usage rate of 84 persons per 1,000. This figure is derived from a strong reliance on nursing homes (55 per 1,000), a lesser reliance on board and care homes (4 per 1,000), and moderate reliance on home health care (25 per 1,000). The South had a usage rate of 73 persons per 1,000 and was close to the national average on all three individual usage factors. The West was significantly below the national rate at 57 persons per 1,000, and considerably below the Northeast rate. Western seniors used board and care homes, but avoided nursing homes and home health care.

Table 11. Number of residents 65 years and over in nursing homes, board and care homes and receiving home health care per 1,000 population 65 years and over by geographic region: United States, 1991

	Nursing Homes[2]		Board & Care Homes[3]		Home Health Care		Total[1]	
	Number (000s)	No. per 1,000 Pop.	Number (000s)	No. per 1,000 Pop.	Number (000s)	No. per 1,000 Pop.	Number (000s)	No. per 1,000 Pop.
United States	**1,318**	**42**	**207**	**7**	**918**	**29**	**2,443**	**77**
Northeast	295	42	51	7	295	42	642	91
Midwest	429	55	31	4	201	26	662	84
South	421	39	62	6	321	29	803	73
West	168	29	63	11	101	17	336	57

Source: Sirrocco 1994.

10. SUMMARY AND CONCLUSION

In order to provide benchmark data for developers and investors, 1991 NHPI data was presented on a state-by-state basis for nursing homes and board and care homes. The data provided state-level information on numbers of homes, beds, residents, size of homes by bed numbers, ownership, occupancy, and beds per 1,000 persons over age 65. The data showed significant variation in usage of the homes by seniors according to state and region of the country.

In conclusion, future studies should utilize state-based data to examine the relationship between nursing home usage, board and care home usage, and home health care usage. Nationally, 78 percent more people used home health care than board and care homes. But in certain parts of the country, board and care homes were chosen more frequently.

Additional research using multivariant analysis should more rigorously explore states with higher levels of nursing occupancy, board and care occupancy, and home health care usage. There is also a need for qualitative exploration to address why these relationships exist.

REFERENCES

Delfosse, R., Hospice and Home Health Agency Characteristics: 1991 National Health Provider Inventory, National Center for Health Statistics. Vital Health Statistics. In Preparation.

Sirrocco, A., Nursing Homes and Board and Care Homes. Advanced data from vital and health statistics: No 244 Hyattsville, MD: National Center for Health Statistics 1994.

13

FORECASTING SENIORS HOUSING DEMAND

Robert H. Edelstein
Professor, Haas School of Business,
Co-chair, Fisher Center for Real Estate & Urban Economics
University of California, Berkeley

Allan J. Lacayo
Ph.D. Research Fellow
Fisher Center for Real Estate & Urban Economics
and Economics Department
University of California, Berkeley

ABSTRACT

While the elderly population (defined as age 65 and older) of the United States is expected to grow substantially over the next 25 years, it is less clear how much and what types of housing demand this diverse group will generate. This is true, in part, because the demand for housing by the senior population is jointly dependent upon the type and level of personal services the householder requires, which in turn is dependent upon household location, gender, and age, among other variables. Applying a nested multinomial logit model to U.S. Census data and demographic forecasts, a set of demand forecasts for seniors housing through 2020 is created. In brief, the forecasts indicate that overall seniors housing demand will grow substantially, but differentially by product type (i.e., nursing homes, bed and care, congregate care, and assisted living) over the next 25 years. The largest growth in demand will occur for assisted living seniors housing, especially in the second decade of the twenty-first century. The growing demand will average a little less than 10% annually of the existing seniors housing each year over the next 25 years.

1. INTRODUCTION

Households of all ages must make the fundamental decision of housing choice. Throughout life, changing circumstances affect the individual's decision on housing consumption. Factors that affect these decisions include job changes, income, health, marriage, children, divorce, and so forth. Although these changes affect people of all ages, seniors are more likely to make housing changes due to circumstantial changes such as retirement, changing financial well being, or health status. Ultimately, these housing choices are intertwined with and affected by ethnicity, economic situations, family circumstance, and personality differences.

Seniors comprise the fastest growing sector of the U.S. population between the present and 2020. For this reason, it is important to understand the pattern of future seniors housing needs. This study will take a first step in this direction by developing a set of seniors housing demand forecasts through 2020.

This analysis is different from traditional housing tenure choice models because housing services demanded by the elderly include specialized personal services related to "needs" or "wants" not commonly observed in younger age groups of the population. "Needs" for nontraditional housing services are related to health status or lifestyle changes that occur as individuals age, whereas "wants" for nontraditional housing services are rooted in the cultural, social, and economic issues that relate to lifestyle changes that are highly correlated with advancing age. In specifying the model, housing choices are classified by the extent to which individuals in such housing arrangements need care, want nontraditional housing (i.e., personal) services, or choose to live independently.

In the next section, seniors housing choice—as used in this study—is defined. The specific stratification scheme used corresponds closely to industry classifications for seniors housing and is, in part, dependent upon the idiosyncrasies of the available data. Section III follows with a description of the statistical model and the database—the Public Use Microdata Samples (PUMS).[1] The 1990 PUMS contains unique housing unit and personal data sampled statistically from the full U.S. Census. As such, it provides a relatively large sample for the senior population by gender, by geographic area, and by age group. Section IV describes the early 1990s benchmark derived from the U.S. Census and other contemporary survey data for the housing and sociodemographic status of seniors. Based upon the PUMS database and U.S. Census population projections, the model in Section V contains forecasts of demand for seniors housing in five-year intervals through 2020. The final section provides a summary of the study, conclusions, an overview of seniors housing public policy issues, and the challenges of future research.

---

[1] PUMS is described in more detail in Appendix A.

2. SENIORS HOUSING CHOICE CATEGORIES

Utilizing the 1990 Bureau of the Census PUMS survey, seniors housing choices can be classified into six categories. These housing choice alternatives developed from the PUMS survey are:[2]

- Nursing Home (NH): Seniors choosing to live in group quarters, institutions, or facilities housing elderly with physical or mental limitations are classified as NH. Ownership of the facility may be public (federal, state, county, or city) or private (for profit or nonprofit), and the set of available services varies significantly from home to home.

- Assisted Living (AL): Seniors choose assisted living arrangements when they have personal care physical limitations or mobility limitations that do not allow them to perform activities of daily living (ADLs) such as minimal hygiene and personal care functions without assistance. However, the limitations are generally not as severe as those found in seniors living in a nursing home.

- "Stay At Home" Care Services (SAHCS): This classification includes seniors who require assisted living services, but maintain their place of residence. Most of these people own their residences, but some are renters, or live with relatives or friends.

- Congregate Care/Continuing Care Retirement Communities (CC/CCRC): These group housing facilities provide amenities such as meals, transportation, security, medical, and other services to the tenants. The individual households in the community may have kitchenettes in their units and be self-sufficient.

- Independent Living, Rent (ILR): These housing choices relate to renters who live on their own and purchase no special senior care personal services.

- Independent Living, Own (ILO): These housing choices relate to elderly individuals who own a home, whose spouses own a home, or who live with a relative who owns a home. The home may be single or multifamily, attached or detached. In addition, the elderly household members do not purchase special senior care personal services.

Housing choices are the result of a two-step process, represented in Figure 1. First, the senior respondent's wants or needs for specialized personal care services are identified. If a need or desire for elderly housing services is needed critically _and_ chronically, the demand is classified NH. If the services are needed chronically, the demand is classified AL. If the services are received by the elderly in their homes, the demand is SAHCS. Thus, SAHCS is usually classified as a form of AL. If the service is wanted more than needed, the demand is classified CC/CCRC. People who neither

---

[2] See Appendix B for detailed specifications of housing categories derived from PUMS.

need nor want any of the personal care services that are provided through institutional housing settings are identified as independent living home owners and renters (ILO or ILR, respectively).[3]

Figure 1. Housing Choices of the Elderly Under P.U.M.S.

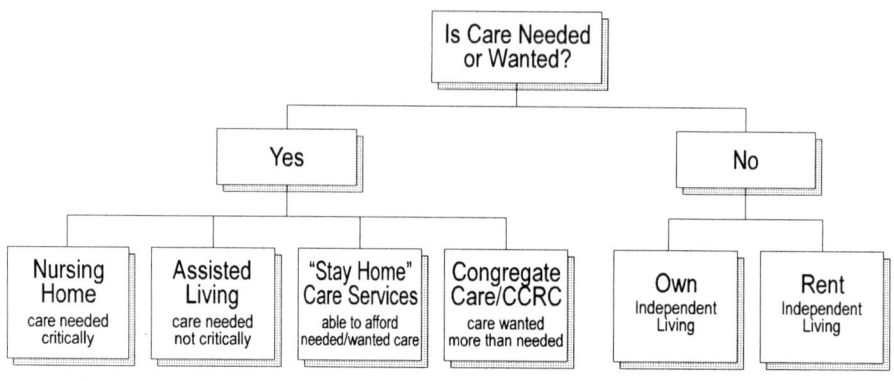

3. MODELING SENIORS HOUSING

Figure 2 delineates the multinomial nested logit (MNL) model specification used in this study to identify the determinants of seniors housing demand. In estimating the logit specifications, the forecasts are calibrated by taking into account four sets of factors that are described in charts 1 through 4: economic, demographic, sociological, and health factors, respectively.

The 1990 U.S. Bureau of the Census PUMS was used to estimate the multinomial nested logit model. The PUMS contains relatively large samples over all relevant stratifications of elderly groups by geographic regions and by level of urbanization.[4] The data also provide representative seniors population in terms of variation in

---

[3] For example, physical or mental incapacitation/deficiencies that are positively correlated with increasing age give rise to the need for individual daily care or infrequent care. Some individuals will choose to live in institutional or group settings which deliver the needed services in an affordable, effective, and efficient manner (NH or AL). However, the demand for these health-related services in institutional settings may be abated by sociological and economic factors that enable individuals to have greater flexibility in their selection of a housing arrangement.

Given the data sample, sometimes it is difficult to distinguish whether the observed housing choice is at-home care services, congregate care/CCRC, or assisted living facilities. This is because survey responses do not always clarify whether the source of elderly housing services (meals, security, common areas, etc.) coincides with the owner of the housing unit itself. Such observations have been removed from the sample because they cannot be assigned to any of the six categories of housing choices with certainty. This procedure may bias the sample because it eliminates observations from AL, CC/CCRC, and SHCS in greater proportion than from NH, or the two independent living alternatives.

[4] The PUMS data consists of several million observations, of which this study employs approximately 300,000.

Figure 2. Structure of Housing Demand Model

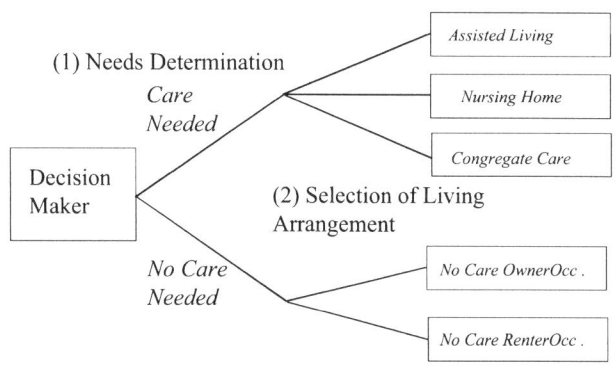

marital and family status, age and gender, health and disability status, and economic characteristics.

The MNL model was calibrated utilizing the PUMS data. The dependent variable relates to the housing choices shown in Figure 2. The explanatory variables are related to the four sets of factors described in Charts 1 through 4.[5] In brief, the statistical results indicate that no single factor stands alone in influencing the observed seniors housing choice in 1990.

Separate logit models are developed for each of seven states (Arizona, California, Florida, Kansas, Nevada, New Jersey, and Texas) and the District of Columbia. As discussed in Appendix A, these geographic areas represent a nationally-representative mix of sociodemographic and housing choices for the elderly. These eight separate logit models are then combined with independent population projections from the U.S. Census by state, by gender, and by age groups over time to generate a set of forecasts for the demand for various seniors housing choices.

4. CURRENT AND ANTICIPATED STATUS OF SENIORS POPULATION AND HOUSING

In 1990, the over-65 population comprised about 12.6 percent of the U.S. total population.[6]

In the past decade, this group has increased at a rate twice as fast as that of the general population. More than two thirds of all Americans who have *ever* lived to be 65 are currently alive. This trend is especially intriguing because the first wave of

---

[5] The structure and statistical details of the Nested Logit model are beyond the scope of this study. A companion research paper, "A Nested Logit Model for Estimating Seniors Housing Demand," currently in preparation by the authors, focuses on the statistical and structural modeling issues. For a discussion of multinomial nested logit models, see McFadden (1987), McFadden (1976), and Thiel (1969). Appendix C provides a brief introductory discussion about logit models.

[6] Porter (1995).

Chart 1. Economic Factors Influencing Housing Choice Decisions

- Total Income and Amount by Sources—Wages, Pension, SS, Dividends, Capital Gains, Annuity, etc.
- Ratio of Income to Poverty Level Income
- Ratio of Rental/Mortgage Payment to Income
- Labor Market Factors—Participation, Skills, Education, Duration, etc.
- Tastes Regarding Living Space

Chart 2. Demographic Factors Influencing Housing Choice Decisions

- Age of Individual
- Gender
- Migration
- Location: Central City/Noncentral City/Rural?

Chart 3. Sociological Factors Influencing Housing Choice Decisions

- Marital Status
- Presence and Age of Children in the Household
- Presence and Age of Other Family Members in the Household
- Presence and Age of Nonfamily Members in the Household or Group Quarters

Chart 4. Health Factors Influencing Housing Choice Decisions

- Presence and Severity of Disabilities or Difficulties Requiring Basic Care or Extended Care
- Presence and Severity of Disabilities or Difficulties Affecting Ability to Work
- Mobility Limitations

baby boomers will not turn 65 until the year 2011, at which point the elderly population will swell.[7] The seniors consumer group generates highly-specific types of demand for goods and services. Pharmaceuticals enterprises, medical service providers, and perhaps most of all, real estate developers and investors confront an unusual opportunity because of the expected seniors population increase. The seniors population boom is about to happen, and will continue to be a major force affecting the U.S. economy for many decades to come.

A. Seniors Demographic Trends

The seniors market is heterogeneous and changing in terms of age groups. The current distribution of the seniors population by age as of 1993 is shown in Table 1.

Table 1. 1993 Age Distribution of the Seniors Population

Age Group	% of U.S. Population	% of Seniors Population
65–74	7.3	57.9
75–79	2.5	19.8
80–84	1.6	12.8
85+	1.2	9.5

Source: Porter, 1995.

For the next three decades, the Census Bureau expects that the 75-84 population will increase by 45%, and the 85+ group by 104%. By 2000, 21% of Americans will be 65 years or older.[8] The 85+ group is expected to double in size between 1990 and 2010, from 3 million to 6 million, and will double again between 2010 and 2040. By then, this group's share of the seniors population will also nearly double to 17.3%. By 2050, it is expected that more than 1 million Americans will be 100+, compared to fewer than 50,000 in 1996, and the 65+ group—"The Seniors Collective"—will total about 69 million.[9]

Another way in which the seniors population is heterogeneous is in its needs for services. As the size of each elderly group increases, incidence of chronic illness will also increase. Thus, care for the frail elderly becomes an increasingly pressing concern. Using the 1990-1995 experience, by age 85, nearly 33% of all seniors need help with ADLs, but less than 3% of people in their late 60s need such assistance, and about 10% in their late 70s.[10]

---

[7] Bogorad and Kaufman (1993).
[8] Bradford (1995).
[9] Collins (1995).
[10] Bogorad and Kaufman (1993).

B. Seniors Mobility and Migration

There are some salient features of the seniors population which are more qualitative in nature. For example, it is widely accepted that seniors have very strong preferences against moving.[11] Retiree magnets like Florida and California have lost some ground recently in attracting seniors, but remain the two most frequent destinations for retirees on the move. The top states for elderly populations include Florida, California, Arizona, and Texas, followed by North Carolina, Pennsylvania, New Jersey, Washington, Virginia, and Georgia. Table 2 contains data on the geographic distribution of the elderly population as of 1990.[12]

During the last five years, over half of all moving retirees have moved to just eight states.[13] In a recent survey, however, it was made clear that the elderly do not like to move: 84% of those surveyed (55 or older) by the AARP said that they would like to never move again.[14] Overall, the 60+ group is half as likely to move as the rest of the population.[15]

C. Seniors Socioeconomics

There are many other important features of the elderly population that are likely to affect seniors housing demand and related policy issues. Currently, women outnumber men by 33%. A man is almost twice as likely to live with his spouse as a woman, and this ratio increases at higher ages. Unmarried men who move into retirement communities are likely to be married within a year or two. On the other hand, women are twice as likely to live with other elderly women or relatives. Only about 5% of all seniors live in a nursing home or a personal care facility.

Seniors households are diverse, especially by senior age group. In the early 60s age group, two thirds of households are married couples, as compared with one third of 75+ households. The death of a spouse will often trigger housing changes. Home ownership rates peak at 55-64 and decline somewhat after that, but most seniors *continue* to live in their current homes for the rest of their lives. The elderly are also more educated than in the past. The seniors population is now more ethnically diverse than it once was. Many will enjoy financial security, but many—especially minorities and those who live alone—are likely to confront poverty.[16] In fact, elderly poverty, a topic beyond the scope of this study, but clearly related to housing choice, is a major policy issue as the elderly group grows in the next century.

Income characteristics of the market are also of great interest. The percentage of Americans who are poor is actually lower for the 65+ age group than for those

---

[11] Bogorad and Kaufman (1993).
[12] The source for Table 2 is the U.S. Census and Taeuber (1991).
[13] Longino (1994).
[14] Porter (1995).
[15] Longino (1994).
[16] Bradford (1995).

FORECASTING SENIORS HOUSING DEMAND

Table 2. Elderly Population, By State, 1990

State	Overall Rank[1]	Rank %-chg 1980-1990	Rank % of total for state	Rank 1990	1990 65+	1990 % (65+/total)	1980-1990 %-chg
United States					31,241,831	12.6	22.3
Florida	1	6	1	2	2,369,431	18.30	40.40
Pennsylvania	2	28	2	4	1,829,106	15.40	19.50
New Jersey	3	26	16	9	1,032,025	13.40	20.00
Massachusetts	4	41	13	10	819,284	13.60	12.80
Missouri	5	47	10	12	717,681	14.00	10.70
Ohio	6	25	22	7	1,406,961	13.00	20.30
Iowa	7	48	3	26	426,106	15.30	9.90
Oregon	8	17	11	29	391,324	13.80	29.00
Arizona	9	4	20	22	478,774	13.10	55.80
New York	10	49	20	3	2,363,722	13.10	9.40
Connecticut	11	22	13	25	445,907	13.60	22.20
Wisconsin	12	34	17	16	651,221	13.30	15.40
West Virginia	13	40	4	34	268,897	15.00	13.00
Rhode Island	14	31	4	38	150,547	15.00	18.60
Arkansas	15	44	6	30	350,058	14.90	12.00
North Carolina	16	10	31	11	804,341	12.10	33.30
Illinois	17	37	27	6	1,436,545	12.60	13.80
Indiana	18	29	27	13	696,196	12.60	18.90
Tennessee	19	27	25	17	618,818	12.70	19.60
Alabama	20	30	23	20	522,989	12.90	18.90
Kansas	21	45	11	31	342,571	13.80	11.90
Michigan	22	23	34	8	1,108,461	11.90	21.50
Oklahoma	23	42	15	27	424,213	13.50	12.80
Nebraska	24	50	9	35	223,068	14.10	8.50
California	25	15	45	1	3,135,552	10.50	29.90
Washington	26	11	35	18	575,288	11.80	33.30
South Dakota	27	43	7	45	102,331	14.70	12.40
North Dakota	28	39	8	46	91,255	14.30	13.20
Maine	29	33	17	36	163,373	13.30	15.90
Kentucky	30	36	25	24	466,845	12.70	13.90
Minnesota	31	35	29	19	546,934	12.50	14.00
Montana	32	20	17	44	106,497	13.30	25.90
Virginia	33	13	43	14	664,470	10.70	31.50
Texas	34	21	47	5	1,716,576	10.10	25.20
South Carolina	35	7	37	28	396,935	11.40	38.10
Maryland	36	14	41	21	517,482	10.80	30.80
Georgia	37	19	47	15	654,270	10.10	26.60
Louisiana	38	32	40	23	468,991	11.10	16.00
Mississippi	39	46	29	33	321,284	12.50	11.00
Delaware	40	9	31	47	80,735	12.10	36.40
Idaho	41	16	33	43	121,265	12.00	29.40
Hawaii	42	3	38	42	125,005	11.30	64.20
New Mexico	43	5	41	37	163,062	10.80	40.70
Nevada	44	1	44	40	127,631	10.60	94.10
D. C.	45	51	24	48	77,847	12.80	4.80
New Hampshire	46	24	38	41	125,029	11.30	21.40
Colorado	47	12	49	32	329,443	10.00	33.20
Utah	48	8	50	39	149,958	8.70	37.30
Vermont	49	38	35	49	66,163	11.80	13.70
Wyoming	50	18	46	50	47,195	10.40	27.00
Alaska	51	2	51	51	22,369	4.10	93.70

[1] Overall rank is a weighted average of % change, % of state total, and absolute 1990 rank with weights of 15%, 50%, and 35%, respectively.

younger than 65. This is, in part, true because so many children live in poverty. Older seniors (75 plus) are more likely to be poor than the 65-74 group. Per capita, average after-tax income of seniors is about 9% higher than that of the rest of the population, but total income per household is lower. Most seniors actually do not live on fixed incomes. Careful studies indicate that their incomes are actually better shielded against inflation than the incomes of nonseniors. Despite a common perception that elderly people must live much more frugally than when they were younger, more than 80% of seniors actually can consume at similar preretirement rates. Some seniors are not retired, which means that these households will continue to receive significant wage income. Many seniors households are also well invested, which provides non-pension, nonwage income. Seniors can be expected to pay from 50-59% of their incomes on a retirement housing package. In 1992, at least 46% of 70+ households could afford to pay $900-1450 per month for single units, and $1100-1800 per month for double occupancy, which makes the potential market for these services roughly 5.5 million households.[17]

Starting with the second half of the 1990s, demand for seniors housing will grow substantially. This growth will continue, and in fact, accelerate, in decades to come. Moreover, seniors housing demand is, and will continue to be diverse and complex.

5. FORECASTS FOR SENIORS HOUSING DEMAND THROUGH 2020

In this section, a set of forecasts for seniors housing demand through 2020 is developed, and is based upon the multinomial nested logit model described in Section 3. The estimates are generated for five-year intervals from 1995-2020. To create the forecasts, the estimated MNL model is combined with the Census forecasts of population by gender, age group, and geographic location. While the model recognizes that individuals located in different states with differences in age group or gender will have different probabilities of choosing each of the six housing categories, the forecast model assumes that the 1990 choices by locale, gender, and age group are representative, stable, and unchanging over the forecast horizon. To the extent that there are dynamic housing demand behavior changes after 1990, the forecasts will necessarily be in error. Conceptually, the seniors housing demand forecasts should be considered a benchmark, rather than the definitive distribution of future housing demand. On balance, the forecast model is likely to provide a set of reasonable national aggregate estimates of likely seniors housing demand in the future. The remainder of this section is divided into four subsections: Census Demographic Forecasts, Seniors Demand for Nursing Home and Board and Care, Seniors Demand for Congregate Care, and Seniors Demand for Assisted Living.

---

[17] Bogorad and Kaufman (1993).

A. Census Demographic Forecasts

The statistical results of the nested logit model have been combined with the U.S. Census Preferred Series of Population by geographic locale, age group, and gender to generate the forecasts for seniors housing demand in five-year intervals. Figures 3 and 4 summarize the fundamentals of the Census forecasts. Figure 3 displays the U.S. population by age group and shows the projected levels of population growth by age groups through 2020. From 1990-2020, the 65+ age population is expected to increase from over 30 million to close to 55 million people. The 65-84 age segment represents the preponderance of the elderly, and, as you would expect, is larger than the 85+ age group by a factor of 5.

Figure 4 arrays the population growth rates for the elderly in five-year intervals for 1990-2020. From 1990 to 2010, the rate of growth of population for the 84+ age group (though the total population of this group is small) will be substantially faster than that of the 65-84 group. However, in approximately 2010 the post-war baby boomers will begin to be classified as elderly (defined as 65 and above). At that point, the rate of population growth for the 65-84 group will be substantially greater than that of the 85+ population. Hence, the real challenge for seniors housing providers over the next 25 years is to find products that are appropriate for the 65-84 age group. This age group will tend to be healthier and exhibit greater longevity than its predecessors. Seniors housing demand, therefore, will shift away from the intensive personal service nursing home toward the less personal-service-intensive congregate care and assisted living housing types.[18]

B. Nursing Homes and Board and Care[19]

Nursing homes and board and care facilities constitute people living in group quarters, such as licensed nursing homes and a variety of specialty hospitals and care facilities. Using the Preferred Census forecasts through 2020 and the statistical analysis based on the MNL model, and aggregating the United States data by age and state, Figure 5 shows the total population that is expected to live in nursing homes and board and care facilities between 1990 and 2020, by five-year intervals. Figures 6 and 7 illustrate respectively the implied percentage changes in the demand for nursing homes and board and care homes and the corresponding net change in total seniors housing demand by five-year intervals for 1990 through 2020. The rate of growth and the maximum number of people that will enter nursing homes (net change) peak in approximately 2010. This is, in part, due to the relatively rapid growth of the over 85 age group through 2010. The "old" seniors age group requires nursing facilities to a greater extent than younger seniors age groups. These estimates

---

[18] The reduced usage of high cost nursing home facilities is likely to occur anyway in order to increase efficiency and reduce costs for providing seniors housing because of reforms taking place in the general medical care system.

[19] Nursing homes and board and care facilities have been combined as a single category for seniors housing because it is not practical to separate these categories within the Census data.

of the demand for nursing home and board and care facilities by seniors may be on the high side because of the movement toward improved cost efficiency, which is driven by reform in medical care, including services provided to the elderly. Hence, forecasts for nursing home demand are likely to represent higher-than-expected levels, reflecting the assumed 1990 behavior imbedded in the PUMS database and the logit modeling.

Figure 3. U.S. Population by Age Group—Actual and Projected: 1990–2020

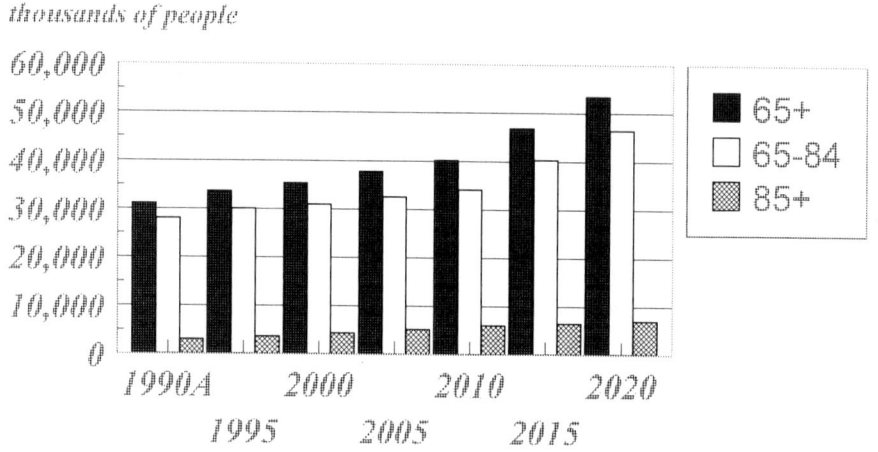

Source: Fisher Center for Real Estate and Urban Economics, based on Preferred Series Forecast, U.S. Census Bureau.

Figure 4. U.S. Population Growth Rates by Age Group: 1990–2020

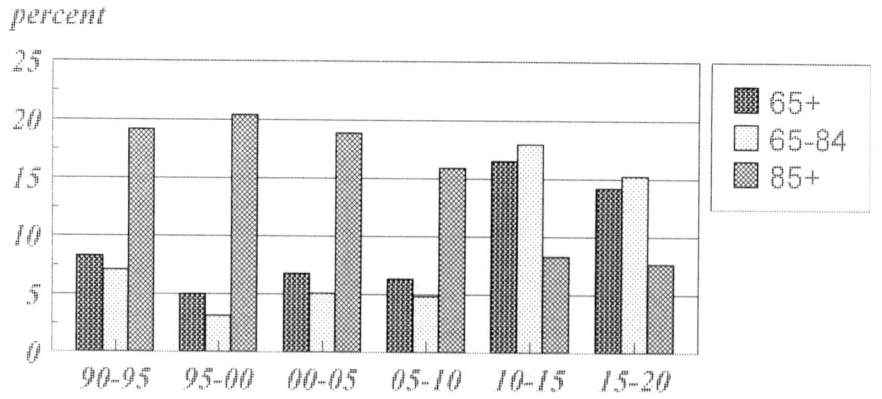

Source: Fisher Center for Real Estate and Urban Economics, based on Preferred Series Forecast, U.S. Census Bureau.

FORECASTING SENIORS HOUSING DEMAND 217

Figure 5. Nursing Home Plus Board and Care: 1990–2020

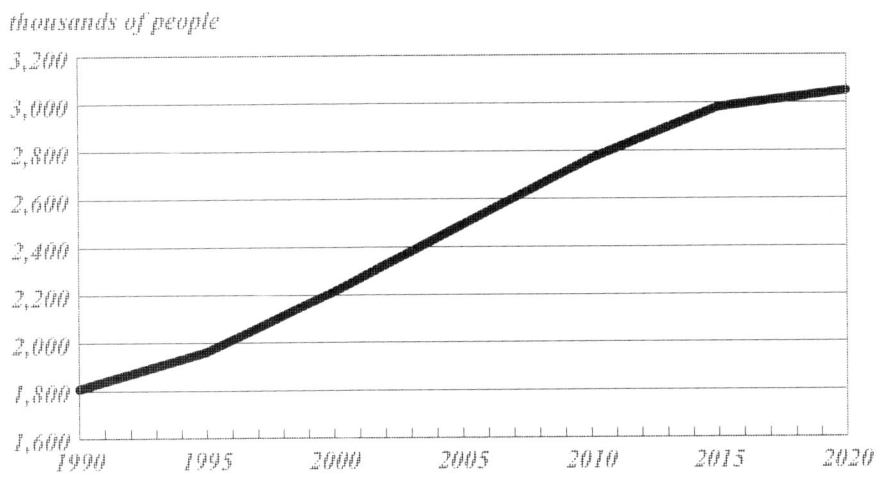

Source: Fisher Center for Real Estate and Urban Economics.

Figure 6. Percent Change in Nursing Home plus Board and Care Population: 1990–2020

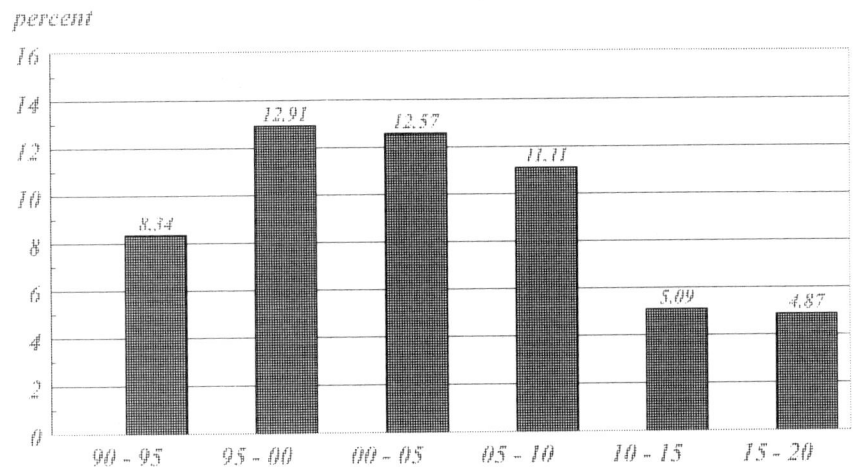

Source: Fisher Center for Real Estate and Urban Economics.

Figure 7. Net Change in Nursing Home plus Board and Care Population: 1990–2020

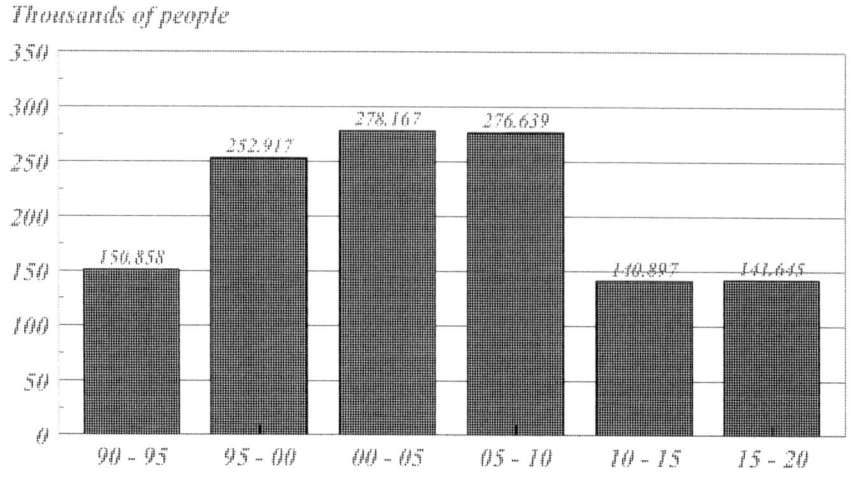

Source: Fisher Center for Real Estate and Urban Economics.

C. Congregate Care

Congregate care housing comprises a multiunit residence with private sleeping quarters, perhaps kitchenettes, and some basic living services, such as meals, transportation, healthcare, and security. These services are typically included in the rental payment or in an ownership-related maintenance fee.

Figures 8, 9, and 10 provide projections for seniors' demand for congregate care between 1990 and 2020. Figure 8 shows the total U.S. congregate care population. Demand for congregate care housing will increase from approximately 1.5 million people to 2.6 million people over the thirty year period. Figure 9 shows that the percentage change in congregate care population (i.e., growth rate) will peak before the 21st century at almost 13%, and will fall to less than half of that rate of growth by the second decade of the 21st century. Figure 9 provides the net population demand change for congregate care.[20]

Along the spectrum of seniors housing options, congregate care housing is probably too close to the nursing home and board and care sector; a sector that is likely to

---

[20] Congregate housing experienced considerable growth during the 1980s. Private sector involvement dramatically expanded in response to the demand for seniors housing alternatives. Financially sound real estate opportunities and a simultaneous increase in elderly consumer demand for more supportive housing settings without overly institutional environments combined to engender a market for congregate care housing. Expectations that this option would be attractive to the younger elderly, however, proved to be incorrect. It has appealed mostly to persons in their late 70s and older. Misjudgment of the size of the market, the length of time a congregate care project would take to fill, the service needs of the elderly occupants, and the costs of development and management have contributed to financial failures of many congregate housing developments.

face a diminishing demand in the early part of the next century. Therefore, while the demand for congregate care housing will grow, the growth is unlikely to be rapid.

Figure 8. Congregate Care Population Projections: 1990–2020

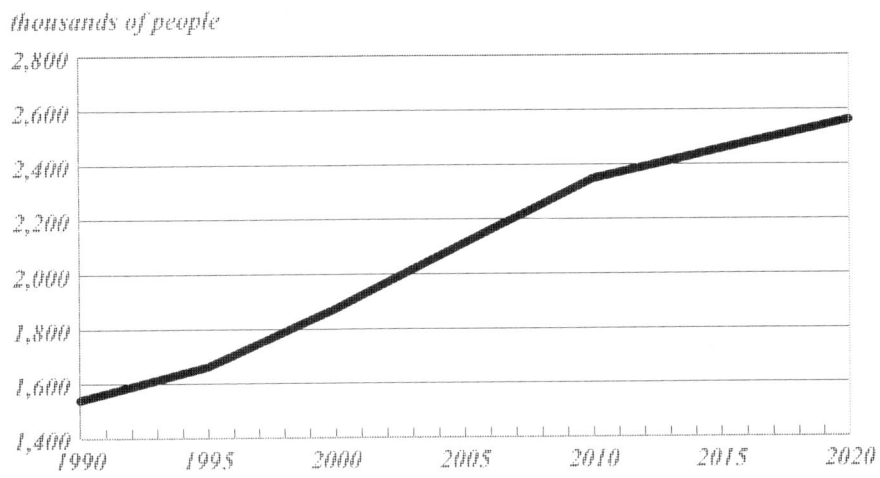

Source: Fisher Center for Real Estate and Urban Economics.

Figure 9. Percent Change in Congregate Care Population Projections: 1990–2020

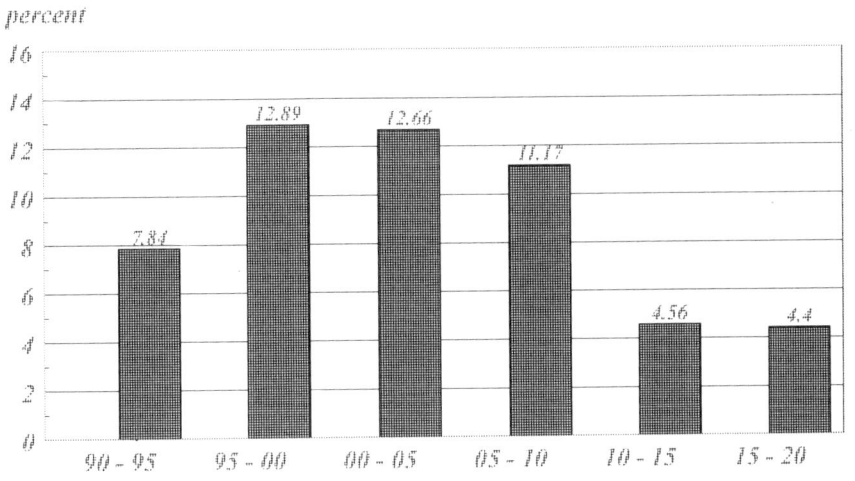

Source: Fisher Center for Real Estate and Urban Economics.

Figure 10. Net Change in Congregate Care Population: 1990–2020

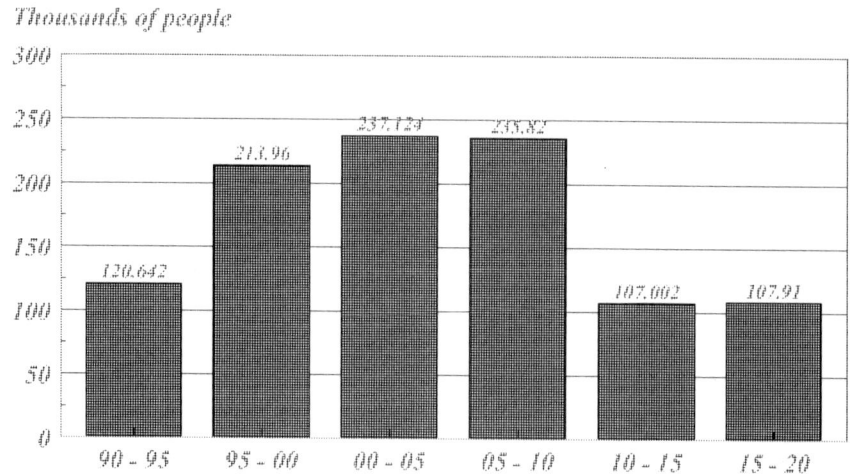

Source: Fisher Center for Real Estate and Urban Economics.

D. Assisted Living

Assisted living is a broad housing category in which people obtain some kind of personal care because of physical or mental deficiency, degradation, or disability. Most individuals in such housing are single and live in multifamily private residential housing that is owned or rented by the occupant. Group living does occur in assisted living facilities, and historically has comprised 10-15% of the total assisted living population.

Continuing care retirement communities (CCRC)—which comprise much of this housing category—are also known as lifecare communities and offer essentially an administered continuum of shelter and care accommodations within the same facility. In this form, CCRCs would be classified as assisted living facilities. According to the Consumer Guide Book published by the American Association of Homes for the Aging (1990), "as a continuing care resident you can enjoy a comfortable independent lifestyle, secure in the knowledge that if you become frail or ill as you grow older, your needs will be met in a familiar environment." Over a course of residency in the CCRC, an older occupant could conceivably occupy a rental apartment in the independent accommodations of congregate housing facilitates, a room in a semidependent assisted living center, and a bed in a skilled nursing home. However, the bulk of CCRC housing would be classified under assisted living.

Figures 11, 12 and 13 represent projections from 1990 to 2020 for seniors demand for assisted living housing. Figure 11 contains the forecasts for the total seniors demand for assisted living between 1990 and 2020. The assisted living seniors population is expected to increase from under 7 million in 1990 to approximately 12 million

FORECASTING SENIORS HOUSING DEMAND

Figure 11. Assisted Living Population Projections: 1990 to 2020

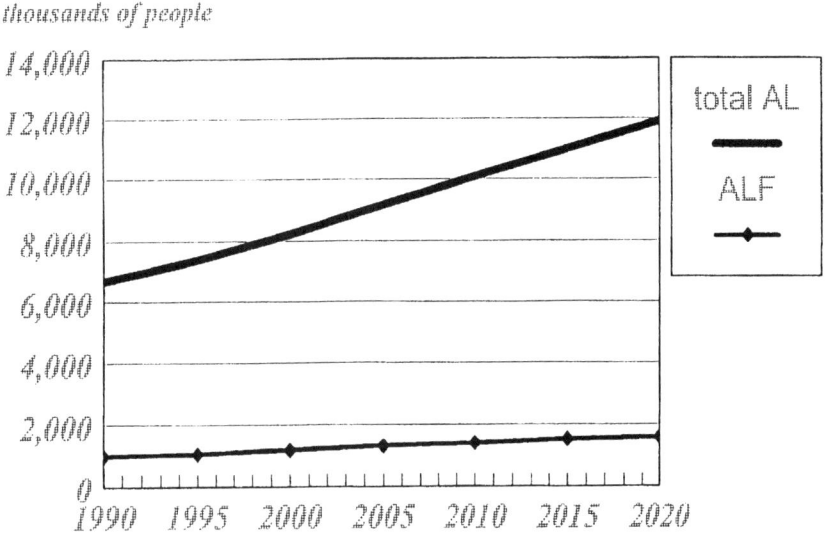

Source: Fisher Center for Real Estate and Urban Economics

Figure 12. Percent Change in Assisted Living Population—Projections: 1990–2020

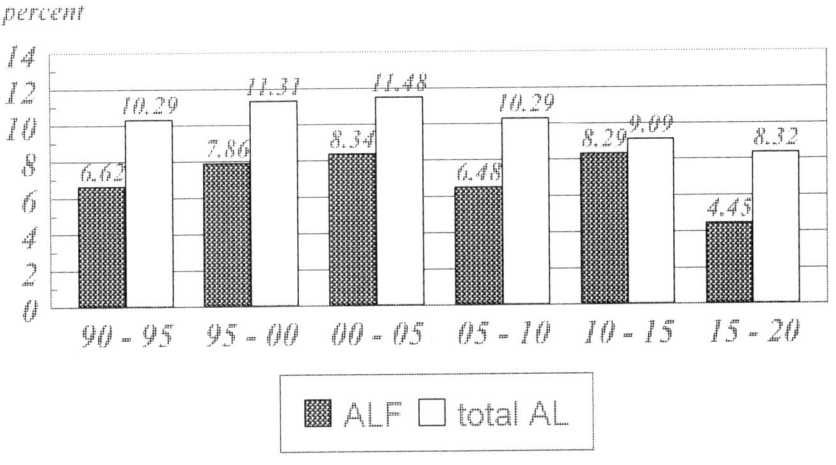

Source: Fisher Center for Real Estate and Urban Economics.

by 2020. During this time period, the demand for assisted living facilities—the group quarters version of assisted living—will increase from 1 million to 1.8 million. The relatively small growth in the demand for assisted living facilities is caused by seniors' preferences not to move (i.e., seniors like to age in place). Obviously, the original residence is the best place for a senior to age in place. There is also an aversion

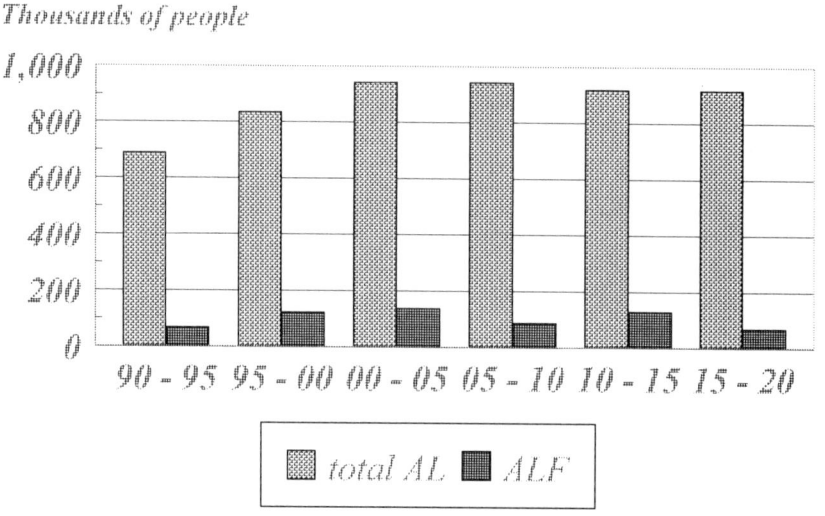

Figure 13. Net Change in Assisted Living Population—Projections: 1990–2020

Source: Fisher Center for Real Estate and Urban Economics.

among seniors to move into institutional settings, no matter how attractive they may be. Part of this aversion may stem from financial concerns in addition to foregoing the familiar surroundings of their own abode. Figure 12 demonstrates how the total demand by seniors for assisted living is expected to grow over the 30-year period from 1990 to 2020. The demand for assisted living housing will grow approximately 20% faster than the institutional component (assisted living facilities populations). This implies that most assisted living takes place in private residential settings.

Figure 13 shows the projected net absolute change in the seniors population in assisted living housing quarters in five-year intervals from 1995 through 2020. Only a small fraction of the 800,000 person net population change in each five-year interval ends up in institutional assisted living facilities.

6. SENIORS HOUSING CONCLUSIONS: DEMAND, SUPPLY, PUBLIC POLICY ISSUES, AND RESEARCH PROSPECTIVES

In order to determine the required net additional supply of seniors housing, a comparison of seniors housing demand and existing supply is required. The difference between stock demand and stock supply represents the vacancy. Adjusting for normal vacancy and for housing stock depreciation, an estimate of how much additional housing supply will be needed over time can be generated.

A. Understanding Seniors Housing Demand

The demand for housing by seniors is complex because it combines traditional demand for shelter with varying degrees of nonhousing personal services. These nonhousing personal services encompass a significant array of goods and services, including meals, transportation, housekeeping, and medical care. Seniors housing demand is different from that of any other age group because of the nonhousing personal services required. Put somewhat differently, demand for seniors housing is generally dependent upon the type of and level of housing and the nonhousing personal services the household requires which, in turn, is functionally dependent upon household location, household head, gender, age cohort, and physical and mental conditions, among other variables.

While the seniors population of the United States is expected to grow substantially over the next 25 years, it is less apparent what types of housing demand this diverse group will generate. Besides the complexity of the housing and personal services, it also appears that demand for housing and personal services by these various subgroups of seniors is probably in flux. In order to capture the essence of this multifaceted decision, this study develops a nested multinomial logit model. The housing tenure decision is estimated statistically as being nested within the level and types of personal services demanded by the household. This estimate is then utilized to forecast total U.S. seniors housing demands for five year intervals through 2020.

In brief, using the statistical model, the forecasts indicate that seniors housing demand by product type (i.e., nursing homes, board and care, congregate care, and assisted living) will grow substantially, but differently by type of product and by subtime interval over the next 25 years. The fastest growing portion of the demand for seniors housing will be assisted living. This group tends to need relatively low levels of nonhousing personal services and it tends to age in place. Only 10% of this group chooses to live in an assisted living institutional housing environment. The assisted living group represents the bulk of the seniors market growth, and, therefore, it is the focal point for housing providers, businessmen, and government policy makers.

B. Estimating Additional Seniors Housing Demand

Table 3 contains an estimate of the supply of nursing homes and assisted living facilities as of 1994. As of that time, estimated totals were 17,000 nursing homes with 1.7 million beds. Of course, not all of these beds were occupied by highly-dependent nursing home patients. Similarly, assisted living facilities (group quarters only) comprised 35,000 to 40,000 facilities nationwide. These assisted living facilities had the capacity to house between 600,000 and one million people.

Table 3. Estimated Supply of Nursing Homes and Assisted Living Facilities, 1994

	Nursing Homes	Assisted Living Facilities (Group Quarters Only)
Facilities	17,000	35,000–40,000
Capacity	1,700,000 Beds	600,000–1,000,000 People

As Table 3 implies, differences in definition and surveying of these housing industries are not as statistically reliable as one might wish, and therefore are best estimates. Assuming that the growth in seniors housing demand will, in the long run, be accommodated by supply within five-year periods, then taking the projections developed in Section 5 and adjusting for a normal vacancy factor and housing stock depreciation rate, it is possible to estimate the required supply of housing for seniors between 1990 and 2020. Figure 14—using the assumption that supply ultimately fulfills demand—estimates the required additions to the supply of nursing homes, board and care homes, and assisted living facilities (group quarters). The assisted living housing choice will be the fastest-growing numerically over the next thirty years. However, because most people wish to age in place, they will choose independent living outside of group facilities. For this reason, assisted living facilities will need to provide—from 1995 through 2020—somewhere between 70,000 and 150,000 beds per five-year period, even though the total assisted living population will grow in each of these five year periods by about 800,000. On the other hand, nursing homes and board and care homes, though slower-growing housing choices than assisted living, will, through 2010, grow substantially, needing to accommodate as many as 600,000 seniors in the first decade of the 21st century. This will decline to half that number by the second decade of the 21st century.

Figure 14. Required Additions to the Supply of Housing for Senior Living: 1990–2020

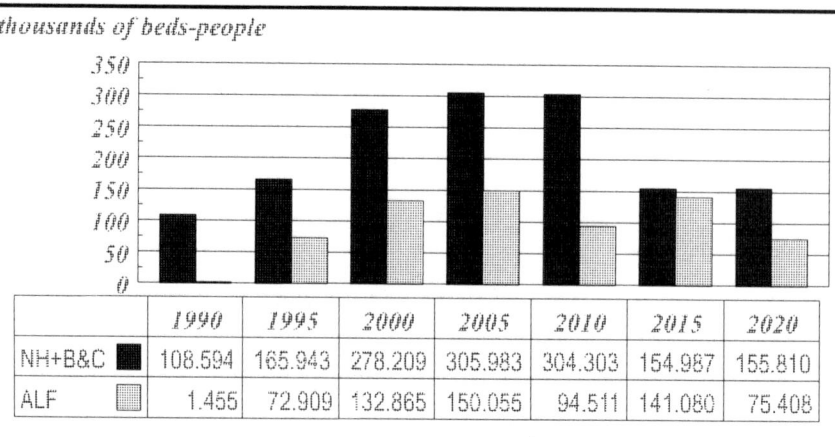

	1990	1995	2000	2005	2010	2015	2020
NH+B&C	108.594	165.943	278.209	305.983	304.303	154.987	155.810
ALF	1.455	72.909	132.865	150.055	94.511	141.080	75.408

No. of additional beds needed every 5 yrs. NH + B&C and ALF mean Nursing Home plus Board and Assisted Living Facilities, resp.
Source: Fisher Center for Real Estate and Urban Economics.

C. Public Policy Issues

The derived forecasts for additional required seniors housing supply should be an important policy focus issue for our society. Government policy must take heed of these changing demographics and the associated seniors housing demand. As the U.S. population ages, many facets of the U.S. economy besides housing will be affected. To the extent that seniors housing demand substantially changes where and how seniors live over the next 25 years, the growth in demand may require substantial reallocations of national resources. The seniors housing forecasts developed here indicate that on average, a little less than ten percent of the current annual home-building activity will need to be redirected to satisfy seniors housing demand. This translates into an average of between 100,000 and 150,000 housing units per year for the next 25 years.

D. Research Prospectives

Research that improves the understanding of the forces that drive the economic decision making regarding seniors housing choice is surely needed. Behavioral research of seniors housing choice, using microdata, is required in order improve the current ability of researchers to forecast and evaluate seniors housing demand. The forecasting analyses presented in this study are predicated on the assumption that the future behavior of seniors within each cohort will reflect the underlying behaviors of the past. For the modeling used in this study, 1990 behavior is imprinted on the forecasting through 2020. Of course, all researchers understand that this is an assumption of convenience, and any changes in these implied behavioral assumptions—without guidance from additional research—would be speculative.

Economists have promulgated the life-cycle hypothesis, which suggests that over a household's life cycle there is a wealth accumulation/housing consumption pattern. Specifically, the life-cycle theory claims that seniors should reduce their housing consumption and be considerably more mobile than they appear to be. In reality, seniors tend to age in place and stay in current domiciles longer than the theory predicts.

It is time to modify and test the life-cycle theory with additional theoretical visions of behavior. As a starting point, the life-cycle theory should be combined with the notion that housing wealth is held in the portfolio to meet a precautionary or bequeathal motive. Housing assets would serve other specialized behavioral motives, such as bequeathal and risk reduction, with respect to other portions of a household's wealth. This notion is advocated elsewhere,[21] and a careful study of it is a needed next step if seniors housing demand analysis is to improve.

---

[21] Jones (1995).

APPENDIX A: *WHAT IS PUMS?*

The Public Use Microdata Samples (PUMS) contain housing unit and personal records drawn from the full census population. Each sampled record contains information coded from the long form questionnaire—a more detailed survey than the general census survey used for the entire U.S. population. The file is hierarchical in structure: a housing unit record is followed in sequence by records for the persons living in that housing unit. The household variables used in this study include:

- Group Quarters Institution: whether residents are institutionalized or not;

- Units in Structure: contains the following categories—mobile home or trailer, one-family house detached, one-family house attached, and apartment (with the following subdivisions: 2, 3-4, 5-9, 10-19, 20-49, 50 or more);

- Rooms: how many rooms are in a structure (from 1-9, and then 9 or more);

- Tenure: whether a unit is owned with debt, owned free and clear, rented for cash rent, or no cash rent;

- Business or Medical Office on Property: a dichotomous yes/no variable;

- Property Value: the value in dollars in ranges between 10,000 (or less) and 40,000 (or more);

- Monthly Rent: the value in dollars in ranges between 80 (or less) and 1,000 or more;

- Meals Included in Rent: a dichotomous yes/no variable;

- House or Apartment Part of Condominium: a dichotomous yes/no variable;

- Mortgage Status: whether a residence has a mortgage, deed of trust, a contract to purchase, or none;

- Mortgage Payment: the value in dollars in ranges between zero and 2,001 or above;

- Farm/Nonfarm Status: whether the household is urban, rural farm, or rural nonfarm;

- Gross Rent as a Percentage of Household Income in 1989: in ranges from 0% to 100% or more;

- Family Income: the value in dollars in ranges between -9,999,999 and 9,999,999;

- Household Income: the value in dollars in ranges between -9,999,999 and 9,999,999;

- Household/Family Type: whether the household is vacant, married-couple family, male householder family, female householder family, male householder living alone nonfamily, male householder not living alone nonfamily, female householder living alone nonfamily, or female householder not living alone nonfamily.

Several personal variables utilized in the study include:

- Relationship: the categories are householder, husband/wife, son/daughter, stepson/stepdaughter, brother/sister, father/mother, grandchild, other relative, not related (roomer/boarder/foster child, housemate/roommate, unmarried partner, other nonrelative), group quarters (institutionalized person, other persons in group quarters);

- Sex: a male/female identifier;

- Age: the value in ranges between less than one year and 90 or older;

- Marital Status: the categories are now married (except separated), widowed, divorced, separated, never married, under 15 years old;

- Married: Spouse Present/Spouse Absent: the categories are now married/spouse present, now married/spouse absent, widowed, divorced, separated, never married;

- Presence and Age of Own Children: the categories are with own children under 6 years old only, with own children 6 to 17 years only, with own children under 6 years and 6 to 17 years, no own children;

- Person Poverty Status Recode: the percentage above or below the poverty line in a range from 1% to 501% or more;

- Mobility Status (lived here on April 1, 1985): whether or not the individual lived in the same residence for the 1985-1990 period;

- Migration—State or Foreign Country Code: two-digit code of the location the individual moved from;

- Migration PUMA (state dependent): five-digit code of the PUMA the individual moved from;

- Work Limitation Status: whether or not an individual is limited in kind or amount of work;

- Work Prevented Status: whether or not an individual is prevented from working;

- Mobility Limitation: whether or not an individual has a mobility limitation;

- Personal Care Limitation: whether or not an individual has a personal care limitation;

- Employment Status Recode: the categories are civilian employed/at work, civilian employed/with a job but not at work, unemployed, armed forces/at work, armed forces/with a job but not at work, not in labor force;

- Hours Worked Last Week: the value in ranges from 1 to 99 or more;

- Total Person's Earnings: the value in dollars in ranges from -19,996 or less to 284,001 or more;

- Total Person's Income: the value in dollars in ranges from -29,997 or less to 401,001 or more;

- Interest, Dividends, and Net Rental Income in 1989: the value in dollars in ranges from -9,999 or less to 40,001 or more;

- Social Security Income in 1989: the value in dollars in ranges from zero to 17,001 or more;

- Public Assistance Income in 1989: the value in dollars in ranges from zero to 10,001 or more;

- Retirement Income in 1989: the value in dollars in ranges from zero to 30,001 or more.

This study uses the 5% PUMS for seven states and the District of Columbia to estimate the housing choice models. The seven states considered in the analysis are Arizona, California, Florida, Kansas, Nevada, New Jersey, and Texas. These eight geographic areas comprise a balanced blend of nationwide seniors population attributes. The sample includes

(a) states that cover the entire country,

(b) urban/rural breakdown of the observed housing arrangements of the elderly population (using the "farm" dummy enables one to distinguish among people living in a rural setting), and

(c) a mix of states that includes both elderly migration destination and departure states.

Even though the data are cross-sectional and not panel, the focus of the study is not migration behavior, per se. However, by ensuring that the samples include both destination and departure states, the sample will not improperly reflect differences in seniors housing demand caused by migration effects.

APPENDIX B: PUMS VARIABLE SPECIFICATION AND SENIORS HOUSING DEMAND

Housing choice categories are discussed in Section II of the paper. The statistical MNL model is calibrated, using five-year age cohorts for seven representative states and the District of Columbia in 1990, to develop forecast housing demands through 2020.[22]

The population control forecasts are derived from the U.S. Census Bureau, Preferred Series Forecast of the Population of the United States, pp. 25-1111. The Census provides forecasts by five-year cohorts of the entire United States and forecasts of the age cohorts 2-65 and 65+ for each state, but does not contain forecasts of five-year cohorts for each state. Therefore, we interpolate, applying the shares of the population made up by each state for the two broad age cohorts to the population forecasts for the entire United States by our nine five-year cohorts. The nine cohorts are 45-49, 50-54, 55-59, 60-64, 65-69, 70-74, 75-79, 80-84 and 85+. This census dataset provides, after one simple transformation, the estimated fraction of the total population of the U.S. by State. Since the U.S. forecasts from the Census Bureau are available by age cohorts, the State projections can be translated by age cohorts as well.

The PUMS 5% sample data sets are the product of the U.S. Census Bureau. Using the multinomial logit model, housing choice parameters are estimated for each age group and for each geographic area (7 states and DC) separately. Since computer hardware storage capacity is limited, datasets range in size from 12,000 to over 300,000 people—2MB to 300MB. Therefore, the model for each of the 7 states and for the District of Columbia is estimated separately.

Utilizing the five-year cohort population estimates by state described above, for each age group in each state, the population is allocated for housing categories based upon the state characteristics and the parameters of the MNL model.[23]

---

[22] Age cohorts are five year age intervals, beginning with 45-49, ..., 80-84, and 85+.
[23] These weights are a function of the statistical proximity or likeness of the non-PUMS states to the PUMS states employed in calibrating MNL. We split non-PUMS states into two cohorts: "destination

Finally, the database is aggregated across all age cohorts and all states in order to generate the seniors housing forecasts and the implied U.S. Census projections by housing categories y={1,2,3,4,5}, for 1990-2020.

Definition of Housing Demand Categories: PUMS Algorithm

1. Assisted Living:

People in this category choose to demand services not provided in standard housing arrangements. These are people who need some kind of personal care due to a physical or mental deficiency, degradation, or disability. However, these people need not live in group quarters or institutions. In fact, the great majority live in their own (rented or owned) residence; single or multiunit, detached or attached.

> **CONDITION:** If perscare = 1, then y = 1.0 which means AL is the identified housing choice. Otherwise, y = 0.0. Perscare = 1 implies that the person in question has personal care limitations.

2. Congregate Care:

Out of the remaining non-AL PUMS sample (y = 0.0 from Step (1)), if these people choose {to live in multiunit residences[24] which have meals included in gross rent} or {community use facilities are present in these multiunit residences} then we conclude that they are living in some kind of Congregate Care (CC) arrangement.

> **CONDITION:** if meals = 1.0 & commuse = 1.0 then y = 2.0. Otherwise, y remains at 0.0.

3. Nursing Homes:

Excluding the PUMS sample already defined by y = 1.0 or y = 2.0, determine the fraction of the remaining sample who choose nursing homes (NH) as the living arrangement. In order to do this, select {the population living in group quarters (GQ/Institutionalized)} *and* {who also have a physical or mental deficiency, degradation, or disability which prevents them from participating in the labor force}. Two choices exist for the second condition: the choice employed is "have you had a physical disability for more than six months from the time of the Census form filing." The employed condition is likely to reflect the objective of the NH choice, i.e., counting people in nursing homes and some types of board and care facilities.

---

states" and "all others." The migration destination states are CA, HI, NM, TX, and UT. To those states, the mean parameter coefficients from the MNL model from CA, NJ, FL, and AZ are applied. Other states received the mean coefficient from the six representative locales, excluding CA, FL, and AZ.

[24] These multiunit residences may or may not have private sleeping quarters and kitchens.

CONDITION: if gqinst = 1 & disabl1 <2.0, then y = 3.0. Otherwise, y = 1.0 (for those individuals choosing AL) or y = 0.0 for people still with unidentified housing choice, according to the algorithm.

4. No Care, Owner Occupied:

People in this category receive no special personal care (y = 0.0) and {who claim real property ownership in the PUMS census form}.

CONDITION: if tenure <3.0 then y = 4.0.

5. No Care, Renter Occupied:

Are the people we have not selected through the above four sampling conditions in the algorithm.

CONDITION: if is still y = 0.0, then y = 5.0.

REFERENCES

"A Place to Grow Old," New York: Columbia University Press, 1984.
American Association of Homes for the Aging: Continuing Care retirement Communities. An Industry in Action, Washington, DC: American Association of Homes for the Aging, 1989.
American Association of Homes for the Aging, Continuing Care Retirement Communities: An Industry in Action, Washington, DC: American Association of Homes for the Aging, 1989.
American Association of Homes for the Aging, The Continuing Care Retirement Community: A Guidebook for Consumers, Washington, DC: American Association of Homes for the Aging, 1990.
American Association of Retired Persons, Understanding Seniors Housing for the 1990s, Washington, DC: American Association of Retired Persons, 1990.
American Society on Aging, The Aging Connection, Vol. 10, No 3, 1989.
Anderson, Katherine, "Growing Old Purposefully," *Journal of Property Management*, March/April 1995.
Boersch-Supan, Axel et al., "Health, Children and Elderly Living Arrangements: A Multiperiod Multinomial Probit Model with Unobserved Heterogeneity and Autocorrelated Errors." Working Paper No. 3343, NBER, April 1990.
Bogorad, Leonard and Gadi Kaufmann, "Retirement Housing Market Opportunities," *The Real Estate Finance Journal*, Spring 1993.
Bradford, Susan, "Spotlight on Seniors," *Builder*, May 1995.
Bradsher, Julia E., Charles F. Longino, Jr., David J. Jackson, and Rick S. Zimmerman, "Health and Geographic Mobility Among the Recently Widowed," *Journal of Gerontology*, Vol. 47, No. 5, 1992.
Braun, K. L., and C.L. Rose, "Goals and Characteristics of Long-term Care Programs: An Analytic Model," *Gerontologist*, Vol. 29, 1989.
Cantor, M.H., "Life Space and the Social Support System of the Inner-City Elderly of New York," *Gerontologist*, Vol. 15, 1975.
Cohen, Robin A. and Joan F. Van Nostrand, Trends in the Health of Older Americans: United States, 1994, National Center for Health Statistics, Vital Health Statistics, Series 3: No.30, 1995.

Collins, David P., "Graying of America Leads to Senior Housing Shortage," *The Real Estate Finance Journal*, Spring 1995.

Cuba, Lee and Charles F. Longino, Jr. "Regional Retirement Migration: The Case of Cape Cod." *Journal of Gerontology*, 1991, Vol. 46, No. 1, pp. S33-42.

Dey, Achintya N. "Characteristics of Elderly Men and Women Discharged From Home Health Care Services: United States, 1991-92." National Center for Health Statistics, Vital Health Statistics, March 1995, No. 259, pp. 1-8.

Diamond, L.M. (1990). "Self-insurance versus Private Insurance: A New Option for Life-care Communities." In R. D. Chellis & P. J. Grayson (Eds.), *Life care: A long-term solution?* (pp. 251-260). Lexington, MA: Lexington.

Edmonds, Helen L. and Dwight H. Merriam. "Zoning and the Elderly: Issues for the 21st Century," *Land Use Law & Zoning Digest*, March 1995, pp. 3-7.

Evans, Mariwyn. "Seniors Housing Finally Scores," *Journal of Property Management*, May/June 1994, pp. 28-32.

—"Seniors Housing Finally Scores," *The Mortgage and Real Estate Executives Report*, Vol. 26, No. 4, April 15, 1993, pp. 2-3.

Feinstein, Jonathan and Daniel McFadden. "The Dynamics of Housing Demand by the Elderly: Wealth, Cash Flow, and Demographic Effects." NBER Working Paper #2471, Massachusetts Institute of Technology, December 1987.

Fournier, Gary M. "Multilevel Determinants of Elderly Migration: Methodological Reservations." *Social Science Quarterly*, Vol. 74, No. 2, June 1993, pp. 416-419.

Golant, Stephen M. (1975). "Residential Concentrations of the Future Elderly. *Gerontologist*, Vol. 15, pp. 16-23.

— (1976). "Intraurban Transportation Needs and Problems of the Elderly." In M. P. Lawton, R. J. Newcomer, & T. O. Byerts (Eds.), *Community Planning for an Aging Society*, (pp. 282-308). Stroudsburg, PA: Dowden, Hutchinson, & Ross.

— (1980). "Locational-Environmental Perspectives on Old-Age Segregated Residential Areas in the United States." In D. T. Herbert & R. J. Johnston (Eds.), *Geography and the Urban Environment* (pp. 257-294). New York: John Wiley.

— (1984a). "The Effects of Residential and Activity Behaviors on Old People's Environmental Experiences." In I. Altman, M. P. Lawton, & J. Wohlwill (Eds.) *Elderly People and the Environment*, (pp. 239-278). New York: Plenum.

— (1984b). "A Place to Grow Old." New York: Columbia University Press.

— (1985). "In Defense of Age-Segregated Housing." *Aging*, 348, 22-26.

— (1986). "Subjective Housing Assessments By the Elderly: A Critical Information Source for Planning and Program Evaluation." *Gerontologist*, 26, 122-127.

— (1987). "Residential Moves by Elderly Persons to U.S. Central Cities, Suburbs, and Rural Areas," *Journal of Gerontology*, 41, pp. 534-539.

— (1990). "The Metropolitanization and Suburbanization of the U.S. Elderly Population: 1970-1988." *Gerontologist*, 30, pp. 80-85.

— "City-Suburban, Metro-Non-metro, and Regional Differences in the Housing Quality of U.S. Elderly Households." *Research on Aging*, Vol 16, No. 3 (September 1994), pp. 322-346.

Gollub, J. O., and T.J. Chmura. (1986). "Using Public and Private Policy Options to Meet the Housing Needs of the Aged." In R. J. Newcomer, M. P. Lawton, & T. O. Byerts (Eds.), *Housing an aging society*, (pp. 210-216). New York: Van Nostrand Reinhold.

Gyourko, Joseph, Peter Linneman and Susan Wachter. "Analyzing the Relation Among Race, Wealth, and Homeownership in America." Working Paper, (April 30, 1996).

Gyourko, Joseph and Peter Linneman. "The Changing Role of Age and Aging on Homeownership." Working Paper, (June 28, 1995).

Hausman, Jerry A. and Paul A. Ruud. "Specifying and Testing Econometric Models for Rank-Ordered Data." *Journal of Econometrics*, 1987, Vol. 34, No.1/2, pp. 63-82.

Hazelrigg, Lawrence E. and Melissa A. Hardy. "Older Adult Migration to the Sunbelt." *Research on Aging*. Vol. 17, No. 2, pp. 209-234.

Hogan, Timothy D. and Donald N. Steinnes. "Toward an Understanding of Elderly Seasonal Migration Using Origin-Based Household Data." *Research On Aging*, Vol. 16, No. 4, December 1994, pp. 463-475.

Jackson, David J., Charles F. Longino, Jr., Rick S. Zimmerman, & Julia E. Bradsher. "Environmental Adjustments to Declining Functional Ability, Residential Mobility and Living Arrangements." *Research on Aging*, Vol. 13, No. 3, September 1991, pp. 289-309.

Jones, Lawrence D. "Testing the Central Prediction of Housing Tenure Transition Models," *Journal of Urban Economics*, Vol. 38, No. 1, July 1995, pp. 50-73.

— "The Tenure Transition Decision for Elderly Homeowners." Working Paper, (September, 1995).

Kallan, Jeffrey E., "A Multilevel Analysis of Elderly Migration," *Social Science Quarterly*, Vol. 74, No. 2, June 1993, pp. 403-416.

Kenney, Genevieve M. "Is Access to Home Health Care a Problem in Rural Areas?" *American Journal of Public Health*, Vol 83, No. 3, March 1993, pp. 412-414.

Litwak, E., and C.F. Longino. (1987). "Migration Patterns Among the Elderly: A Developmental Perspective. *Gerontologist*, Vol. 27, pp. 266-272.

Longino, C. F. (1990). "Geographical Distribution and Migration." In R. H. Binstock & L. K. George (Eds.), *Handbook of Aging and All the Social Sciences* (3rd ed., pp. 45-63). New York: Academic Press.

— "From Sunbelts to Sunspots," *American Demographics*, November 1994, pp. 22-31.

Longino, Jr., Charles F., David J. Jackson, Rick S. Zimmerman, and Julia E. Bradsher. "The Second Move: Health and Geographic Mobility." *Journal of Gerontology*. 1991, Vol 46, No. 4, pp.218-224.

McFadden, Daniel. "Properties of the Multinomial Logit (MNL) Model." Working Paper No. 7617, Institute of Transportation Studies, University of California, Berkeley. 1976.

— "Regression-Based Specification Tests for the Multinomial Logit Model." *Journal of Econometrics*, 1987, Vol. 34, pp. 63-82.

McKay, Niccie L. "An Econometric Analysis of Costs and Scale Economies in the Nursing Home Industry," *The Journal of Human Resources*, Vol. XXIII, No. 4, 1988, pp. 57-74.

McLeister, Dan. "Seniors' Housing Market Undergoes Dramatic Change," *Professional Builder and Remodeler*, December 1993, p. 20.

Moore, Jim. "Back to Basics," *Multi-Housing News*, Summer 1992, pp. 20-23.

Mullen, A. J. (1991). "The Assisted Living Industry: An Assessment." *Retirement Housing Report*, 5, pp. 6-7.

Ols, J. M. (1990, April 27). "Low-income Housing Tax Credit Utilization and Syndication." Testimony to U.S. Senate, Committee on Banking, Housing, and Urban Affairs.

Ourand, Chris. "Bigger.And Better," *Spectrum*, September/October 1993. p. 7.

Porter, Douglas, R. "Developing Housing For Seniors," *Urban Land*, February 1995, pp. 17-22.

Progressive Architecture. "Housing for the Elderly. (Assisted Living Housing for the Elderly Project)." Progressive Architecture Awards for Architectural Research, *Progressive Architecture*, Vol. 75, No. 7, July 1994, pp. 94-96.

Pynoos, J. (1984). "Setting the elderly housing agenda." *Policy Studies Journal*, 13, pp. 173-184.

Pynoos, J. (1990). "Public policy and aging in place: Identifying the problems and potential solutions." In D. Tilson (Ed.), *Aging in place* (pp. 167-208). Glenview, IL: Scott, Foresman.

Redfoot, D. L., and K.S. Sloan. (1991). "Realities of Political Decision-making on Congregate Housing." *Journal of Housing for the Elderly*, 9 (1 & 2), 97-108.

Reschovsky, J. D., and Newman S. J. (1990). "Adaptations for Independent Living By Older Frail Households." *Gerontologist*, Vol. 30, pp. 543-552.

Rivlin, A. M., and Wiener, J. M. (1988). "Caring for the Disabled Elderly: Who Will Pay?" Washington, DC: Brookings Institution.

Salive, Marcel E., Karen S. Collins, Daniel J. Foley, and Linda K. George. "Predictors of Nursing Home Admission in a Biracial Population," *American Journal of Public Health*, Vol. 83, No. 12, December 1993, pp. 1765-1767.

Schick, Frank L. and Renee Schick, Eds. (1994) *Statistical Handbook on Aging Americans*. (pp. 1-30). Phoenix, AZ: Oryx Press.

Sirrocco, Al. "Nursing Homes and Board and Care Homes, Data from the 1991 National Health Provider Inventory." National Center for Health Statistics, Vital Health Statistics, (February 1994), No. 244, pp. 1-8.

Sloan, Frank A. and May W. Shayne. "Long-term Care, Medicaid, and Impoverishment of the Elderly," *The Milbank Quarterly*, Vol. 71, No. 4, 1993, pp. 575-597.

Steinnes, Donald N., & Hogan, Timothy D. "Take the Money and Sun: Elderly Migration as a Consequence of Gains in Unaffordable Housing Markets." *Gerontology*, Vol. 47, No. 4, July 1992, pp. S197-204.

Stegman, M. A. (1986). "Urban Displacement and Condominium Conversion." In R. Newcomer, M. P. Lawton, & T. Byerts (Eds.), *Housing an Aging Society,"* (pp. 151-160). New York: Van Nostrand.

Struyk, R. J. (1985). "Future Housing Assistance Policy for the Elderly." *Gerontologist*, Vol. 25, pp. 41-46.

Struyk, R. J., and Katsura, H. M. (1987). "Aging at Home: How the Elderly Adjust Their Housing Without Moving." *Journal of Housing for the Elderly*, Vol. 4, pp. 1-175.

Struyk, R. J., Page, D. P., Newman, S., Carroll, M. Ueno, M., Cohen, B., & Wright, P. (1989). "Providing Supportive Services to the Frail Elderly in Federally Assisted Housing." Washington, DC: Urban Institute Press.

Struyk, R. J., and B. J. Soldo. (1980) "Improving the Elderly's Housing." Cambridge, MA: Ballinger.

Struyk, R. J., M.A. Turner & M. Ueno. (1988). "Future U.S. Housing Policy." Washington, DC: Urban Institute Press.

Theil, Henri. "A Multinomial Extension of the Linear Logit Model." *International Economic Review*, October 1969, Vol. 10, No. 3, pp. 251-259.

Taeuber, C. M. (1991). [U.S. Bureau of the Census tabulations]. Mimeo.

U.S. Bureau of the Census. (1989). *Current Population Reports* (Series P-20 data for 1987-1988, unpublished). Washington, DC.

U.S. Bureau of the Census. (1990a). "American Housing Survey for the United States in 1987" *Current Housing Reports* (H-150-87). Washington, DC: U.S. Government Printing Office.

U.S. Bureau of the Census. (1990b). "Household Wealth and Asset Ownership: 1988." *Current Population Reports* (Series P-70, No. 22). Washington, DC: U.S. Government Printing Office.

U.S. Bureau of the Census. (1991). "Marital Status and Living Arrangements: March." *Current Population Reports* (Series P-20, No. 450). Washington, DC: U.S. Government Printing Office.

U.S. Conference of Mayors. (1986). "Adaptive Reuse for Elderly Housing." Washington, DC: U.S. Conference of Mayors.

U.S. Conference of Mayors and National Association of Counties. (1988). "Graying of Suburbia: Policy Implications for Local Officials." Washington, DC.

U.S. Congressional Budget Office. (1988). "Current Housing Problems and Possible Federal Responses." Washington, DC: Superintendent of Documents.

U.S. General Accounting Office. (1988b). "Long-term Care for the Elderly: Issues of Need, Access, and Cost." Washington, DC: General Accounting Office.

U.S. General Accounting Office. (1988a). "Rental housing: Housing Vouchers Cost More Than Certificates But Offer Added Benefits." Washington, DC: General Accounting Office.

U.S. General Accounting Office. (1991). "Older American Act: Promising Practice in Information and Referral Services." Washington, DC: General Accounting Office.

U. S. Senate, Special Committee on Aging, American Association of Retired Persons, Federal Council on the Aging, & U.S. Administration on Aging. (1991). "Aging America: Trends and Projections." (DHHS Publication No. 91-28001). Washington, DC: U.S. Department of Health and Human Services.

Varady, D.P. (1988). "Elderly Independence: Promise & Reality. *Journal of Housing*, Vol. 45, pp. 289-295.

Varady, D.P. (1991). "Planning Housing and Social Service Options for the Community Resident Elderly in a Racially and Religiously Diverse Area" (Final Report to Cincinnati Department of Neighborhood Housing and Conservation Ohio Board of Regents). University of Cincinnati, School of Planning.

Varady, D.P., and C.T. Birdsall (1991). "Local Housing Plans. *Journal of Planning Literature*, 6, 115-135.

Wills, Hugh. "A Note on Specification Tests for the Multinomial Logit Model." *Journal of Econometrics*, 1987, Vol. 34, pp. 263-274.
Winklevoss, H.E., and A.V. Powell. (1984). "Continuing Care Retirement Communities." Homewood, IL: Richard D. Irwin.

The Relationship between Healthcare REITs and Healthcare Stocks

Darcey D. Terris*
F. C. Neil Myer*

Abstract. A two-factor regression model was used to examine the relationship between returns on healthcare equity REITs (EREITs) and healthcare stocks from 1985 to 1992. General stock indices were incorporated in the model to account for the influence of the market. Multiple positive contemporaneous relationships were found between six of the seven REITs studied and portfolios of other healthcare stocks. Furthermore, in four of the six REITs with positive results, significant correlations were evident between individual REIT portfolios and the SIC indices with which they showed a significant relationship. These results are consistent with a common factor or factors affecting the returns of both healthcare EREITs and stocks.

The relationships found between returns on healthcare EREITs and healthcare stocks, especially the correlation between the classification of the EREIT portfolios and SIC indices, indicate the importance of real estate management for healthcare firms and asset subclassification choice for the real estate manager. Although this study specifically investigated healthcare EREITs and healthcare stocks, the results may be more widely applicable to other single-property-type EREITs.

Introduction

An estimated 25% of a corporation's value, as reported by Zeckhauser and Silverman (1983), is vested in the firm's real estate. As discussed by Myer and Webb (1993, 1994), this suggests that at least a portion of the variance of a stock's return can be explained by variation in the value of corporate-owned real estate. From the opposite perspective, equity REITs (EREITs) appear to behave much more like the returns on common stocks, than like the returns on unsecuritized real estate. EREITs are probably more like stocks than unsecured real estate for several reasons. First, EREITs are traded on exchanges that are very different from unsecuritized real estate markets. In addition, EREIT stock returns are transaction based, whereas the returns on unsecuritized real estate are appraisal/accounting based.

The empirical studies of Gyourko and Keim (1992) and Myer and Webb (1994), however, provide significant evidence that real estate stock returns contain economically important and timely information concerning unsecuritized real estate markets. Lagged EREIT returns have been shown to have the ability to predict current returns of the Russell-NCREIF Property Index, especially prior to the fourth quarter which is the period of greatest appraisal activity. This implies that the stock market signals changes in

---
*Department of Finance, James J. Nance College of Business Administration, Cleveland State University, Cleveland, Ohio 44115.
Date Revised—May 1995; Accepted—June 1995.

the appraisal value of real estate, as given in Russell-NCREIF returns, prior to any accounting activity generated by the increase in appraisal values. Appraisal-based data is currently not available, but is needed, for unsecuritized healthcare real estate.

This study employs a methodology similar to a detailed study by Myer and Webb (1994) of the relationship between retail stocks and securitized and unsecuritized retail real estate. The results of the Myer and Webb study, after accounting for the market return, showed evidence of a positive contemporaneous relationship between retail stocks and retail EREITs. Myer and Webb argue that the provision for percentage rents in retail REIT lease contracts links the financial success of the retail properties more closely to the success of tenants operating retail facilities. Percentage rent clauses are also standard in healthcare EREIT sale/leaseback arrangements. This provision may provide for a closer relationship between healthcare stocks and healthcare EREITs.

Healthcare REITs, as a subclass, gained popularity with investors in 1986 and 1987 due to the Tax Reform Act of 1986 (Lutz, 1989). During this period the REIT structure was also a much talked about alternative for financing from the healthcare provider's perspective (Monroe and Peach, 1987). Most healthcare trusts were spin-offs from large, for-profit healthcare companies. Healthcare chains typically sold a small portion of their assets in order to raise capital and fund expansion programs. EREITs were an attractive source of capital because they provided funds equal to 100% of the facility's market value and acted as an off balance sheet source of capital. In addition to using REITs to raise capital, hospital companies also typically established subsidiaries to advise the REITs, which led to additional income for the healthcare chain, and commonly owned stock in the REIT, up to 10% of the outstanding shares (Lutz, 1989).

Literature Review

Gyourko and Nelling (1994), in their study of systematic risk and diversification in association with EREITs, warn investors to interpret the higher returns on retail properties over recent years as compensation for greater systematic risk. EREITs investing primarily in retail properties tended to have a *beta over* 50% larger than EREITs specializing in industrial properties. Gyourko and Nelling argue that the percentage rent clauses included in most retail leases creates systematic risk as the REIT shares in their tenant's cash flow risk. Healthcare EREITs, which were also included in the Gyourko and Nelling study, were found to have the second highest *beta* of the six property types studied.

Healthcare REITs have historically invested solely in healthcare properties. The singular nature of the healthcare REIT holdings, in addition to the nature of healthcare leases, make healthcare real estate a more appropriate classification than retail for studying the relationship between REITs and stocks. Healthcare REITs also provide historical single-property-type REIT data, providing insight into the performance of recent single-property-type REIT IPOs.

Healthcare EREIT Lease Agreements

As outlined by Monroe and Peach (1987), sale/leaseback agreements are the standard method for a healthcare company to obtain equity financing through a REIT. A healthcare institution sells a property to a REIT, generally for 100% of the facility's fair market value, and then leases the property from the trust. Typical leases are triple net and long-term, ten to fifteen years, with options every five years after the initial lease period to renew the lease or repurchase the facility at the current market price.

The base rent for the lease is determined by the healthcare company's financial condition and the purchase price of the facility, but commonly ranges between 10% and 15% of the initial purchase price. The base rent must be paid over the lifetime of the lease, usually regardless of the occupancy of the facility. Typically, lease payments are required to be guaranteed through the sponsoring company or a lending institution by a letter of credit.

In addition to base rent, it is standard for the lessee to pay percentage, or participating rent. After the first year, every year that the operator's gross revenues increase, a percentage of the increase in revenues is paid to the REIT. Initial percentage rents range from 5% to 9%, depending on the type of facility. A transition level of gross revenues is also usually specified, after which percentage rents on additional revenue are in the range of 1% to 2%. Percentage rents are commonly paid on a quarterly basis and adjusted annually. The provision for percentage rents in healthcare REIT lease contracts should link the financial success of the healthcare properties more closely to the success of the healthcare providers operating the facilities.

Under typical sale/leaseback agreements, the healthcare provider is responsible for, and has control of, all operations of a facility. However, if a prospective change in operations will have significant impact on revenues for the property, or capital improvements are sought, the lessee must negotiate such changes with the REIT. Capital additions may be financed by the REIT, resulting in additional rents. Once any REIT-financed capital changes have been made they commonly become the property of the REIT upon termination of the lease. The lessee's control over the sale of a property to a third party when the lease expires is usually limited to rights of first refusal to repurchase or renew the lease at the third party-negotiated rates.

Data and Research Design

Selection Criteria

Although a significant positive relationship was found between the index of retail EREITs and three indices of retail stocks in the Myer and Webb study (1994), a significant positive relationship was found for only two of the eight individual retail EREITs studied. In the Myer and Webb study, retail EREITs were identified from the 1992 *REIT Sourcebook* published by NAREIT. This method of identification may have been a weakness with the investigation. Although the EREITs chosen had a least 80% of their investments in equity retail at the time the data were collected by NAREIT for publication in the 1992 *Sourcebook*, the composition of the REITs' portfolios over the period of the study (1983 to 1991) was unknown.

Healthcare EREITs included in this study were initially identified from the 1991 and 1992 *REIT Sourcebook* and then tracked through the annual reports of each trust. A REIT was considered to be a healthcare EREIT if 100% of its portfolio was in healthcare and at least 75% of investments were equity. As shown in Exhibit 1, seven REITs were identified for inclusion in the study. They are American Health Properties, Health and Rehabilitation Properties Trust, Health Care Property Investors, Health Equity Properties, Medical Properties, Nationwide Health Properties, and Universal Health Realty Income Trust. A brief description of each healthcare EREIT is included in Appendix B.

Exhibit 1
List of Healthcare Equity REITs

Company Name	Start Date	Last Date	Perm Number
American Health Properties	3/87	12/92	71300
Health & Rehabilitation Properties Trust	1/88	12/92	70703
Health Care Property Investors	6/85	12/92	67598
Health Equity Properties	1/88	12/92	70340
Medical Properties	4/87	10/92	72274
Nationwide Health Properties	1/86	12/92	68312
Universal Health Realty Income Trust	2/87	12/92	72864

Company Name	1985	1986	1987	1988	1989	1990	1991	1992
American Health Properties	0.0	0.0	100.00	82.22	75.00	81.03	84.51	92.34
Health & Rehabilitation Properties Trust			<75.00	82.82	77.14	<75.00	89.87	87.72
Health Care Property Investors	84.62	91.40	91.80	93.53	91.28	86.40	89.97	84.98
Health Equity Properties				100.00	100.00	100.00	100.00	100.00
Medical Properties			100.00	100.00	100.00	100.00	100.00	100.00
Nationwide Health Properties		100.00	100.00	100.00	100.00	100.00	100.00	100.00
Universal Health Realty Income Trust			100.00	93.04	not available	not available	91.39	96.57

(% Equity Healthcare)

Research Design

In order to investigate the relationship between returns of the healthcare EREITs and returns of healthcare stocks, the following two-factor multiple regression model was employed:

$$r_{r,t} = a_r + br_{m,t} + cr_{s,t} + e_{r,t}, \qquad (1)$$

where:

a_r = the intercept of the returns,
$r_{r,t}$ = the dependent variable; the return on an individual healthcare REIT at time t,
$r_{m,t}$ = an independent variable; the return on a market index at time t (the S&P 500, CRSP equally weighted or CRSP value weighted),

$r_{s,t}$ = an independent variable; the return on a stock index at time t (based on SIC classifications of healthcare stocks),
$e_{r,t}$ = a random error term, and
b and c are constants.

By including a market index as a contemporaneous term in the model, the relationship between the healthcare EREITs and healthcare stocks can be examined directly since the effects of the stock market in general have been controlled.

Data

The S&P 500, CRSP equally weighted and CRSP value-weighted stock indices were used as a proxy for the market in the model just explained. As shown in Exhibit 2, equally weighted portfolios of healthcare stocks were formed on the basis of their industry group SIC classification for use as stock indices in the model. Health services firms, as a group, are classified under the 8000 SIC heading. Industry groups, such as "Nursing and Personal Care Facilities" and "Hospitals," are designated by the second digit from the right in the group SIC classification. For example, Nursing and Personal Care Facilities are found within the 8050 to 8059 SIC classification while Hospitals are classified within 8060 to 8069. SIC code ranges for the industry groups are referred to as 805X and 806X, respectively, in the following discussion of this study.

Indices of the industry groups 802X (Offices and Clinics of Dentists), 803X (Offices and Clinics of Doctors of Osteopathy) and 804X (Offices and Clinics of Other Health Practitioners) were not included in the study because these classifications contained three or fewer firms over the study period (1985 to 1992). An index of the industry group 801X (Offices and Clinics of Doctors of Medicine) was also not included in the study due to the limited amount of data available. The number of firms included under the other SIC indices are listed in Exhibit 2. Brief descriptions of the SIC industry group indices included in the study are given in Appendix A.

Return data for the healthcare EREITs selected, the market indices, and the SIC code stock indices were taken from the CRSP NYSE/AMEX monthly tape from 1985 to 1992. The relationship between individual healthcare EREITs, the market, and the SIC indices was examined for different time periods based on the status of the REIT during the study period and the availability of data. Healthcare EREITs were included when initiated as a REIT and were dropped from the study if they changed their equity status. Missing data points for the EREITs were also not included in this study.

Exhibit 2
List of Healthcare Stock Indices

SIC Code	Description	Count
80XX	Health Service	92 (total)
805X	Nursing and Personal Care Facilities	16
806X	Hospitals	21
807X	Medical and Dental Laboratories	11
808X	Home Health Care Services	7
809X	Miscellaneous Health and Allied Services	27

Results

The results of estimating the relationship between individual healthcare EREITs and an equally weighted portfolio of healthcare EREITs and healthcare stocks are shown in Exhibit 3. As expected, multiple positive contemporaneous relationships were found for six of seven of the individual healthcare EREITs studied and various healthcare stock indices. Only one significant positive relationship was found for Health Care Property Investors. American Health Properties, Health and Rehabilitation Properties Trust, Health Equity Properties, Medical Properties, Nationwide Health Properties, and Universal Health Realty Income Trust all had several significant relationships with healthcare stock indices. The equally weighted portfolio of healthcare EREITs also demonstrated multiple positive contemporaneous relationships with the healthcare stock indices.

To further highlight the relationships demonstrated between the healthcare EREITs and healthcare stocks, the portfolios of the EREITs can be unbundled down to their SIC classification of the facilities. Of the six EREITs that had multiple significant positive relationships with the SIC indices, four show a significant correlation between the classification of their portfolios and their SIC indices.

Universal Health Realty Income Trust (UHRIT) showed a significant positive relationship with the 806X (hospital) index using all three market indices (at confidence levels of 1% and 5%) and a significant positive relationship with the 809X (outpatient) index using two of the market indices (with a confidence level of 1% for both models). UHRIT had equity investments in six acute care, two rehabilitation and two psychiatric hospitals in 1992, representing 96.6% of its total investment. UHRIT's facilities would most probably be classified under the 806X SIC code for hospitals, and would most probably provide significant outpatient services, as described under the 809X index.

Similarly, American Health Properties (AHP) showed a significant positive relationship with the 809X (outpatient) index using all three market indices (at a confidence level of 1% for all three models). AHP had equity investments in ten acute care hospitals, three rehabilitation facilities and three psychiatric hospitals in 1992, representing 92.3% of its total investments. Again, these facilities would most probably provide significant outpatient services, as described under the 809X index.

Health and Rehabilitation Properties Trust (HRPT) also showed a significant positive relationship with the 806X (hospital) index using all three market indices (at confidence levels of 5% and 10%) and a significant positive relationship with the 809X index using all three market indices (at confidence levels of 1% and 5%). In 1992 HRPT had equity investments in twelve rehabilitation facilities and two psychiatric hospitals, representing 29.1% of its total investments. HRPT's equity investments in rehabilitation facilities and psychiatric hospitals would most probably be classified under the 806X SIC code for hospitals and would most probably provide significant outpatient services.

Finally, Health Equity Properties (HEP) showed a significant positive relationship with the 805X (skilled nursing) index using all three market indices (at confidence levels of 5% and 10%). HEP had equity investments in seventy-four nursing homes and two personal care facilities in 1992, representing 100% of its investment. HEP's investments would most probably be classified under the 805X SIC code for skilled nursing facilities.

The two exceptions in looking at correlations between EREIT portfolio composition and significant SIC indices are Medical Properties (MP) and Nationwide Health Properties (NHP). MP had a significant positive relationship with the 808X (home

Exhibit 3

	805	S&P 500	806	S&P 500	807	S&P 500	808	S&P 500	809	S&P 500	800's	S&P 500
American Health Properties												
Coefficient of Index	−.035	.562***	.195	.306	.037	.481**	.059	.409*	.294*	.195	.293*	.160
P-Value of t-Test	(.7063)	(.0083)	(.1431)	(.1807)	(.5922)	(.0147)	(.4440)	(.0792)	(.0234)	(.3779)	(.0848)	(.5532)
Health and Rehabilitation Properties Trust												
Coefficient of Index	−.058	.447***	.176*	.197	.073	.320**	.006	.373**	.238**	.166	.222*	.138
P-Value of t-Test	(.3951)	(.0040)	(.0826)	(.2417)	(.1656)	(.0231)	(.9132)	(.0277)	(.0150)	(.2822)	(.0844)	(.4725)
Health Care Property Investors												
Coefficient of Index	.000	.206	.075	.128	.036	.173	−.028	.248*	.101	.118	.100	.101
P-Value of t-Test	(.9993)	(.1041)	(.3604)	(.3558)	(.4391)	(.1414)	(.5428)	(.0575)	(.1622)	(.3462)	(.3425)	(.5159)
Health Equity Properties												
Coefficient of Index	.303	−.001	.246	.043	−.065	.327	.136	.070	.327	.085	.477*	−.204
P-Value of t-Test	(.0199)	(.9987)	(.2111)	(.9131)	(.5256)	(.3422)	(.2183)	(.8560)	(.1341)	(.8395)	(.0605)	(.6302)
Medical Properties												
Coefficient of Index	.026	.280	.394	−.106	.267	.063	.518***	−.620	.397	−.115	.875***	−.712
P-Value of t-Test	(.9116)	(.5989)	(.2588)	(.8560)	(.1258)	(.8956)	(.0072)	(.2594)	(.2623)	(.8451)	(.0427)	(.2864)
Nationwide Health Properties												
Coefficient of Index	.015	.398**	.090	.320	.007	.408**	.031	.366*	.251**	.181	.222	.176
P-Value of t-Test	(.8610)	(.0290)	(.4652)	(.1144)	(.9174)	(.0160)	(.6478)	(.0544)	(.0295)	(.3272)	(.1529)	(.4359)
Universal Health Realty Income Trust												
Coefficient of Index	.101*	.262*	.241***	.110	.045	.333***	.075	.243*	.189**	.175	.316***	.006
P-Value of t-Test	(.0813)	(.0508)	(.0047)	(.4446)	(.3220)	(.0093)	(.1339)	(.0984)	(.0354)	(.2371)	(.0038)	(.9720)
Equally Weighted Portfolio of Healthcare EREITs												
Coefficient of Index	.063	.268**	.162**	.165	.430	.294***	.089**	.200*	.146**	.206*	.295***	.022
P-Value of t-Test	(.2207)	(.0139)	(.0203)	(.1558)	(.2858)	(.0041)	(.0258)	(.0677)	(.0188)	(.0531)	(.0009)	(.8644)

Of the three market indices used in the model (S&P 500, equally weighted CRSP and value-weighted CRSP), only the results obtained with the S&P 500 are shown. The results obtained with the CRSP indices were omitted for brevity as they did not differ significantly from the S&P 500 results. 805, 806, 807, 808, 809, and 800's refer to indices of healthcare stocks. Asterisks to the right of the index coefficients and p-value indicate the level of significance: *indicates significance at the 10% level, **indicates significance at the 5% level and *** indicates significance at the 1% level.

Exhibit 4
Correlation Matrix for Healthcare Stocks and S&P 500 Indices

	805	806	807	808	809	800's	S&P 500
805	1.00						
806	.436	1.00					
807	.253	.417	1.00				
808	.428	.465	.349	1.00			
809	.446	.568	.380	.506	1.00		
800's	.683	.764	.634	.759	.795	1.00	
S&P 500	.491	.615	.361	.533	.500	.712	1.00

health) index with two of the market indices at a significance level of 1% for both models. MP's holdings, however, include two acute care hospitals and one medical office building, with little chance of overlap with the home healthcare industry. (It should be noted that MP is unique within the healthcare EREIT sample group due to the limited nature and poor performance of its portfolio.) NHP had a significant positive relationship with the 809X (outpatient) index with all three market indices at significance levels of 5% and 10%. However, NHP's properties have almost exclusively been long-term care facilities (111 facilities out of 113 in 1992, representing 95.48% of total equity investment) which would fall within the 805X (skilled nursing) classification and would most probably offer little or no outpatient services.

A correlation matrix for the various healthcare stock indices and the S&P 500 is given in Exhibit 4. The correlations shown, in general, are not large enough to cause significant multicollinearity problems. Multicollinearity, if it affects the data analysis described in this study, would cause the reported results to be less significant that they truly were, not more significant. Therefore, at a minimum, multiple positive contemporaneous relationships were found between six of the seven REITs studied and portfolios of other healthcare stocks, and in four of the six REITs with positive result, significant correlations were evident between individual REIT portfolios and the SIC indices with which they showed a significant relationship.

Summary and Conclusions

A two-factor regression model was used to investigate the relationship between returns on healthcare equity REITs and healthcare stocks from 1985 to 1992. General stock indices were incorporated in the model to account for the influence of the market. As expected, multiple positive contemporaneous relationships were found between six of the seven REITs studied and various healthcare stock indices. Furthermore, of the six EREITs that had multiple significant positive relationships with the healthcare stock indices, four show a significant correlation between the classification of their portfolios and their SIC indices. The best example of this is Health Equity Properties, which invests exclusively in equity holdings of long-term care facilities and exhibited a strong positive relationship with the 805X SIC index composed of skilled nursing facility stocks.

These results are consistent with the argument that a common factor, or factors, affects the returns of both healthcare equity REITs and stocks. Although a previous study by Myer and Webb (1994) investigating the connection between retail EREITs and stocks also seems to confirm this idea, significant positive relationships were found for only two of the eight individual retail EREITs in their study. Healthcare EREITs' homogeneous nature, in addition to the provision for percentage rents in healthcare REIT leases, may create a closer link between the financial success of the healthcare facilities and the healthcare providers than other categories of real estate.

The relationships found between returns on healthcare equity REITs and healthcare stocks, especially the correlation between the classification of the EREIT portfolios and SIC indices, indicate the importance of real estate management for healthcare firms and asset subclassification choice for the real estate manager. Although this study specifically investigated healthcare EREITs and healthcare stocks, the results may be more widely applicable to other single-property-type EREITs.

Appendix A
SIC Index Descriptions

805X SIC Index: Nursing and Personal Care Facilities

Firms represented in this industry group provide inpatient nursing and health-related personal care, but not hospital services. Examples of facilities included in this index are convalescent homes (including psychiatric convalescent hospitals), nursing homes and personal care facilities.

806X SIC Index: Hospitals

Firms represented in this industry group provide diagnostic services, extensive medical treatment, surgical services, and other hospital services in addition to continuous nursing care. Examples of facilities included in this index are general medical and surgical hospitals, psychiatric hospitals, rehabilitation hospitals, substance abuse hospitals, and other specialized centers.

807X SIC Index: Medical and Dental Laboratories

Firms represented in this industry group provide professional analytical diagnostic services. Examples of facilities included in this index are blood analysis laboratories, x-ray facilities and dental laboratories.

808X SIC Index: Home Health Care Services

Firms represented in this industry group provide skilled nursing or medical care in the home setting, under supervision of a physician. Visiting nurse associations are an example of firms included in this classification.

809X SIC Index: Miscellaneous Health and Allied Services, Not Elsewhere Classified

Included in this industry group are firms that provide specialized outpatient services and other allied health services. Examples of firms listed under this classification are kidney dialysis centers, outpatient substance abuse programs, blood banks and health screening services.

Appendix B
Healthcare EREIT Descriptions
(summarized from Annual Reports and 10-Ks)

American Health Properties: American Health Properties' initial public offering (IPO) was held in February of 1987. The IPO raised over $200 million and was the second largest REIT equity offering to that date. The proceeds of the offering were used to purchase seven acute care hospitals from American Medical International, Inc. (AMI). AMI initially retained a 9.8% interest in the EREIT, served as an advisor to the trust and continued to operate the facilities for American Health Properties (AHP). AHP terminated its advisor relationship with AMI in 1988. In 1992, the EREIT's portfolio included twenty-one healthcare facilities, including ten acute care hospitals, three rehabilitation facilities, six psychiatric hospitals and two development projects. The properties were located in thirteen states and were operated by twelve hospital management companies. In 1992, after a $45 million devaluation of the psychiatric hospitals, AHP owned over $552 million in equity assets, representing 92.3% of total investment. On average, the AHP has been moderately leveraged with a debt-to-total asset ratio of 44.0%.

Health and Rehabilitation Properties Trust: Health and Rehabilitation Properties Trust's IPO was held in December of 1986 and raised approximately $63 million. The EREIT purchased several of its original properties from Greenery Rehabilitation Group, Inc. (GRG) and Continuing Health Care Corp. (CHC). GRG and CHC retained interests in the EREIT totalling 12.4%, served as advisors to the trust and continued to operate the facilities purchased by Health and Rehabilitation Properties Trust (HRPT).

In 1992 CHC became the focus of a congressional hearing on fraud and abuse in the healthcare industry. Due to concern about the effects of its association with CHC or HRPT's stock price, the trust divested $130 million of investment in CHC, including sale or releasing of CHC-operated facilities, redemption of CHC's stock in HRPT and termination of the advisory relationship between CHC and HRPT. GRG, however, continues in its advisory capacity.

At the year end 1992, HRPT owned equity interests in forty-seven properties operated by various management companies. The properties, including twelve rehabilitation facilities, thirty-three long-term care facilities and two psychiatric hospitals, are located in twelve states. HRPT owned over $280 million in equity assets in 1992, representing 87.7% of total investment. On average, HRPT has been moderately leveraged with a debt-to-total asset ratio of 39.6%.

Health Care Property Investors: HCPI was the first major health service company-sponsored REIT to go public, the first to diversify through operators other than the sponsor and the first to obtain an investment grade bond rating from both Moody's and Standard & Poor's (unusual even for the general REIT industry). Health Care Property Investors' IPO was held in May of 1985 and raised approximately $90 million. The proceeds from the offering were used to purchase interests in forty-two properties, including thirty-eight long-term care facilities, one rehabilitation hospital, two acute care facilities and one psychiatric hospital. A 9.8% stake in the EREIT was retained by National Medical Enterprises, Inc. (NME), advisor to the EREIT and operator of a majority of facilities purchased by Health Care Property Investors (HCPI). HCPI ended its advisor relationship with NME in 1987.

In 1992, HCPI owned over $497 million in equity assets, representing 85.0% of total investment. Property holdings included 138 long-term care facilities (nursing homes), five acute care hospitals, nine congregate care/assisted-living facilities, one psychiatric hospital, six rehabilitation facilities and six medical office buildings. The properties continued to be geographically diversified and were operated by thirty hospital management companies. On average the EREIT has been moderately leveraged with a debt-to-total asset ratio of 52.3%.

Health Equity Properties: Health Equity Properties was originally formed as a Master Limited Partnership in 1986 under the name Angell Care Master Limited Partnership. Angell reorganized as an EREIT under the name Angell Real Estate Company in late 1987 and changed its name again, to Health Equity Properties (HEP), in 1990. The trust posted a net profit in 1992 for the first time since changing its status to an EREIT. In 1992 HEP owned interests in seventy-four nursing home properties and two personal care facilities, totalling over $124 million in equity assets and representing 100% of total investment.

Health Equity Properties was highly leveraged from 1988 to 1990, with an average debt-to-total asset ratio of 74.8%. The REIT's debt-to-total asset ratio decreased in 1991 to 47.0% and further decreased in 1992 to 26.5%. The dramatic drop in HEP's debt-to-asset ratio was accomplished through a major restructuring of the EREIT's debt in 1991.

Medical Properties: Medical Properties (MP) was formed in October of 1986 as a captive EREIT sponsored by Nu-Med, Inc. (NM). In formation, MP issued common stock to NM in exchange for two acute care hospitals and one medical office building located in California. NM retained an 8% stake in MP, served as an advisor to the EREIT and operated the three healthcare facilities. By 1990 the NM-operated facilities were unable to make lease payments. Although NM originally guaranteed the leases, the company has not been able to fulfill the guarantee since 1991.

MP terminated its advisor relationship with NM in 1991 and filed for protection under Chapter 11 of the Federal Bankruptcy Code in October of 1992. In 1992, after devaluation of the MP properties by more than $22 million, the EREIT owned less than $20 million in equity real estate, representing 100% of total investment. MP's debt-to-total asset ratio was low from 1988 to 1990, averaging 37.9%, but rose dramatically due to the property devaluation to 86.6% in 1992. To avoid foreclosure on the properties, MP entered into a standstill agreement with its lender in February 1993, pledging "furniture, furnishings, fixtures, inventory, supplies and equipment" owned by NM as collateral.

Nationwide Health Properties: Nationwide Health Properties was originally organized as an EREIT under the name Beverly Investment Properties. Beverly Investment Properties' IPO was held in October of 1985 and raised over $104 million. Proceeds from the offering were used to acquire thirty-nine long-term care facilities (nursing homes) from Beverly Enterprises. As the initial sponsor of the EREIT, Beverly Enterprises retained a 5% interest in Beverly Investment Properties, served as an advisor to the trust and operated all of the Beverly Investment Properties' facilities. Beverly Investment Properties terminated its advisor relationship with Beverly Enterprises in 1988 and changed its name to Nationwide Health Properties (NHP) in 1990.

By 1992, NHP owned equity investments in 113 properties, including 111 long-term care facilities and two rehabilitation hospitals. The properties continued to be geographically diversified and were leased to twenty-one hospital management companies. Equity assets for NHP totalled more than $344 million in 1992, representing 81.5% of total investment. On average, NHP has been modestly leveraged, with a debt-to-total asset ratio of 32.2%. NHP received an investment grade bond rating from Standard and Poor's and Duff and Phelps in 1992.

Universal Health Realty Income Trust: Universal Health Realty Income Trust (UHRIT) was established in December of 1986 as a captive EREIT for Universal Health Services, Inc. (UHS). Shares in the trust were exchanged for ten properties and related debt financing from UHS. UHS retained a 6% interest in the EREIT; it served (and continues to serve) as an advisor to the trust and operated the facilities exchanged in the formation.

In 1992 UHRIT owned equity interests in ten facilities, including six acute care hospitals, two rehabilitation facilities and two psychiatric hospitals. All but one of these properties were operated by affiliates of UHS. Lease payments from UHS and affiliates accounts for 89.0% of UHRIT's total revenues for 1992. Although two of the EREIT's properties have been experiencing operating difficulties, UHS, as guarantor, has continued to make lease payments. In 1992 UHRIT equity interests totalled over $137 million, representing 96.6% of total investment. On average UHRIT has been modestly leveraged, with a debt-to-total asset ratio of 32.6%.

References

Dine, D. D., REITs Court Not-for-Profit Providers in Attempt to Expand Their Portfolios, *Modern Healthcare,* 1986, 18:11, 54–8.

Executive Office of the President, Office of Management and Budget, *Standard Industrial Classification Manual,* Washington, D.C.: 1987.

Gyourko, J. and E. Nelling, Systematic Risk and Diversification in the Equity REIT Market, working paper, April 1994.

Gyourko, J. and D. B. Keim, What Does the Stock Market Tell Us About Real Estate Returns?, *Journal of the American Real Estate and Urban Economics Association,* 1992, 20:3, 457–85.

Lutz, S., Healthcare LBO Bid Not Your Usual Deal, *Modern Healthcare,* 1989, 19:18, 60–62.

Monroe, S. M. and P. R. Peach, Are Healthcare REITs a Cheap Source of Capital?, *Healthcare Financial Management,* 1987, 41:4, 88–92.

Myer, F. C. N. and J. R. Webb, 1994. Retail Stocks, Retail REITs, and Retail Real Estate, *Journal of Real Estate Research,* 1994, 9:1, 65–84.

———, Return Properties of Equity REITs, Common Stocks, and Commercial Real Estate: A Comparison, *Journal of Real Estate Research,* 1993, 8:1, 87–106.

National Association of Real Estate Investment Trusts, Inc. *REIT Sourcebook: A Complete Guide to the Modern Real Estate Investment Trust Industry,* Washington, D.C.: NAREIT, 1992.

———, *REIT Sourcebook: A Complete Guide to the Modern Real Estate Investment Trust Industry,* Washington, D.C.: NAREIT, 1991.

Zeckhauser, S. and R. Silverman, Rediscover Your Company's Real Estate, *Harvard Business Review,* 1983, 61, 111–17.